AF674173

Human Resource Management

Priyanka Goel

ATLANTIC
PUBLISHERS & DISTRIBUTORS (P) LTD

Published by
ATLANTIC
PUBLISHERS & DISTRIBUTORS (P) LTD

7/22, Ansari Road, Darya Ganj, New Delhi-110002
Phones : +91-11-40775252, 23273880, 23275880, 23280451
Fax : +91-11-23285873
Web : www.atlanticbooks.com
E-mail : orders@atlanticbooks.com

Branch Office
5, Nallathambi Street, Wallajah Road, Chennai-600002
Phones : +91-44-48531784, 28411383
E-mail : chennai@atlanticbooks.com

Copyright © Priyanka Goel, 2017, 2019

All rights reserved. No part of this publication may be reproduced, stored in a retrieval system, transmitted or utilized in any form or by any means, electronic, mechanical, photocopying, recording or otherwise, without the prior permission of the copyright owner. Application for such permission should be addressed to the publisher.

Disclaimer

The author and the publisher have taken every effort to the maximum of their skill, expertise and knowledge to provide correct material in the book. Even then if some mistakes persist in the content of the book, the publisher does not take responsibility for the same. The publisher shall have no liability to any person or entity with respect to any loss or damage caused, or alleged to have been caused directly or indirectly, by the information contained in this book.

The publisher has fully tried to follow the copyright law. However, if any work is found to be similar, it is unintentional and the same should not be used as defamatory or to file legal suit against the author/publisher.

If the readers find any mistakes, we shall be grateful to them for pointing out those to us so that they can be corrected in the next edition.

All disputes are subject to the jurisdiction of Delhi court only.

Printed in India at Nice Printing Press, A-33/3A, Site-IV, Industrial Area, Sahibabad, Ghaziabad, U.P.

Preface

Human Resource Management (HRM or HR) can be defined as a function in organizations designed to maximize the performance of employees in service of an employer's strategic objectives. It focuses on policies and systems and is primarily concerned with the management of people within organizations. A number of activities are undertaken by HR departments and units in an organization, including job design and analysis, workforce planning, recruitment and selection, training and development, performance appraisal, and rewarding, among others. HR also concerns itself with organizational change and industrial relations, viz. the balancing of organizational practices with requirements arising from collective bargaining and from governmental laws and established practices.

The book throws light on various aspects of HRM, giving definitions of important terms from management experts, and explaining them with examples. Enumeration of important points or factors has also been used in almost every chapter to apprise the readers with related aspects. This will widen their horizon on the topic covered as also help them at the time of revision. Many structures and designs of pertinent topics have been elucidated with the help of diagrams and tables.

The book takes up all the important topics in HRM, including human resource planning, job analysis, job design, recruitment, psychological tests and interviews, placement and induction, training of the employees, management development, career development and employee empowerment, succession planning, morale and productivity, performance appraisal and employee counselling, job changes, voluntary retirement scheme and job change, employee compensation, job evaluation, incentives to employees who perform better, employee benefits, industrial relations, employee health and safety, employee welfare and social security, workers' participation in management, and grievance handling and redressal. Exclusive chapters have been devoted to Human Resource Information System (HRIS), International Human Resource Management and Workforce Diversity, and Human Resource Accounting and Audit. Likely questions from the topics covered have been given at the end of each chapter from the students' point of view so that they can work on specific areas in preparation for the examination. This will also help them in doing focused study.

The book is the result of interaction with experts in the field. Some authentic sources, including online sources, have also been consulted for preparing of the book. These sources have been duly acknowledged, but if any source has been left out, it incidental, not intentional. These sources can also be consulted by the readers for further study or research.

The book will be useful to the students pursuing courses in management, especially Human Resource Management at graduate as well as postgraduate level. It will also help those preparing for competitive examinations in management as all the core concepts on HRM have been covered in it. Since a number of practical aspects on HRM have been covered in the book, it will serve as an ideal reference source for HR departments or units in organizations. It will also help professional managers in their job.

It is a matter of great satisfaction to bring out the present edition of *Human Resource Management*. I have always drawn great inspiration from my respected guide-cum-mentor, Dr. S.K. Khandelwal a great visionary and institutional builder. I owe deep sense of gratitude to my father Dr. R.A. Goel for his constructive cooperation. Comments and suggestions for the improvement shall be highly appreciated and duly acknowledged.

Priyanka Goel

Contents

Chapter 1

Introduction to Human Resource Management

Human Resources are the most important asset of any organization. Out of all the factors of production like land, capital, fixed assets, etc., human factor is the only living factor which activates the other passive factors of production. In today's highly competitive world, the achievement of organizational goals rests completely in the hands of the people working in the organization. A company may have the most sophisticated machinery, equipment and technology, but in the absence of human elements, these resources cannot be utilised. Having superior production facilities is not enough to ensure the long-term sustainability of any organization. The attainment of organizational goals and success of organization depends upon the productivity and efficiency of the company's workforce. A competitive organization must have highly skilled and knowledgeable workers. That is why the need for proper management of human resources arises. Management of human resource refers to the policies and practices involved in carrying out the human resource aspects of a management position, including recruitment, screening, training, rewarding and appraising.[1]

Some definitions of human resource management:

1. Human resource management is the planning, organizing, directing and controlling of the procurement, development, compensation, integration, maintenance

and separation of human resources to the end that individual, organizational and societal objectives are accomplished.[2] The management of human resources is viewed as a system in which participants seek to attain both individual and group goals.[3]

2. Human resource management is the recruitment, selection, development, utilization of and accommodation in human resources by organizations. The human resources of an organization consist of all individuals regardless of their role, who are engaged in any of the organization's activities.[4]

Characteristics of Human Resource Management (HRM)

1. Comprehensive function: HRM covers all levels (lower, middle and top) and all categories (unskilled, skilled, clerical, technical, managerial and professional) of employees. It applies to workers, officers, supervisors, managers, executives and other types of personnel.
2. **Definite principles and policies:** HRM applies definite principles and policies for managing and developing the workforce.
3. **Integral part of management process:** The process of HRM is not an isolated function of management. It is an integral part of the management process as a whole. It is embedded in the organization structure. HRM is pervasive in nature since employees are a vital resource of each organizational department.
4. **People orientation:** Workers are considered as human beings with emotional, behavioural and social aspects. The whole philosophy of HRM is based on the fact that the worker is a human being. It emphasizes on motivating and developing the worker in the best interests of the organization.
5. **Individual oriented:** The development of an individual worker's skills, capacity, knowledge and potential is given utmost importance. HRM aims to achieve

organizational growth by facilitating the personal growth and satisfaction of the individual.

6. **Continuous process:** HRM is a continuous and ongoing process. Management of human beings is dynamic in nature because the motivation, desires, knowledge and skill levels of employees are ever changing. HRM requires constant awareness about human nature to motivate and develop the employees.
7. **Pervasive function:** HRM is applicable to all types of organizations, whether corporations, not for profit sectors, religious institutes, educational institutes, armed forces, sports organizations, etc. as recruitment, selection, training and development of workforce is essential for all types of workforce.

Functions of Human Resource Management

The functions of Human Resource Management can be divided into two categories: Managerial functions and Operative functions.

1. Managerial Functions

(i) **Planning:** It is the main function of management. It is concerned with manpower planning, studying labour turnover rate, forecasting future personnel requirement and planning for selection and training procedures, etc.

(ii) **Organizing:** It is the process of establishing harmonious authority-responsibility relationships among the members of the organization. The network of authority-responsibility is called the organization structure. This structure serves as a framework within which people can work together for attainment of organizational goals.

(iii) **Staffing:** It is the process concerned with filling all the positions in the organization with adequate and qualified personnel. It is the responsibility of the human resource department to recruit, select, train, place, compensate, maintain, promote, and retire the employees of the organization at the appropriate time and in the most effective manner.

(iv) **Direction:** This is the function of guiding, motivating, supervising and leading people towards the attainment of planned targets of performance. Direction is concerned with the execution of plans, which involves issuing instructions to the workers, supervising people, motivating them and influencing employees' behaviour.

(v) **Controlling:** Controlling means measurement of actual performance, comparing it with the set standards, finding deviations if any, and taking corrective actions. This process ensures that everything is moving according to the plans.

2. Operative Functions

The managerial functions are common to all types of managers. On the other hand, operative functions are the specialised functions related to a specific field. The operative functions of Human Resource Management are:

(i) **Procurement:** It is concerned with obtaining the proper kind and right number of personnel at the right time and at the most economical rates. It deals specifically with the determination of manpower requirement, recruitment, selection, induction and placement.

(ii) **Development:** Various training and development programmes are to be provided to the employees to develop their skills and increase their productivity. This function also includes framing of promotion policy, determining the basis of promotion and making performance appraisals.

(iii) **Compensation:** Compensation means determination of adequate and equitable remuneration of personnel for their contribution to organization objectives. The importance of monetary compensation cannot be underestimated even though non-financial incentives also play an important role in raising the morale of employees. The compensation function includes job evaluation, remuneration policy, incentive and premium plans, etc.

(iv) **Integration:** It deals with the integration of individuals, societal and organizational goals. This function mainly focuses on employee satisfaction, grievance handling, and maintenance of discipline and free flow of communication at all levels.

(v) **Maintenance:** This function deals with sustaining and improving of already established conditions. This function is concerned with the establishment of proper health, medical and safety measures. Arrangement and proper maintenance of health and safety standards are essential for providing working environment which is conducive to the organization.

(vi) **Good industrial relations:** The human resource manager has to see that harmonious relations are maintained between the management and the workers. Good industrial relations are intended to reduce conflict, promote industrial peace, provide fair deal to workers and establish industrial democracy.

(vii) **Record keeping:** The personnel manager has to collect and maintain information concerned with the staff of the organization. It is essential for every organization as it assists in decision-making such as in case of promotion.

(viii) **Separation:** Separation refers to the process by which the employees leave the organization and return to the society. The final function of Human Resource Management is to assist the employees in separating themselves from the organization smoothly. This function deals not only with resignations and retirements, but also with retrenchment, lay-off, etc.

Relevance of HRM

1. **Attracting the best employees:** It is the responsibility of HR department to recruit and select the most suitable employees. HR places the right person on the right job.
2. **Promote team spirit:** HRM encourages team spirit among workers and motivates them to work towards

the common organizational goals. Goodwill and understanding is created among all members of the organization.

3. **Develop loyalty and commitment:** HRM treats human beings as invaluable assets of the organization. The emotional and motivational needs of the employees are cared for. This develops employee loyalty.
4. **Retention of employees:** One of the big problems facing companies now-a-days is the high rate of employee turnover. Good HRM helps to retain talented employees by developing loyalty and by ensuring that employees are satisfied with their jobs.
5. **Creation of employment opportunities:** The emergence of HRM as a separate field of management has created many job opportunities. Professional courses in HRM are conducted to equip interested candidates with a relevant degree so that they can enter this field as employees.
6. **Improve productivity:** HRM matches the employee's abilities, interests and skill levels with job profiles before placing him on the most suitable job. When a worker is entrusted with a job that interests him, then he is likely to be more productive.
7. **Employee job satisfaction:** HRM recognizes the worker as a human being and treats him with respect and dignity. Payment of suitable salary, good working conditions, friendly atmosphere and timely redressal of grievances are provided to him. This results in higher job satisfaction.
8. **Good employer–employee relations:** HRM provides for an understanding environment and democratic set up in the organization. Open communication between the management and workers is encouraged and workers are free to list their grievances, if any. Efforts are always made to maintain cordial relations between all levels of employees.

9. **Development of skills and talents:** The individuals are trained to enhance their skills and develop their talents. Many training and development programmes are held regularly for employees at all levels. This helps to increase their productivity and boost their self-esteem.

Evolution of Human Resource Management

1. **Early philosophy (before 1900):** The history of modern Human Resource Management began with the efforts of Robert Owen. Owen is called the founder of Human Resource Management. In 1813, he wrote a book, *A New View of Society*. In it he propounded the need for better industrial relations and improvements in the service conditions. His attitude towards workers was very cordial, liberal and paternalistic. He got good houses constructed for his workers by the side of his factory. He eliminated child labour and provided healthy working conditions. J.S. Mill, Andrew Yule and Charles Bewarage, contemporaries of Robert Owen, developed Human Resource Management as a science and supported the idea of wage incentives, profit sharing and labour welfare, etc.
2. **Efficiency and productivity movement (1900-1920):** During the last year of the 19th century arrived the age of efficiency and productivity movement. The two decades from 1900 to 1920 were the years of scientific management movement. Taylor's Scientific Management Thought was accepted during this period. Taylor opposed the idea of trade unionism and workers' organization. The main contribution of these two decades has been the increase in the size of units, introduction of scientific thinking into actions, job analysis, standards costing, scientific selection and training of workers and the idea of mental revolution.
3. **Period of welfare-ism and industrial psychology (1920-1930):** Up to 1925, the Human Resource Management had taken a definite form. Staff line organization became the basis of Human Resource Management.

The opposition of scientific management movement by workers introduced the need of industrial psychology. Industrial psychologists developed many new techniques like psychological testing, interviewing, workers training and non-financial incentives. They helped to give a professional form to Human Resource Management. The Human Resource Management began to be realized as a profession and a specialist's function.

4. **Period of human relations (1930-1950):** When Prof. Elton Mayo and his companions conducted Hawthorn experiments, it was the beginning of recognition of the fact that human resources have greater influence on production than other psychical resources. A worker must be treated as a human being. His social, psychological and moral instincts should be fully recognized by the management. Due to these experiments the commodity concept of labour changed to social concept. The decade of 1940-1950 was very important for the development of Human Resource Management. During that decade, many new techniques were developed for the selection, training and induction of workers. The human resource philosophy became people-oriented. Trade unions flourished and provision of fringe benefits for the workers became common.
5. **Modern times (After 1950):** The history of Human Resource Management since 1950 up to current times is the age of modern developments. It is the period of the citizenship concept of labour where the workers have full right to be consulted in determining the rules and regulations under which they work. The concept of industrial democracy has imposed many new responsibilities upon the human resource managers of industrial houses. In modern times, Human Resource Management is widely accepted as an independent discipline. One finds two important developments during this period: After 1960, the Human Resource Management began to be realized as a behavioural science which centred completely on human elements

with the study of organizational behaviour as its main crux. After 1970s the belief of 'open social and industrial system' became very popular for business organizations. In modern times, Human Resource Management is fully recognized as a profession dealing with the management of human resources. These developments widened the scope of Human Resource Management.

Development of Human Resource Management in India

The development of Human Resource Management in India can be studied under two heads:

I. Development before Independence

1. **Appointment of labour welfare officers:** Before Independence nothing commendable was done either on the part of employers or on the part of government for the development of industrial relations. The development of Human Resource Management in India was as late as in 1920 when labour welfare activities were initiated by some Indian business enterprises like Tata Group, British India Corporation, Calico Mills, Empress Mill, etc., who appointed labour welfare officers to look after the interest of the working people and of the enterprise in relation to the human problems.
2. **Industrial unrest:** The year 1920 was the year of industrial unrest. Employers and the government took various steps to resolve better industrial relations including the recognition of trade unions. But satisfactory progress in industrial relations could not be seen on the whole.
3. **Governmental efforts:** Before and during World War II, the government (central and states) was the leading agency in India to develop and improve the labour relations in Indian industries. In 1934 with the efforts of Bombay Government, the appointment of the labour welfare officers was made compulsory in industries employing 500 or more workers throughout Bombay (now Mumbai) to resolve the labour disputes with labour

commissioner as the chief conciliation officer. Industries in other states also appointed the labour officers.

4. **Royal Commission on labour:** In 1939, Royal Commission on Labour recommended the appointment of labour officers so that the labour problems might be reconciled amicably. The Union Government convened a tripartite labour conference to discuss the extent of labour laws in Indian industries, to evolve a system of grievance handling and to establish conciliation system in industrial matters.

II. Development in Post-independence Period

1. **Labour legislations:** Government of India did commendable work in this direction. On the recommendations of the Central Labour Investigation Committee 1946, several labour legislations were enacted, such as Labour Disputes Act, 1947, Industrial Employment Act, 1946, Factories Act, 1948, etc. The Factories Act, 1948 provided the appointment of a labour welfare officer in every industry employing 500 or more workers for the purpose of helping the management in providing welfare measures to the workers as enunciated in the Act. Now the urgency of appointing human resource or labour officer is being felt even in such industries where there is no legal compulsion to appoint welfare officer as there is a need of such agency to guide the management in tackling the ticklish labour problems by providing specialised services. The services of these labour welfare officers are not up to the mark even now because of their taking a biased view. While dealing with the workers, they consider themselves as agents of management.
2. **Training:** The Government arranged for the training of workers and management of human resource in India and started several training centres and institutes for imparting training in industrial relations. In 1949, for the first time in independent India 'Xavier Institute of Labour Relations' was established. Several other

institutions were started later on such as Indian Institute of Personnel Administration, Kolkata, Indian Labour Management Institute, Mumbai, Institute of Industrial Relations, Bangalore, Federation of All India Labour Welfare Officers, and Indian Productivity Councils, Shri Ram Centre for Industrial Relations and Human Resources at Delhi.

3. **Reforms during emergency:** In the middle of 1975, the government proclaimed the state of emergency in India and took several administrative steps to eradicate the system of bonded labour, to give momentum to the scheme of workers' participation in management in Indian industries and to extend the scheme of apprenticeship.
4. **Post-emergency labour legislation:** In 1978, a comprehensive Industrial Relation Bill was introduced in Parliament in order to improve the labour relations in industries through collective bargaining by consolidating Trade Union Act, 1926; Industrial Employment (Standing Order) Act, 1946 and the Industrial Disputes Act, 1947. But due to dissolution of Lok Sabha in 1979 the bill could not be passed. In 1981 the President promulgated an ordinance giving powers to the Government to ban strikes in essential services for six months. The essential services include Railways, Post and Telegraph, Telephone, Docks, Airports, Banks, Petroleum, Water and Sewage Disposal, Defence and Hospitals. The Government was empowered to declare any service as an essential service. In 1982, Government amended several labour laws, including Industrial Disputes Act, Industrial Employment (Standing Order) Act, 1946. The Government also amended the Employees State Insurance Act in 1984.

Scope of HRM

HRM is very wide in scope. It includes all the major activities in the working life of an individual starting from his entry into the organization till he leaves the organization.

Traditionally, Human Resource Management was a simpler process but with increase in industrialisation, it has grown to be a much specialised field. The scope of HRM may be classified under the following heads:

1. **HRM in Personnel Management:** This aspect of HRM deals with manpower management. HRM strives to achieve organizational development through individual growth and development of workers. It includes the following functions:
   - (i) *Manpower planning, recruitment and selection*: It is the responsibility of the HR department to plan for future manpower requirements, recruit candidates and select the most suitable candidate for the job vacancy.
   - (ii) *Induction and orientation*: The newly joined employees have to be introduced into the organization and made familiar with the workplace and other employees in order to help them in adjusting to the new surroundings.
   - (iii) *Training and development*: This is the function of training the employees to develop their skills, knowledge and capabilities so that they become more productive.
   - (iv) *Transfer and promotion*: The employees of an organization may be transferred to other branches or promoted to a senior level based on the organizational requirements.
   - (v) *Compensation*: The HR department decides the method of rewarding the employees for their contribution to the organization. The compensation should be able to attract and motivate the employees towards giving their best.
   - (vi) *Lay-off and retrenchment*: The functions of HR include not just the recruitment and selection of staff, but also lay-off and retrenchment of workers, i.e. discharge of workers from the organization, either temporarily or permanently during times of economic difficulties.

(vii) *Performance appraisal*: The performances of the employees at all levels have to be assessed to measure their efficiency and to motivate them towards better performance. This is another important function of HRM.

(viii) *Career development*: HRM helps the employees to plan and develop their career. They are provided career counselling and informed of new opportunities for growth inside the organization.

2. **HRM in Employee Welfare:** Employee welfare deals with the working conditions and facilities at the work place. The aim of employee welfare is to take care of employees' safety and medical needs and provide them comfortable working conditions. It includes:

   (i) *Medical facilities*: It is mandatory that the employees of an organization be provided with medical care and sickness benefits whenever required.

   (ii) *Eliminating workplace hazards*: Safe working conditions should be provided to the employees. Any machinery or equipment that might cause physical injury should be removed from the workplace.

   (iii) *Proper ventilation and lighting*: Good working conditions are conducive to employees' physical health and productivity. The work premises should be properly ventilated and well lit for their comfort.

   (iv) *Sanitation facilities*: Hygienic washroom facilities are to be maintained to protect the employees' health and well-being.

   (v) *Safeguarding machinery*: Machineries should be equipped with enough safety mechanisms so that no one is injured while operating them.

   (vi) *Employment injury benefits*: In case any worker gets injured or disabled in the factory premises while working, he should get the necessary injury benefits that he is entitled to.

(vii) *Maternity benefits*: Female employees should be allowed maternity leaves and other benefits as per the legal requirements.

(viii) *Canteen facilities*: Mess and canteen facilities where employees can get eatables and drinks should be available at the workplace.

(ix) *Crèches*: This is applicable at workplaces where a large number of women are employed. There should be crèche facility for safely leaving small kids while the mothers are busy working.

3. **HRM in Industrial Relations:** Industrial relations refer to the collective relationship between management, employees and government in any organization. For the maintenance of harmonious industrial relations it is necessary to have frequent interactions with labour unions, address their grievances and settle the disputes effectively. The problems should be solved with joint consultations and collective bargaining. Mutual understanding and goodwill should be promoted between the employer and the unions. It is about establishing open communication and industrial democracy to safeguard the interests of both the management and the employees.[5]

Human Resource Development

Human Resource Development (HRD) is that part of Human Resource Management which specifically deals with the training and development of employees. It helps the employees in developing their knowledge, skills and abilities to achieve self-fulfillment and aid in the accomplishment of organizational goals. HRD can be defined as organized learning activities arranged within an organization in order to improve performance and/or personal growth for the purpose of improving the job, the individual, and/or the organization.[6] HRD includes the areas of employee training, career development, performance management, coaching, mentoring, key employee identification, talent development and organization development. Developing a highly productive and superior workforce is the aim of HRD activities. The role of human beings in an organization's success is deeply recognized. Many formal and informal methods are used for developing the employees. HRD strives for the improvement of not just the individual workers, but for the growth of the group and organization as a whole.

Components of HRD

HRD includes the development of employees at the individual and organizational level. It also comprises career development. The crux of HRD is that organizational growth can be achieved only through the personal and collective development of the individual employees. The main components of HRD are:

1. **Individual development:** It refers to the development of new skills, knowledge and improved behaviour that contribute to his productivity. As a result of this training, his job performance is improved. Individual development mainly takes place through informal activities like coaching or mentoring by an experienced senior. Some companies, may, however provide formal programmes for such training.
2. **Career development:** It is an approach to match employee goals with the requirements of the organization. The interests, values, abilities and competencies of the individuals are identified to analyse how their skills can be developed for future jobs. At an individual level, career development includes career planning and career awareness. Mentoring, providing career counselling, career development workshops, human resource planning are the steps the organization takes for career development.
3. **Organizational development:** Organizational development means an organization wide effort to enhance organizational effectiveness. It includes making improvements to the organizational structure, culture, processes, etc. through activities like performance

evaluation, change management, succession planning, process analysis and team building. The first step in organizational development is to discover its internal problems and weaknesses, and then work towards solving them. The organization should try to become a more functional unit by fostering a close relationship among its various units.

Nature of HRD

1. **Learning:** The essence of HRD is learning. The very purpose of HRD is to make the employees acquire knowledge, learn newer concepts and develop their skills. The core of HRD is to enhance the quality of workforce by creating an environment which fosters constant learning.
2. **Career development:** HRD helps in the career development of individuals by matching employee characteristics with job requirements. Growth of the organization is achieved through growth and development of individual employee.
3. **Specific duration:** Any particular HRD programme would have a specific duration. It could be for a short, medium or long duration.
4. **Improves performance:** The performance of employees is improved as a result of HRD. The training programmes enhance the capabilities of employees and improve their productivity.
5. **Organizational development:** HRD aims at not just the development of the human resources, but at the progress of the organization as a whole. Positive changes in work culture, processes and organizational structure are made.
6. **Long-term benefits:** HRD is a very future oriented concept. The results of HRD can be experienced only after some time following its implementation. But it benefits the employee and the organization for a long time in the future.

7. **Continuous process:** HRD is a continuous process. Different HRD programmes are to be implemented in the organization according to changes in the work environment. Human behaviour needs to be monitored regularly to enable them to adjust themselves according to environment dynamics.
8. **Employee welfare:** The organization attempts to provide all the facilities which are vital for the physical and mental well-being of the employees to facilitate HRD. Measures like canteen facilities, crèche, medical insurance, etc. are provided as part of employee welfare.
9. **Development of team spirit:** HRD creates a healthy work environment which helps to build team spirit and coordination among various groups and the department. Team spirit is necessary for fostering loyalty and belongingness among employees.

Need and Importance of HRD

1. HRD is needed to develop a workforce that is capable of functioning productively even during changing market conditions and intense competition.
2. HRD boosts employee morale, builds their confidence and helps them derive more job satisfaction.
3. HRD helps to maintain and retain efficient employees.
4. It is the HRD process which trains employees to adopt modern technological innovations.
5. HRD is necessary to utilise the skills, knowledge and talents of the human resource in the best possible way.
6. HRD helps in business diversification by preparing the employees to take on additional duties and responsibilities in different areas of work.
7. HRD treats human beings with dignity and cares for their safety and emotional health, thereby giving them psychological satisfaction and self-esteem.
8. It provides a cordial work environment and promotes teamwork and cooperation between employees.

9. HRD seeks to provide maximum opportunities for personal and career growth of the employees and makes them an invaluable asset of the organization.
10. HRD helps the organization to achieve its goals and objectives by linking employee growth with organizational development.

Organization of the HR Department

An organization can work more effectively if the personnel know the part they are to play in any collaborative endeavour and how their roles relate to each other. An organization structure should be so designed as to clarify the job positions so that everyone knows who is to do what and who is responsible for what results. The position of the HR department in the overall organization structure depends upon the size of organization, i.e. small or large one.

Organization structure of a small scale organization

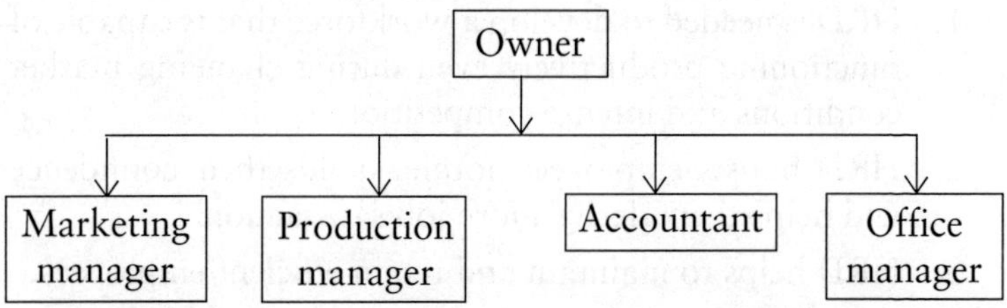

In case of small scale organizations, there is usually no separate department of HRM. There may not be a HR manager. Sometimes, services of outsiders are availed for the maintenance of accounts and records of employees at nominal fees. Otherwise, an employee of the organization may be entrusted with HR responsibilities.

With the passage of time, increasing complexities, rising status of HR department, things have improved over the years. Realizing the importance of human resources along with physical resources, organizations have started providing separate department for HR activities.

Organization structure of a large scale organization

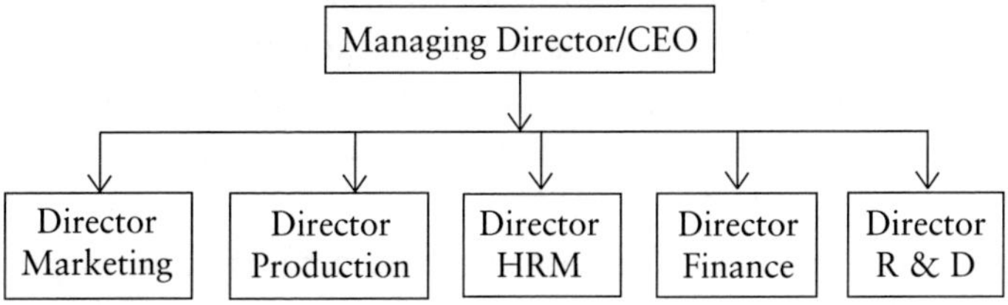

Large organizations have an HR department for dealing with specific HR issues. The composition of the HR department depends upon the scale of operations and the management's attitudes towards its employees.

Administration manager is in charge of the canteen, medical, transport facilities etc. The personnel manager takes care of human resource planning, recruitment, selection, job analysis, compensation, placement and induction. The training and development requirements, counselling and performance appraisal are duties of the HRD manager. The responsibilities of the Industrial relations manager include health, safety and welfare functions.

Role of the HR Manager

HR manager plays a variety of roles in the organization. Earlier, the main role of HR manager was to procure and maintain a committed workforce. But with the passage of time, increasingly critical nature of problems and challenges in the effective utilisation of human beings has elevated the status of HR manager. The different roles played by the HR manager are as follows:

1. **The counsellor:** HR manager acts as a counsellor for the employees facing problems related with health, work, colleagues, family, supervisors, financial concerns, children's education, etc. Employees can freely discuss their problems with HR manager and he offers suitable suggestions to solve their problems.
2. **The advisor:** HR manager advises the management regarding human resource planning, recruitment,

selection, training and development, appraisal, compensation, integration, separation, etc. HR manager plays a dual role in case of industrial disputes—he advises the top officials and provides assistance to the workers by conveying their problems to the management.

3. **The mediator:** In case of some conflicts and disputes, HR manager plays the role of peacemaker between management and employees.
4. **The conscience role:** This role is that of a humanitarian who advises management of its moral and ethical obligations to its employees.
5. **The liaison role:** Generally, HR manager acts as a spokesman for or representative of the organization.
6. **The change agent:** He acts as a catalyst in introducing new changes in the organization.
7. **The problem solver:** Problems related with HR in any part of organization are tackled by HR manager.
8. **The welfare role:** As per The Factories Act, 1948, where 500 or more workers are employed, one welfare officer should be appointed. Otherwise, HR manager acts as a welfare officer. He is concerned about facilities like crèche, canteen, shelter, lunch and restrooms, etc.
9. **The legal role:** HR manager plays a vital fire-fighting role during grievance handling procedure, settlement of industrial disputes, collective bargaining, handling disciplinary action, joint consultation, etc.

Competencies of HR Manager

HR manager should be a blend of many talents such as good negotiator, psychologist, strategist, adviser, statistician, etc. The various competencies of a HR manager should include:

1. **Intelligence:** It is concerned with mental ability, tactfulness while dealing with others, etc.

2. **Educational skills:** He should possess learning and teaching skills, as he himself has to learn and teach workers about organization's growth and development.
3. **Communication skills:** HR manager should have good command of the language, especially the local language, listening skills, interpretation skills, etc.
4. **Executive skills:** This refers to the speedy and accurate execution of management policies and programmes by HR manager.
5. **Human skills:** This refers to the HR manager's successful dealing with employees.
6. **Leadership skills:** This includes ability to motivate, direct and create enthusiasm among employees.
7. **Decision skills:** HR manager should possess analytical ability, good judgement, etc.
8. **Free from bias:** HR manager should be free from bias. He should be neither pro-workers nor pro-management. He should be a well-balanced and an honest person.

QUESTIONS

1. Explain the nature and scope of HRM.
2. Describe the various stages in the evolution of HRM.
3. What is the scope of HRM?
4. Write a note on the development of HRM in India.
5. What do you mean by Human Resource Development?
6. Diagrammatically explain the structure of HR department in a large organization.

NOTES

1. Gary Dessler. *Human Resource Management*. Pearson Education, Ninth ed., Delhi, 2004.
2. Edwin Flippo. *Personnel Management*, Sixth ed., McGraw-Hill, New York, 1984, p. 5.
3. Dale Yoder. *Personnel Management and Industrial Relations*. Prentice-Hall of India, New Delhi, 1975.

4. Wendell French. *The Personnel Management Process: Human Resources Administration*. Houghton Mifflin Company, New York, Third ed., 1974, p. 3.
5. http://www.managementstudyguide.com/scope-of-human-resource- management.htm
6. J.W. Gilley and S.A. Eggland. *Principles of Human Resource Development*. Addison-Wesley, NY, 1989, p. 5.

Chapter 2

HR Policies

The concept of HR policy in India derives its philosophy and content from the Directive Principles of the Constitution and has been evolving in response to specific needs of the situation to suit requirements of planned economic development and social justice. It has been envisaged that growth of the economy would not only increase production but also absorb the backlog of unemployed and underemployed labour and a substantial proportion of the additional labour force. Starting from the Seventh Five Year Plan, much emphasis has been laid on harnessing the country's abundant human resources and improving their capabilities for development. HR policies are part of labour policies. According to Edwin B. Flippo, "A policy is a man-made rule or predetermined course of action that is established to guide the performance of work towards the organization. It is a type of standing plan that serves to guide subordinates in the execution of their task."[1] Policies are statements of the organization's overall purposes and its objectives in the various areas with which its operations are concerned—HR, finance, production, marketing and so on.[2]

Need for HR Policies

1. **To achieve the objectives of the organization:** Policies guide the employees to take action for achieving the objectives of the organization. Hence, they must be

known and well understood by everyone in order to concentrate efforts on the objectives.

2. **To bring uniformity in decisions:** HR policies furnish the general standard on which decisions are taken. Various line authorities take decisions in an organization keeping in view the HR policies. Thus, uniformity of action is maintained in similar cases. If the person in authority is transferred and some other person takes charge of the office the decisions to be taken by the new authority are similar to those which have already been taken in comparable circumstances by the former authorities due to the predetermined policies of the organization. This brings simplicity and uniformity in action.
3. **To delegate authority:** HR policies make delegation of authority possible, which means assigning the work to others and give them authority to do it. HR policies help executives at various levels of decision centres to act with confidence without consulting the superiors every time. HR policies give a manager liberty to choose the alternatives provided and to decide upon the action.
4. **To achieve better control:** HR policies specify relationships among organization, management and workers. Therefore, each group works for the achievement of the larger objectives of the organization without any policy conflicts. Thus, HR policies provide better control.
5. **To evaluate efficiency:** HR policies serve as standards in execution of work. Efficiency of a group may be evaluated by its performance in the light of the policy. After assessing whether organization has achieved the desired results set in the policy, HR policy may be amended or a new policy may be formulated in the light of the actual performance.
6. **To create confidence among employees:** HR policies provide the workers a security against exploitation and create confidence in employees who may know where they stand in the organization.

7. **To motivate:** HR policies introduce the employees to the objectives of the organization. It guides the workers in achieving the objectives. They work enthusiastically and with loyalty to get those objectives.
8. **To guide the management:** HR policies provide guidance to management in relation to the HR problems. HR policies decide how to get the work done by the people or how to behave with them.

Principles of HR Policies

1. **Common interest:** The principle of common interest must be given due recognition in designing HR policies. Factors like economic success of the enterprises, the interest of the employer and the employees should all be taken into account. It should benefit all the concerned parties—employees, employer and the government. Employees must have a chance for a better standard of living, better security and opportunity for living a fuller and better life. In return, the employer must be able to get the maximum possible regain. A successful business enterprise contributes substantially to the national exchequer and creates propriety all around.
2. **Development:** The organization must provide ample opportunities for the growth of employee's personality. People want to improve their status, to earn more, and to shoulder higher responsibility. HR Policies should lay down rules for the opportunities for development to those who are willing to contribute something to the prosperity of the organization and to sacrifice their time and efforts for undergoing training to improve themselves on the job.
3. **Recognition of work and accomplishment:** There must be a direct relationship between work and accomplishment. A job should provide for sufficient wages and benefits that will enable an employee to lead a comfortable life. The HR policies should take into consideration the employee's expectations such

as reasonable security on the job against accidents, sickness and old age.

4. **Recognition of trade unions:** As the trade unions play an important role in the development of industrial relations, therefore, the management must recognize them. The HR policies should incorporate the clause for amicable settlement of disputes with the trade unions through negotiations and collective bargaining.
5. **Participation in management:** Employees' representatives should be given participation in decision-making bodies of the organization so that they may realize their responsibilities towards the management and workers. The success of any programme or policy depends considerably upon its wilful acceptance by the employees. If the decisions regarding HR affairs are taken in the presence of workers' representatives, there shall be better employees' satisfaction and morale. It will also minimise resistance to change.
6. **Facing the changes:** Employees always resist changes that may seem inconvenient or unpleasant to them. Changes may relate to loss of income, loss of status, transfers, reassignment or retraining activities and broken friendships. Therefore, the employees should be prepared by the management well in advance to face the change as and when warranted. This may be done through bulletin boards, company magazines and newspapers, committee meetings, union-management meetings, broadcasting system and so forth. In this regard management's viewpoints should be reflected in HR policies.

Steps in Formulation of HR Policies

1. **Identify the areas:** The areas where HR policies are needed are to be identified. Important areas of HR like recruitment, selection, training, compensations must have specific policies clearly spelt out. If need arises, additional policies may have to be formulated for dealing with newer HR issues.

2. **Collecting data:** After selecting the areas, relevant information should be collected for facilitating policy formulation. The company's records, past practices, industry practices and top management policies should be studied. The organizational culture and employee aspirations should also be taken into account while formulating policies.
3. **Evaluating alternatives:** Once data have been collected, various alternative policies can be designed. Each alternative has to be evaluated in terms of their contribution towards the desired objectives. The policies should be for the betterment of the existing HR system and formulated in congruence with other organizational policies. The policies should be finalised after discussion with those people who are directly affected by its implementation.
4. **Communicating the policy:** The policy details should be conveyed to all the workers throughout the organization. Policy manual, in-house journals, notice boards, intranet, etc. can be used to create awareness among employees at various levels. Special communication programmes can be conducted to inform all the concerned people about the new policy.
5. **Evaluation of the policy:** Policies should be evaluated regularly at periodic intervals to ascertain their effectiveness. The actual policy results should be compared with predetermined standards to check if the policy was successful in achieving its objectives. Policies may be reviewed at the organizational level, or outside experts may be invited to review it. Assessment of existing policies is especially important during crises like labour strikes, lock outs, mass employee grievances, labour union unrest, etc. It is also necessary when company plans to bring about large scale changes like expansion, diversification, adoption of new technology, etc.

HR policies should be designed to promote common interest, create safe and healthy working conditions, give proper recognition for work and accomplishment, recognize impact of change on people, encourage employees' participation and recognize the functions and responsibilities of the trade unions.

QUESTIONS

1. What are HR policies?
2. Describe the principles of HR policies.
3. Give the importance of HR policies.
4. Explain the steps in formulation of HR policies.
5. Why are HR policies important for the firm?

NOTES

1. Edwin B. Flippo. *Personnel Management.* McGraw-Hill, Kogakusha Co. Ltd., Tokyo, 1976, p. 84.
2. James B. Bambrick. "Developing Workable Personnel Policies" in *The Personnel Man and His Job*. D.B. Taraporevala & Sons, Bombay, 1967, p. 88.

Chapter 3

Human Resource Planning

Human resource planning (HRP) is the first step in the HRM process. HRP is the process by which an organization ensures that it has the right number and kind of people, at the right place, at the right time, capable of effectively and efficiently completing those tasks that will help the organization achieve its overall objectives. HRP translates the organization's objectives and plans into the number of workers needed to meet those objectives.[1] The actual HRM process starts with the estimation of the number and kind of people required by the organization for the coming period. HRP is also known by other names such as 'Manpower Planning', 'Employment Planning', 'Labour Planning', 'Personnel Planning', etc. HRP is a sub-system in the total organizational planning. In other words, HRP is derived from the organizational planning just like production planning, sales planning, material planning, etc.

Need and Importance of HRP

The following points highlight the need and importance of HRP in the organizations:

1. **Assessing future personnel needs:** Whether it is surplus labour or labour shortage, it gives a picture of defective planning or absence of planning in an organization. A number of organizations, especially public sector units (PSUs) in India are facing the problem of surplus labour.

It is the result of surplus labour that the companies later on offer schemes like Voluntary Retirement Scheme (VRS) to eliminate surplus staff. Thus, it is better to plan well about employees in advance. Through HRP, one can ensure the employment of proper number and type of personnel.

2. **Foundation for other HRM functions:** HRP is the first step in all HRM functions. So, HRP provides the essential information needed for the other HRM functions like recruitment, selection, training and development, promotion, etc.
3. **Coping with change:** Changes in the business environment like competition, technology, government guidelines, global market, etc. bring changes in the nature of the job. This means changes in the demand of personnel, content of job, qualification and experience needed. HRP helps the organization in adjusting to new changes.
4. **Investment perspective:** As a result of change in the mindset of management, investment in human resources is viewed as a better concept in the long run success of the enterprise. Human assets can increase in value as opposed to physical assets. Thus, HRP is considered important for the proper planning of future employees.
5. **Expansion and diversification plans:** During the expansion and diversification drives, more employees at various levels are needed. Through proper HRP, an organization comes to know about the exact requirement of personnel in future plans.
6. **Employee turnover:** Every organization suffers from the small turnover of labour, some time or the other. This is high among young graduates in the private sector. This necessitates again doing manpower planning for further recruiting and hiring.
7. **Conformity with government guidelines:** In order to protect the weaker sections of the society, the Indian Government has prescribed some norms for

organizations to follow. For example, reservations for SC/ST, BC, physically handicapped, ex-servicemen, etc. in the jobs. While planning for fresh candidates, HR manager takes into consideration all the Government guidelines.

8. **International expansion strategies:** International expansion strategies of an organization depend upon HRP. Under International Human Resource Management (IHRM), HRP becomes more challenging. An organization may want to fill the foreign subsidiary's key positions from its home country employees or from host-country or from a third country. All this demands very effective HRP.
9. **Having highly talented manpower inventory:** Due to changing business environment, jobs have become more challenging and there is an increasing need for dynamic and ambitious employees to fill the positions. Efficient HRP is needed for attracting and retaining well qualified, highly skilled and talented employees.

Objectives of HRP

The main objectives of HRP are:

(i) Proper assessment of human resources needs in future.

(ii) Anticipation of deficient or surplus manpower and taking the corrective action.

(iii) To create a highly talented workforce in the organization.

(iv) To protect the weaker sections of the society.

(v) To manage the challenges in the organization due to modernization, restructuring and re-engineering.

(vi) To facilitate the realization of the organization's objectives by providing right number and types of personnel.

(vii) To reduce the costs associated with personnel by proper planning.

(viii) To determine the future skill requirements of the organization.

(ix) To plan careers for individual employee.

(x) Providing a better view of HR dimensions to top management.

(xi) Determining the training and development needs of employees.

Factors Affecting HRP

1. **Type and strategy of organization:** The nature and scale of organization determines the number and type of human resources required at the managerial and supervisory levels. In case of a manufacturing organization, there will be requirement of more employees as compared to a service organization. Similarly, HRP depends upon the organization's strategy also. If an organization wants to adopt the strategy of internal growth, then more personnel are required. On the other hand, in case of Mergers and Acquisitions (M&As), HR manager must make plans regarding lay-offs, retrenchment, etc. In determining the breadth of the plan, organization can choose a narrow focus by planning in just one or two areas of HR like recruitment and selection. Otherwise, it can choose a broad focus by planning in all HR areas including training and development, compensation, maintenance, etc.
2. **Organizational growth cycles and planning:** Various stages of organizational growth cycles influence the HRP. In the inception stage of the organization, there may not be any personnel planning. When the organization enters the growth stage, then HR forecasting becomes necessary. More people are needed. When an organization becomes mature then growth slows down. There is less flexibility and more formalized plans are there. Organization may be planning about issues like retirement, etc. In the last stage, i.e. the declining stage, the focus of HRP is different. Here, planning is done about lay-offs, retrenchment and offering VRS.

3. **Environmental uncertainties:** An organization does not operate in isolation. Environmental factors such as economic, political, socio-cultural, international conditions, etc. affect all organizations and thus HRP. All this necessitates changes to be made while formulating recruitment, selection and training and development programmes.
4. **Time horizons:** Time factor also affects HRP. Planning about human resources will be different in case of a short-term period (ranging from six months to one year) and in case of a long-term plan (which spread from three to ten years).
5. **Nature of jobs being filled:** Vacancies in the organization may be due to retirement, promotion, transfer, demotion, expansion and diversification decisions. HR manager should be well aware in advance regarding the nature of job. For example, it is relatively easy to fill the vacancies of low-level workers than any managerial position.
6. **Off-loading the work:** Off-loading the work to outside parties through outsourcing, etc. is a regular feature in today's business environment. Thus, it affects decisions like further hiring, offering VRS to surplus labour, etc.

Steps in HRP Process

1. **Analysis of organization's objectives and plans:** Firstly, the HR manager should consider the organization's overall objectives and policies as the HRM objectives are derived from them. HR plans should be aligned with the organization's plans for the success of the organization. Consideration of the factors such as time period, organization's strategic decisions (e.g. growth through M&As or internal growth), flexibility, formality, etc. should be taken into account while formulating HR plans. The ultimate mission or purpose is to relate future human resources to future enterprise need so as to maximize the future return on investment in human resources.[2]

2. **Analysis of HR requirements:** Manpower requirement can be analyzed with the help of information provided by existing job analysis and job design information and future business objectives. The analysis can be divided into 2 parts:

   (a) *Demand forecasting*: It is the process of estimating organization's future quantity and quality of people required. Overall business plans and annual budgets act as a base for demand forecasting. Various other environmental factors are also considered while forecasting such as expansion and growth, management philosophy, business forecasts, government policy, competition, etc.

   The various forecasting techniques are:

   (i) *Managerial judgement*: This is one of the simplest forecasting techniques. In this, the managers judge about the future demand of the personnel. Managers who are experienced, well-acquainted with the requirements of jobs like workload, ability of employees, future capability, etc. discuss together and reach the figure of demand of labour. After the estimation, the lower level managers submit their requirement to the higher level managers for consideration and revision if necessary.

   (ii) *Delphi technique*: In this, estimates of personnel needs are obtained with the help of group of experts. The HR manager obtains the responses from experts and re-considers them and reports back to the experts. Again, the feedback is obtained from the experts through survey method. This technique is considered as qualitative demand forecasting technique.

   (iii) *Work study techniques*: These techniques are more suitable where there is a possibility of work measurement. This is also called as workload analysis. In this, the volume of workload for the forthcoming years are analyzed and on this basis, analysis of personnel requirement is done. Allowances are also made for absenteeism, idle time, labour turnover, etc.

(iv) *Ratio-trend analysis*: In this technique, the past ratios are studied and future ratios are forecast after making some allowances for changes. Availability of past records and estimate of future changes is essential for using this technique.

(b) *Supply forecasting*: Demand forecasting provides the HR manager the estimation of number and type of personnel required. Supply forecast provides information regarding the ability of organization to procure the required number of personnel. It is concerned with the availability of personnel from within and outside an organization. The supply forecast includes:

(i) *HR audits*: This analyses the present employees' skills and abilities. The audits of managers are known as management inventories whereas those of non-managers are called as skill inventories. This gives the HR planners a detailed summary of the capabilities available in the organization.

(ii) *Analysis of internal supply*: The internal supply of labour is affected by the following factors—absenteeism, employee turnover, promotions and productivity. Absenteeism refers to unauthorized absence from the work. In other words, it is the failure of a person to come to work when he is scheduled to work. Turnover is the rate of displacement of the personnel employed due to resignation, retirement, etc. Turnover refers to the movement into and out of an organization by the workforce. It affects the stability of workforce. The productivity levels of the employees also influence HR requirements. Rise in productivity of personnel will reduce the requirement and *vice-versa*. Promotions and transfer of employees from one position to another too will impact the internal availability.

(iii) *Analysis of external supply*: Along with the internal supply analysis, there is a need to look for the prospective employees from the external sources. It is important to have new blood and new experience in the organization. There are numerous sources of external supply such as universities, technical and management institutes, etc.

3. **Development and implementation of HR plans:** After the demand and supply forecast of the personnel, the next logical step is to obtain and maintain a balance between these two. This will ensure that organization fills up its vacancies with the right number and right kind of employees at the right time. This is done by developing HR programmes and implementing them. Implementation refers to converting HR plans into action. As a part of HR plan implementation, there may be series of actions to be taken. Depending upon the situation, programmes like recruitment, selection, training and development, retention, etc. are planned. Planning depends upon the situation. For example, if there is a situation of surplus labour in the organization, then management would not go for fresh hiring but offer schemes like VRS to its employees and plan gradually about retrenchment. On the other hand, if there is a situation of shortage of employees then the organization can proceed for fresh recruitment, hire full-time and contractual employees, ask for overtime, etc.
4. **Control and review:** This is the final phase of HRP process. HRP needs considerable amount of financial resources along with staff and time. Thus, an HR plan should have set targets to be achieved. Regular monitoring will reveal the deficiencies in HR plan so that corrective action should be taken well in time.

Quantitative and Qualitative Dimensions of Human Resource Planning

Human resources have a dual role to play in the economic development of a country. On one hand they are the consumers of the products and services produced by the organizations while on the other hand they are one of the factors of production. Along with capital and other factors of production, human resources can lead to increase in production and economic development. The rate of growth of human resources is determined by two aspects—quantitative and qualitative.

Variables Determining the Quantity of Human Resources

1. **Population policy**: Some population policies operate by influencing the factors responsible for growth such as fertility, marriage and mortality. These are known as population influencing policies. Another category of policies known as responsive policies are implemented to adjust to observed population trends with the help of programmes like health, nutrition, education, housing, etc. The aim of population policies is to achieve an optimum population for enhancing the country's development.
2. **Population structure:** The structure or composition of the population is determined by two factors, sex composition and age composition.
   (i) *Sex composition*: Sex ratio is the ratio of males to females in the population. It is the basic measure of the sex composition of the population of any area. Higher the number of females, higher will be the population growth rate in future.
   (ii) *Age composition*: It is the distribution of population by age groups. Age composition is the result of past trends in fertility and mortality. The supply of labour depends on age composition as economically active population falls in range of 15-65 age groups.

3. **Migration:** Net migration is another factor which causes changes in the population. Age and sex composition determine the natural growth in population, but for calculating the overall changes in population it is important to consider net migration also.

   Net migration = total immigrants – total emigrants

   A positive net migration will lead to a rise in population growth rate while negative net migration will reduce the growth rate of population. Migration can be both inter-regional and international.
4. **Labour force participation:** The population of any country consists of workers and non-workers. The workers are the people, usually in age group of 15-65, who participate in economically productive activities by their mental or physical presence. These include:
   - Employers,
   - Employees,
   - Self-employed persons, and
   - Those engaged in family enterprises without pay.

The others in the population are the non-workers such as students, infants, elderly, beggars, retired people, inmates of jail or mental institutions, unemployed, etc. They do not contribute to any productive economic activity. It is the changes in the working population which affect the growth of human resources. The number of people who are unemployed but available for work also impacts the availability of labour.

Qualitative Aspects of Human Resource Planning

The quantitative dimensions help to ascertain human resources in numbers while the productive power of human resources is assessed by the qualitative dimensions. For example, there may be hundreds of applicants for 20 vacancies, but out of these only a few may meet the quality standards required for the job. Factors which determine the quality of human resources are:

1. **Education and training:** The quantity and quality of education and training received by human resources

impacts their knowledge and skills. Education and training are important for the upliftment of both individual and society. It can be of two types, formal and informal. Formal education is imparted through schools and colleges while informal education and training takes place through on-the-job training methods. Formal education stresses the transfer of theoretical knowledge, while informal education emphasizes on practical application of knowledge.

2. **Health and nutrition:** Health and nutrition along with education are vital for Human Resource Development. Health and nutrition impact the quality of life, productivity of labour and the average life expectancy.

   Health status is determined by:

   - Purchasing power of people.
   - Public sanitation, climate and availability of medical facilities.
   - People's understanding and knowledge of health, hygiene and nutrition.

3. **Equality of opportunity:** Not all segments of people comprising human resources get equal employment opportunities. There is bound to be some discrimination. The most common forms of discrimination are:

   (i) *Social discrimination*: Discrimination on basis of gender, religion or social standing.

   (ii) *Economic discrimination*: Discrimination based on financial positions or possession of wealth by the sections of workforce.

   (iii) *Regional discrimination*: These are in form of discrimination between rural and urban population or between people belonging to different regions/states.

Discrimination affects the quality and productivity of the human resources belonging to different sections of the population. The privileged classes get access to best education, nutrition and health facilities while underprivileged are deprived of their right share in the development process. For the overall, well rounded development of the country's human resources, effective policies need to be implemented to deal with the problem of discrimination.[3]

Prerequisites for Successful HRP

1. There should be a proper linkage between HR plan and organizational plan.
2. Top management support is essential.
3. Proper balance should be kept between the qualitative and quantitative approaches to HRP.
4. Involvement of operating managers is necessary.
5. Proper alignment between short-term HR plans and long-term HR plans should be there.
6. HR plan should have in-built flexibility in order to adopt environmental uncertainties.
7. Time period of HR plan should be appropriate to needs and circumstances of the organization.

QUESTIONS

1. What do you mean by HRP and why is it important?
2. What are the factors that affect HRP?
3. Explain in detail the steps in the process of HRP.
4. How do population structure and migration policy impact the quantity of labour force available?
5. Write a note on the qualitative aspects of HRP.
6. What are the prerequisites for successful HRP?

NOTES

1. David A. Decenzo and Stephen P. Robbins. *Personnel/HRM*, Third Edition. Prentice Hall of India, New Delhi, 1989, p. 79.
2. A.F. Sikula. *Personnel Administration and Human Resource Development*, 1978, p. 148.
3. http://www.egyankosh.ac.in/bitstream/123456789/35832/1/MTM2-02.pdf

Chapter 4

Job Analysis—Job Description and Job Specification

Job analysis is a systematic procedure for securing and reporting the information which defines a specific job. It determines the qualifications required for a job, provides guidance in recruitment and selection, evaluates current employees for transfer or promotion and establishes the requirements for training programmes. It is a foundation for job evaluation. It helps in employee development by means of appraisal and counselling. By establishing improved methods of analyzing problems of health, safety and fatigue, it functions as a guide in connection with discipline and grievances and as a basis for transfers, lay-offs and comparison of the pay rates obtaining in other organizations. It establishes workloads and job assignments.[1]

It helps in redesigning the jobs to improve operational performance or to enrich job content and employee improvement. Managers may develop ways of providing their employees an increased sense of personal accomplishment and control over themselves and their work.

Job Analysis produces four kinds of documentation and procedures crucial to HR activities:

(i) Job descriptions;
(ii) Job specifications;
(iii) Job evaluation; and
(iv) HR assessment.

These are basic inputs for diverse HR functions.

Job Analysis

Job analysis is a procedure by which pertinent information is obtained about a job. It is a detailed and systematic study of information relating to the operations and responsibilities of a specific job.[2] Job analysis includes job description, job specification and job design.

(i) **Job description:** It is a written record of the duties, responsibilities and requirements of a particular job. According to W.D. Scott, "Job description is concerned with the job itself and not with the work."[3] It is a statement describing the job in such terms as its title, location, duties, working conditions and hazards. It tells us what is to be done, how it is to be done, and why it is to be done. It is a standard of function. It defines the appropriate and authorized contents of a job.

(ii) **Job specification:** It is the standard which designates the qualities required for an acceptable performance. It is a written record of the requirements sought from an individual worker for a given job. It refers to a summary of the personal characteristics required for a job. It is a statement of the minimum acceptable human qualities necessary for the proper performance of a job.

(iii) **Job design:** It is the division of the total task to be performed into the manageable and efficient units—positions, departments and divisions—and to provide for their proper integration. The sub-division of work is both on a horizontal scale with different tasks across the organization being performed by different people; and on the vertical scale, in which higher levels of the organization are responsible for the supervision of more people, the coordination of sub-groups, more complex planning, etc.

Job Analysis is a procedure and a tool for determining the specified tasks, operations and requirements of each job. It refers to the anatomy of the job. It is a complete study of the job, embodying every known and determinable factor, including the duties and responsibilities involved in its performance, the conditions under which the performance is carried on, the nature of the task, the qualities required in the worker, and such conditions of employment as pay, hours of duty, opportunities and privileges. Job analysis is the methodical compilation and study of work data in order to define and characterize each occupation in such a manner as to distinguish it from all others. It also emphasizes the relationship of one job with others in the organization.

Contents of Job Analysis

The basic data provided by the job analysis is classified under the suitable sub-heads. Dale Yoder has classified these sub-heads as follows:

(i) The job identification, its title and code number, etc.

(ii) Distinctive features of the job, like its location, physical setting supervision, hazards and discomforts, if any.

(iii) Duties and responsibilities of the workers.

(iv) What materials and equipment are needed?

(v) How the job is performed.

(vi) Required personal qualities.

(vii) Job relationship.

Procedure of Job Analysis

1. **Collection of factual material:** Various approaches are utilized in studying a job and the four most popular are (i) Questionnaires, (ii) narrative descriptions, (iii) observations, and (iv) interviews.

   Two types of information are collected, i.e. (i) information regarding job such as its physical environment (temperature, noise, dirt, comforts and dangers, etc.), its social environment (whether job is in teams, shifts or isolated), financial conditions (wages, bonus, incentive schemes or fringe benefits, etc.), and (ii) information relating to qualities of person holding the job, i.e. his physical demands (muscular energy, hours of work, travel, etc.), intellectual demands (university, technical or professional degrees and problems solving abilities required), skills, experience and personality factors required on the job.

2. **Completion of job description:** After collecting information, the job analyst puts it in a standard job description form as a comprehensive draft. It is a statement showing full details of the activities of the job. Separate job description forms may be used for various activities in the job and may be compiled later on. The job analysis forms may be used as references for the future.
3. **Job specification:** Job specifications are prepared on the basis of information collected. It is a statement of minimum acceptable qualities of the person to be placed on job. It specifies the standard by which the qualities of the person are measured. Job analyst prepares such statements taking into consideration the skills required in performing the job properly. This statement is used in selecting a person matching with the job.
4. **Preparation of report:** On the basis of the information collected mentioning the analysis of various activities on the job and qualities of the individual to be placed on the job, the analyst prepares a report. Such report will be presented before the supervisor and the HR manager for suggestions and comments. The analyst should revise the original report in the light of the suggestions or comments given by the supervisor or the HR manager to make it more correct and informative.
5. **Preparation of final draft:** The complete draft presented by the analyst and approved by the supervisor and HR manager may now be received by the top executive. The office-bearers of the trade unions may also be taken into confidence before approving the draft finally. If union officials have ideas for making changes, the management should consider them as suggestions and incorporate them in the job description and job specification. The

final draft should be approved by the top line executive or by the HR manager who is responsible for making final decisions on the matter.

Significance of Job Analysis

1. **Facilitates manpower planning:** Job analysis is the qualitative aspect of manpower requirements. It determines the demands of the job in terms of responsibilities and duties and then translates these demands into skills, qualities and other human attributes. It determines the quantum of work which an average person can perform on the job in a day. It facilitates the division of work into different jobs. Thus, it is an essential element of manpower planning as it matches jobs with men.
2. **Helps recruitment, selection and placement:** In order to hire the right person on a job, it is essential to know the requirements of the job and the qualities of the individual who will perform it. The information regarding these is procured from job description and job specifications respectively. These help the management in matching the job requirements as closely as possible with workers' aptitudes, abilities, interests, etc. It facilitates the execution of employment programme.
3. **Determines training and development needs:** Job analysis determines the levels of standards of job performance. It helps in administering the training development programmes. Job descriptions and job specifications are written documents. If the contents of these two documents are known to the employees, they will try to acquire the skills and knowledge required to perform the task assigned to them efficiently. They may also prepare themselves for the higher post in the light of the job description and the job specifications. The same information may be used by those who administer the training and development programmes for determining the contents and subject matter needed in such programmes.

4. **Determines job evaluation:** Job evaluation aims at determining the relative worth of the job which helps in determining the compensation of job. These jobs are evaluated in terms of money. An accurate and comprehensive set of job descriptions and the job specifications forms of factual basis for evaluating the worth of the job.
5. **Provides data for performance appraisal:** Job analysis data provide a clear-cut standard of performance for every job. The performance of employee can be appraised objectively with the standard of job performance so established. A supervisor may very easily compare the contribution of each man with the set standards.
6. **Helps job designing:** Industrial engineers may use the job analysis information in designing the job by making the comprehensive study of the job elements. It helps in time and motion study, work-specifications, methods and workplace improvement and work-measurement. Human engineering activities such as physical, mental and psychological actions are studied with the help of job analysis information.
7. **Ensures safety and health:** The job analysis process uncovers the hazardous and unhealthy environmental factors such as heat, noise, fumes, dust, etc. related with the jobs. The management may take corrective measures to minimize the chances of risks to ensure safety to workers and avoid unhealthy conditions.
8. **Maintains discipline:** Job analysis provides the information regarding characteristics of various jobs and the job-holders. It studies the failure of the workman to meet the required standard of performance. Corrective measures may be taken in time to avoid untoward situations. In this way it helps in maintaining the discipline in the industry.

Methods of Gathering Information

1. **Questionnaire or survey method:** In this method a questionnaire is prepared to get the job information

and it is circulated among all job holders. The questionnaire asks the job holder to supply the several types of information sought in job analysis. It may, in addition, ask the immediate supervisor to examine and comment on the replies provided by the job holders. No single questionnaire is appropriate for all types of jobs. However, most of them follow an outline that first identifies the job, seeks information on the principal tasks involved and then ask questions design to discover the mental skill and physical requirements of a satisfactory job holder.

2. **Interview method:** In this method the job analyst interviews the job holders and asks questions from them while observing the following rules:
   (i) Interview should be taken in leisure time.
   (ii) Job analyst must introduce himself to the job holder first and tell him the purpose of the interview.
   (iii) Job analyst must take an interest in job holder and his work.
   (iv) He must concentrate on the job and not on the HR matters.
   (v) The job holder should be motivated to speak more.
   (vi) As far as possible, the atmosphere of interview must remain congenial and conversation must be held in the language of the job holder.
   (vii) An average job holder should be selected for interview. The information will not be useful if the best job holder is contacted.
3. **Observation method:** Here the job analyst observes the work and worker while the worker is involved with the work. An experienced and expert analyst combines interviewing and on-the-job observation to provide a more accurate analysis than is usually secured by the use of either one of the methods.
4. **Record method:** Various types of job information are collected from the old records of the HR department.

The job analyst goes through the records and notes the relevant aspects of job details.

5. **Individual psychographic method:** In this method, the mental peculiarities of an individual successful in a particular kind of job are examined, and a list of these peculiarities is compiled. This list is transcribed in a graph. This provides some standard of judgement in future recruitments for the same job.
6. **Job psychographic method:** According to Viteles, the following three things are essential for the job psychographic method:
   (i) Accurate classification of mental qualities required for the job.
   (ii) Valid method of evaluation.
   (iii) Direct examination or analysis by trained examiners. In this method, some specialist analysts study the work, and they evolve a valid and standard method of evaluation. They prepare a very accurate list in which the various mental qualities required for the job are properly and reliably classified. A graph of these qualities is prepared so that selection of candidates for the job may become easier.
7. **Job analysis by test:** In the test method, some reliable and valid tests are performed on the basis of essential qualities and abilities; the candidates are tested for selection and suitability on the basis of these tests.
8. **Motion study method:** Under this method, the speed of an individual worker in performing some job and time consumed therein are both noted. Similar examinations being performed on other individuals doing the same work, and the results obtained are compared. Such a study of speed and time helps in job analysis and classification of the workers.

Job Description

Job description is an important document that is descriptive in nature. It contains a statement of job analysis. It provides both organizational information such as location in structure, authority, etc. and functional information (what the work is). It defines the scope of job activities, major responsibilities, and positioning of the job in the organization. It provides the worker, analyst, and supervisor with a clear idea of what the worker must do to meet the demands of the job. Job description describes the jobs, and not the job holders. According to Edwin B. Flippo, "The first and immediate product of the job analysis is the job description. As its title indicates, this document is basically descriptive in nature and constitutes a record of existing and pertinent job facts."

Contents of Job Description

1. **Proper job title:** The job title should be short, definite and suggestive of the nature of the job. The desirable qualities of job holder should be clear from the title so that every job can be distinguished from one another. Commerce and industry nomenclature, wherever applicable should always be used while phrasing meaningful job titles.
2. **Job summary:** The findings of the job analysis should be descriptively summarised so that all the necessary facts are incorporated in paragraphs to make it convenient to identify the job. Primary, secondary and other duties to be performed on the job should also be indicated clearly.
3. **Job location:** Job location should be given in the description. It is where, i.e. in what department the job is to be performed.
4. **Duties and responsibilities:** The duties and responsibilities to be performed on the job, arranged in a chronological order with proper classification of duties should be clearly written in the job description. Time taken in performing the job and sub-jobs should also be mentioned.
5. **Degree of supervision:** Certain jobs like unskilled work require close supervision while other jobs like skilled or

supervisory or managerial jobs require less supervision or no supervision. The degree of supervision required on each job should be mentioned in job description.

6. **Requirement of machines, tools and materials:** The machines, tools, equipment and materials required in the performance of each job should also be included in job description to indicate the nature and complexity of the job and help to devise the training programmes.
7. **Description of relation to other jobs:** The job is described in relation to other jobs. This helps to explain the vertical relationship of promotion and horizontal relationship of work flow and procedures.
8. **Description of working conditions:** The working conditions, the job hazards and physical surroundings within the working area should be described. It will be helpful in job evaluation.
9. **Description of amendments:** Job description should be elastic enough so as to incorporate all necessary amendments from time to time to make it up-to-date.
10. **Mention of policies:** The policies for the job holders should be mentioned in the job description.

Uses of Job Description

Job description helps the management in the following:

(i) Job grading and classification.

(ii) Transfers and promotions.

(iii) Adjustments of grievances.

(iv) Defining and outlining promotional steps.

(v) Establishing a common understanding of a job between employers and employees.

(vi) Investigating accidents.

(vii) Indicating faulty work procedures or duplication of papers.

(viii) Maintaining, operating and adjusting machinery.

(ix) Time and motion studies.

(x) Defining the limits of authority.

(xi) Indicating the case of personal merit.

(xii) Facilitating job placement.

(xiii) Studies of health and fatigue.

(xiv) Scientific guidance.

(xv) Determining jobs suitable for occupational therapy.

(xvi) Providing hiring specifications.

(xvii) Providing performance indicators.

Job description helps top executives in jointly discussing one another's responsibilities. Overlapping or confusion can then be pointed out, questions can be raised about the major thrust of each position, and problems of structure can be identified. A job description becomes a vehicle for organizational change and improvement. Some companies have more than one job description for each job. A detailed version may be used in training and in evaluating a job, while a shorter version may be used in planning and hiring of management.

Job Specification

Job specification translate the job description into terms of the human qualifications which are required for a successful performance of a job. They are intended to serve as a guide in job evaluation. As a guide in hiring, they deal with such characteristics as are available in an application blank, with testing, interviews and checking of references. It gives information about what kind of person is to be recruited and for what qualities he should be tested. According to Dale Yoder, "The job specification...as such a summary, popularly described is thus a specialised job description, emphasising personnel requirement and designed especially to facilitate selection and placement."

The items to be included in job specifications vary according to the nature of an organization and the uses to which they are put. However, some items like age, sex, experience, skills, education and personality are invariably included in job specifications. The HR department coordinates the writing of job descriptions and job specifications and secures agreement on the qualifications required.

These specifications relate to the following:

1. **Physical characteristics:** These include health, strength, endurance, age range, body size, height, weight, vision, voice, poise, eye-hand and foot coordination, motor coordination and colour discrimination.
2. **Psychological characteristics:** These include such qualities as manual dexterity, mechanical aptitude, ingenuity, judgement, resourcefulness, analytical ability, mental concentration and alertness.
3. **Personal characteristics or traits of temperament:** These include personal appearance, good and pleasing manners, emotional stability, aggressiveness or submissiveness, extroversion or introversion, leadership, cooperativeness, initiative and drive, skills in dealing with others, unusual sensory qualities of sight, smell, hearing, adaptability, conversational ability, etc.
4. **Responsibilities:** These include supervision of others, responsibility for production, process and equipment, responsibility for the safety of others, responsibility for generating confidence and trust, responsibility for preventing monetary loss, etc.
5. **Other features:** These include features like age, sex, education, experience, etc.

Job specifications are based on the educated guesses of supervisors and HR managers. They give their opinion as to who they think should be considered for a job in terms of education, intelligence, training, etc. Both job description and job specification are important interrelated components of job analysis. They serve as a basis for scientific selection, promotion, training and development programmes. A job description is the standard description of the job, while a job specification is the main specification. Job description tells what is to be done and what is the nature of the job, while job specification tells us what qualities are needed in the prospective job holder.

QUESTIONS

1. Define job analysis. What are its various components?
2. Give the significance of job analysis to the organization.
3. What are the various methods through which data can be collected for job analysis?
4. What are the uses of job description?
5. Write a short note on job specifications.

NOTES

1. R. Calhoon. *Managing the Personnel*, 1964, p. 133.
2. Edwin Flippo. *Personnel Management*, 1980, Fifth ed., p. 110.
3. W.D. Scott, R.C. Clothier and W.R. Spriegel. *Personnel Management*. New Delhi, 1977, Sixth ed., p. 127.

Chapter 5

Job Design

Job design is the process of organizing work into the tasks required to perform a specific job.[1] It involves the conscious efforts to organize tasks, duties and responsibilities into a unit of work to achieve certain objectives. An HR manager should have a keen interest in the design and specification of individual jobs within the organization. The jobs should be designed in such a way that it motivates the employees to execute it in the best possible manner. Excessive specialization and mechanization have made many jobs repetitive and boring, employees performing such dull jobs tend to tire easily. Therefore it is important to design jobs properly so as to increase employee motivation and performance.

Job designs that increase employee access, comfort and flexibility are likely to influence motivation and productivity positively. Job design specifies the work content, i.e. tasks and functions, methods of work, the skills, knowledge and abilities required for performing the jobs, the interrelationship between the jobs, and the rewards the employees will get on the completion of the job.

Principles of Job Design

The main principles of job design are as follows:

1. To influence skill variety, provide opportunities for people to do several tasks and combine tasks.

2. To influence task identity, combine tasks and form natural work units.
3. To influence task significance, form natural work units and inform people of the importance of their work.
4. To encourage autonomy, give people responsibility for determining their own working systems.
5. To influence feedback, establish good relationships and open feedback channels.[2]

Objectives of Job Design

Repetitive and dull jobs that are poorly designed lead to employee dissatisfaction, lower productivity, absenteeism, boredom, insecurity and related issues. A good job design aims to solve this problem by structuring jobs in a way that adds meaning to them so that employees derive maximum job satisfaction from them. The main objectives of job design are:

1. To increase productivity and technical efficiency of employees.
2. To design a job that is psychologically satisfying to the employees.
3. To align the needs of the individual employees with the organizational requirements.

Factors Affecting Job Design

The factors which affect job design can be put into three broad categories: environmental factors, organizational factors, and behavioural factors.

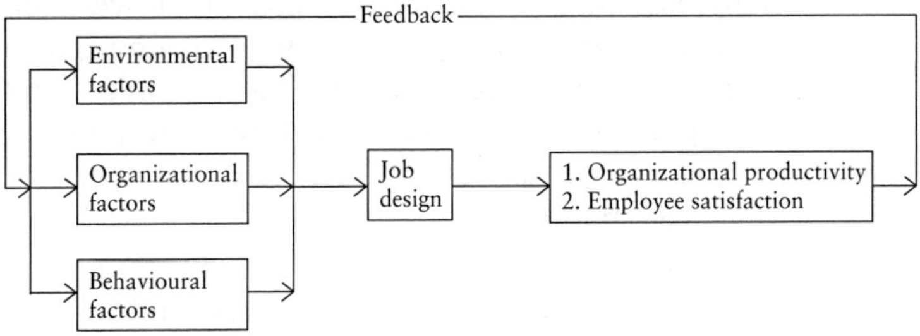

Source: Adapted from *Human Resources and Personnel Management* by William B. Werther and Keith Davis. McGraw-Hill, New York, 1993, p. 147.

1. **Environmental Factors**
   (i) *Availabilities and abilities of employees*: There should be a proper match between efficiency consideration and availability and abilities of employees.
   (ii) *Expectations from the job*: People have lots of expectations from a job and thus the jobs must be designed in order to meet employees' expectations, for example, social and cultural expectations. This includes rest breaks, religious beliefs, vacations, etc.
2. **Organizational Factors**
   (i) *Work flow analysis*: It seeks to ensure that each job in the organization receives as an input, adds value to that work and then passes it on to another worker. During work flow analysis, sometimes a few steps or even jobs are simplified or combined or even eliminated. Work is organized in a manner to meet the organizational production or service goals.
   (ii) *Organization structure*: Individual jobs must be properly fit in the overall organization structure. For example, the autonomous work teams may do well in the decentralized organization rather than the centralized one.
   (iii) *Business strategy*: Overall corporate strategy also influences job designing. For example, emphasis on highly specialized jobs involves more division of labour.
   (iv) *Organizational climate*: It also influences job design. Groups may function well in an atmosphere that encourages participation, job enrichment and autonomous work, while teams may not thrive in an enterprise with an autocratic top-down approach to managerial leadership.
   (v) *Ergonomics*: Ergonomics is the science of adapting working conditions to employee safety and comfort needs. In this, a balance is sought between employee's physical abilities and job requirements.

(vi) *Characteristics of task*: Job design may require the assembly of a number of tasks into a job or a group of jobs. There may be a single main task for an individual to carry out or a variety of task functions divided among team members.

(vii) *Work practices*: These are set ways to perform the work. Work practices may develop from the traditional way of doing work. This limits the job design. Especially when such practices are a part of trade union management relationship.

3. **Behavioural Factors**

(i) *Employee needs*: People having growth and development needs want to have jobs with greater responsibilities, whereas, people having social needs prefer to work in groups/teams.

(ii) *Variety*: There should be variety in jobs, otherwise the employees will get bored.

(iii) *Feedback*: Employees must get regular feedback regarding their job performance. This will motivate them to do better in future.

(iv) *Autonomy*: It refers to freedom to control one's activities. Jobs that give workers authority to make decisions will provide added responsibilities which tend to increase the employee's sense of recognition and self-esteem.

(v) *Abilities*: Individuals must utilize their abilities to the fullest while doing the job. The individual and collective abilities of the employees play an important role in how the jobs are designed.

Techniques of Job Design

Techniques of job design refer to the ways in which the jobs can be restructured and redesigned to enhance the workers' efficiency. Following are some approaches to job design:

1. **Work simplification:** In this technique, work is broken down into simple and repetitive tasks that maximize

efficiency. It standardises the tasks enabling the worker to produce a larger amount of products. Work simplification is appropriate in a stable business environment but is less effective in a changing environment where there is great demand for customised products. But this approach often results in boredom and low job satisfaction.

2. **Job rotation:** It refers to systematic movement of workers from one job to another without disrupting the flow of work. For example, on an auto assembly line, a worker who normally installs carpets can be rotated periodically to a job involving installation of car seats. This technique relieves the employee from boredom, improves worker's skills and abilities, and makes the employee competent in other jobs as well. However, job rotation may not have much impact on employee enthusiasm.
3. **Job enlargement:** It refers to the expansion of job content to include a wider variety. It expands the duties involved in a job. In other words, additional same level activities are assigned to workers. For example, a proof-reader's job could be enlarged to include some elements of copy-editing as well. The philosophy behind this approach is that enlarged jobs will be more intrinsically satisfying to employees than highly specialized jobs. It is horizontal expansion of the job. Some research studies have shown that job enlargement results in reduced absenteeism and lower employee turnover and that greater involvement of employees motivates them. However, certain experts like Herzberg do not agree. According to him, job enlargement is simply "adding zero to zero".
4. **Job enrichment:** Job enrichment puts specialized tasks back together so that one person is responsible for producing a whole product or an entire service.[3] This approach tends to make jobs more interesting and improves employee motivation. Job enrichment refers to the vertical expansion of jobs. In an enriched job, tasks are so organized as to allow the worker to do a

complete activity. The employees are given a higher degree of autonomy and assigned more responsibility. They are given opportunities to provide feedback on their work and improve upon their performances. This is one technique that gives more freedom to workers, provides more scope for development and thus increases job satisfaction. But the successful implementation of this approach to job design is limited by the production technology and the capabilities of the employees who produce the product or service. The merits of job enrichment are improved morale and productivity, increased employee satisfaction, motivation, job involvement and performance and reduced employee turnover and absenteeism. However, job enrichment has limitations too. It involves considerable time and investment. Workers accord more importance to pay and job security rather than the interesting nature of the job. Moreover, it is not practically feasible to implement this technique in the production of goods and services involving a series of complex processes.

5. **Self-managing teams/autonomous work teams:** An autonomous or self-managing team is allocated an overall task. This technique shall focus on giving a team, rather than an individual, a whole and meaningful piece of work to do. Work teams are responsible for a whole work process. Team members plan, execute and control the work processes together. Highly effective teams are composed of groups of committed individuals who trust each other, have a clear sense of purpose about their work, and are effective communicators within and outside the team. In such teams, everyone is involved in the decision-making and planning progress in order to encourage wholehearted participation of each person in the work processes. For the success of a work team, managers should try to ensure that the following conditions are met:

   (i) Individual members have the necessary task related expertise to do their work;

(ii) The group is large enough to perform the work;

(iii) Members possess interpersonal as well as task skills; and

(iv) Membership is moderately diverse in terms of talents and perspectives.[4]

6. **High performance job design:** It involves setting up working groups in environments where high levels of performance are required. It originates from the principle of autonomous group working and develops an approach which enables groups to work effectively together in situations where the role of information is high. Here, operational flexibility is important, and therefore there is need for employees to gain and apply new skills quickly with minimum supervision. High performance work design requires the following steps.[5]

   (i) Management clearly defines what it needs in the form of new technology or methods of production and the results expected from its introduction.

   (ii) Multi-skilling is encouraged—that is, job demarcation lines are eliminated as far as possible and encouragement and training are provided for employees to acquire new skills.

   (iii) Equipment that can be used flexibly is selected and is laid out to allow freedom of movement and vision.

   (iv) Self-managed teams or autonomous working groups are established—each with around a dozen members and with full back-to-back responsibility for product assembly and testing, fault-finding and some maintenance.

   (v) Managers and team leaders adopt a supportive rather than an autocratic style.

   (vi) Support systems are provided for kit-marshalling and material supply, which help the teams to function effectively as productive units.

   (vii) Management sets goals and standards for success.

(viii) The new system is introduced with greater care by means of involvement and communication programmes.

(ix) Thorough training is carried out on the basis of an assessment of training needs.

(x) The payment system is specially designed keeping in mind the needs of employees along with those of the management.

(xi) Payment may be related to team performance (team pay) along with skill-based payment incentives for individuals.

(xii) Peer performance review process may be used which involves team members assessing one another's performance as well as the performance of the team as a whole.

Table 5.1: Positive and negative outcomes of each job design approach

Job Design Approach	*Positive Outcome*	*Negative Outcome*
1. Work simplification	Job is highly specialized so that less trained and lower paid workers can perform	Oversimplification results in boredom with risks of errors and resignation
2. Job rotation	High intrinsic rewards. Enhanced inter- departmental cooperation	Jobs do not improve. Workers may feel rootless and alienated
3. Job enlargement	Claims to have motivational impact	Merely adding one zero to another one—adding one boring task to another likely to be resisted by employees
4. Job enlargement	Increased motivation, reduced absenteeism, psychological needs of employees are met	People may dislike taking new responsibilities. Job enrichment, if not accompanied by other inputs, will fail to achieve its goals

(Contd...)

5. Autonomous work team	There is a greater involvement of employees in planning and decision-making	There is resistance from employees, unions and managers
6. High performance work design	Works in an environment with a high rate of innovation and operational freedom	May not work in large bureaucratic organizations

Source: Aswathappa, *Human Resource and Personnel Management*, Tata McGraw Hill, New Delhi, 2003, pp. 107-08.

QUESTIONS

1. Define job design. What are the principles of job design?
2. What are the various organizational factors influencing job design?
3. Write a note on job enrichment vs. job enlargement.
4. What is high performance job design? What are the steps involved in it?
5. Compare and contrast the various techniques of job design.
6. Which technique of job design is most successful in motivating employees to do better?

NOTES

1. Gomez-Mejia, Balkin and Cardy. *Managing Human Resources*. Third ed., Pearson Education, Delhi, 2003, p. 62.
2. Robertson and Smith. *Motivation and Job Design*, IPM, London.
3. E. Lawler. *High Involvement Management*. Jossey-Bass, San Francisco, CA.
4. Stephen P. Robbins. *Organizational Behaviour*. Tenth ed., Pearson Education, Delhi, 2004, p. 475.
5. D. Buchanan. "Job Enrichment is Dead: Long Live High Performance Work Design", *Personnel Management*. May 1987, pp. 40-43.

Chapter 6

Recruitment and Selection

Recruitment is the process by which a large number of prospective candidates are attracted by various methods to apply for the jobs. It is the process of searching for prospective employees and generating a pool of well qualified candidates for filling the job positions in the organization. The objective of recruitment is to attract a large number of potential candidates for the jobs available. It is considered as a 'positive' concept as compared to selection which is termed as 'negative' because selection tends to eliminate applicants, leaving only the best to be appointed. An organization should have a well-thought and well-laid recruitment policy before actual recruitment begins. A recruitment policy may involve a commitment to broad principles such as filling vacancies with the best-qualified individuals. It may embrace several issues such as extent of promotions and transfers from within, attitudes of enterprise in recruiting its old employees, opinion regarding workplace diversity, etc.

Features of a Good Recruitment Policy

1. It must be based on the organization's objectives, both short-term and long-terms.
2. Job analysis should take place well before recruitment.
3. It should clearly indicate the organization's attitude toward employment of and reservations for women, differently-abled, minorities, etc.

4. It should clearly lay down the long-term career plans for the workers.
5. It should clearly indicate the basis and extent of promotion in the organization.
6. It should indicate the preferred sources of recruitment.

Factors Affecting Recruitment

The factors affecting recruitment may be divided into two categories:

1. **Internal factors**
   (i) Organization's growth and expansion plans.
   (ii) Organization's human resource planning strategy.
   (iii) Recruitment policy of the organization.
   (iv) Cost involved in recruiting employees.
   (v) Organization's size.
   (vi) Role of trade unions.
   (vii) Organizational culture.
   (viii) Company's image.
   (ix) Company's operations.
   (x) Pay package of company.
   (xi) Quality of work life.
   (xii) Geographical spread of operations.
2. **External factors**
   (i) Socio-economic factors.
   (ii) Political and legal considerations like reservations of jobs for minorities.
   (iii) Supply and demand of specific skill in labour market.
   (iv) Employment rate.
   (v) Technological factors.
   (vi) Employment exchanges.

Sources of Recruitment

Recruitment sources can be divided into two groups—internal and external.

1. **Internal Sources**
   (i) *Current/present employees*: Many companies adopt the policy of informing the present employees first about job openings before going for other sources. This results in either promotion or transfer within the organization. However, it also automatically creates another job opening that has to be filled.
   (ii) *Former employees*: These are the persons who were once employees of the company, but were later separated due to resignations, lay-off, retirement, etc. The company may decide to recruit them again. These are safe hires as the employer already has experience with these people.
   (iii) *Referrals from current employees*: Sometimes the companies may allow the current employees to recommend new recruits. This is a good source, as the current employee knows both the company and his acquaintances (family member/friends) and hopefully would try to please both. Employees who are hired through referrals from current employees tend to stay with the organization longer and display greater loyalty and job satisfaction than employees who are recruited by other means.
   (iv) *Previous applicants*: Although not truly an internal source, a database of previous applicants can be maintained by the organization and these people can be contacted when a vacancy comes up.

Advantages of internal recruitment sources:

(i) It is less costly than the external recruiting.
(ii) It raises the morale of employees, as they are preferred than outsiders.
(iii) It promotes loyalty among the employees.
(iv) It provides a sense of job security and opportunities for advancement.
(v) As the present employees are fully acquainted with the company so training can be reduced.

(vi) It gives a sense of recognition for employees.

(vii) As the current employees are tried and tested people so it's easy to rely upon them.

(viii) Internal recruiting has trade union support also.

(ix) It enhances company's social responsibility image.

(x) The company is in a better position to evaluate the performance of present employees before considering them for promotions, thus reducing labour turnover, etc.

(xi) Internal recruiting helps retention.

(xii) It motivates the current employees to prepare themselves for higher posts.

Disadvantages of internal recruitment sources:

(i) Creativity may be hindered by the lack of new talents.

(ii) It limits the choice to few employees only.

(iii) It leads to inbreeding and discourages new blood from entering into the company.

(iv) Sometimes it may be difficult to find the most suitable person from within the company.

(v) There are chances of bias.

2. **External sources**

(i) *Advertisement*: It is the most frequently used method to attract candidates. Companies advertise in newspapers, magazines, trade journals, etc. An advertisement should be well-thought out. Different types of media should be utilized according to the nature of job advertised. Local regional language newspapers would be suitable for targeting clerical and lower level administrative employees. Leading national newspapers and magazines/journals catering to specialized audiences (medical newsletters, legal journals, etc.) can be used to attract applicants for high profile jobs.

(ii) *Employment exchanges*: As per the provisions of the Employment Exchanges (Compulsory Notification of Vacancies) Act, 1959, a number of employment exchanges have been set up all over India. The main functions of employment exchange are registration of job-seekers and their suitable placement. They maintain separate records for non-graduates, graduates and postgraduates. Whenever employers have vacancies in their organizations, they will intimate the exchange and in return, the employment exchange will forward names of suitable candidates to employers.

(iii) *Campus recruitment*: Many companies make special efforts to establish and maintain constructive relationships with professional colleges and universities (e.g. IITs, IIMs, etc.) in order to get qualified personnel. These companies send their representatives to interview the candidates at the campuses. The shortlisted candidates may be further interviewed at the company's premises later on. However, this technique is very expensive.

(iv) *Consultants/private agencies*: There are consulting agencies that act as mediators between the firm and the prospective candidates. Organizations rely on these agencies for recruiting executive and managerial personnel. These agencies will bring together the employers and job-seekers for which they will charge fees either from the employers or the job-seeker or sometimes from both. It costs money, but it can save a lot of time.

(v) *Labour contractors*: Some firms employ contractors to recruit casual workers. This is a commonly used method when the work is of temporary nature.

(vi) *Unsolicited applicants*: Sometimes job-seekers send their applications to company offices without any invitation from the company. Whenever there is vacancy in the company, the recruiter can consider the unsolicited applications.

(vii) *Leasing*: This is commonly used to meet short-term urgent requirements of employees, leasing employees by the hour/day. In this case, the company escapes from the liabilities of making payments for pension, insurance, etc.

(viii) *Data banks*: Company's HR department can collect the biodata of candidates from different sources like employment exchange, campuses, etc. and save them in the form of computer databases. Whenever the need arises, the database will serve as a ready source of recruitment.

(ix) *Competitors*: Organizations may attract suitable candidates from their competitors in the same industry. They may be offered higher pay package or more benefits. This is very common in today's competitive era.

(x) *Internet recruitment*: Using online job portals like naukri.com, monster.com, shine.com, etc. has become a very popular way of recruiting employees. Online ads are cheaper and produce fast results. Moreover, the reach of online media is very vast and a large number of people can be easily recruited this way.

(xi) *Walk-in interviews*: Busy organizations advise candidates to directly attend walk-in interviews on the given date and time. No prior applications are required. This is very economic in nature.

Advantages of external sources of recruitment:

(i) Organization can acquire the right types of candidates with required qualifications in the right number.

(ii) New talent and skill enter into the organization.

(iii) Since the employees are selected from a vast pool of candidates, the best selection is made.

(iv) It is easy to comply with the reservation policy.

(v) Fresh candidates may bring positive changes in the organization.

Disadvantages of external recruitment sources:

(i) It reduces the morale of insiders because outsiders are preferred.

(ii) It may hinder career advancement of existing employees.

(iii) In some cases, outsiders may require initial training which is time-consuming.

(iv) Outsiders need more time to adjust into new environment.

(v) Recruiting from external sources is more expensive as compared to internal sources.

Selection

Selection is the process of putting right men on the right job. It is the procedure of matching the organization's requirements with the skills and qualifications of the candidates. The applicants are differentiated in order to identify and hire those with a greater likelihood of success in a job.[1] Selection is the process of choosing from a pool of candidates, the most suitable person for the current position or for future positions. The concept of selection is often confused with recruitment. However, they are different. Recruitment is a positive process as it motivates more and more candidates to apply for a job, while selection is a negative concept as unsuitable candidates are rejected here. The candidates are properly screened, interviewed and tested during the selection procedure. Selecting the right candidate is very crucial for the organization. By doing so, the organization can ensure high productivity of the employees. On the other hand, selection of the wrong candidate will result in poor job performance and wastage of time and money. Thus, it is very important that the HR manager selects the candidates very carefully keeping in view the organizational requirement and employee characteristics.

The Selection Process

Selection is a long process commencing from the initial contact with the applicants and ending with the contract of employment. All the stages between first and last step seem to be successive hurdles or barriers for candidates. Qualified candidates will go on to next hurdle, while the unqualified are eliminated.

1. **Initial contact/reception of applicants:** Initial contact with the candidates is usually made through their applications for the jobs in the company. Almost every organization maintains a proper record of applications received in their employment office.
2. **Initial/preliminary interview or screening:** This is an introductory interview, which is quite short and just aims at elimination of the obviously unqualified. This is generally done to weed out those who do not possess the minimum requirements laid down for the vacancies. However, care should be taken that this process does not lead to elimination of desirable candidates. In this preliminary interview, on one hand, the applicants are provided with the essential information regarding the nature of jobs in the organization, and on the other hand, necessary information is elicited from the applicants regarding their education, experience, desired salary, reasons for leaving their current jobs, time required to join the job, job interest, etc. If the candidate meets the organization's requirements then he/she will be taken into consideration for further selection phases otherwise he/she would be eliminated at this stage itself.
3. **Application blank/form:** This is one of the most common devices for getting factual information. This is a universally accepted tool for gathering relevant information from the applicant which may be of vital importance to the management for making proper selection. Although the application blanks may differ from organization to organization yet there is high degree of similarity among the application forms of various organizations. Following are the main classes of information usually sought through the application blank:

(i) *Biographical data*: This includes name, father's name, age, sex, nationality, marital status, height, weight, number of dependents and identification marks.

(ii) *Education*: This is information about the courses and subjects studied and grades secured. Organizations look at class, division (first/second/third class) and percentage of marks obtained.

(iii) *Experience*: This refers to the previous work experience of the applicant. It shows the years of experience, nature of duties and responsibilities involved in the previous job.

(iv) *Personal items*: This comprises extra-curricular activities, hobbies, association memberships, etc.

(v) *Salary and other benefits*: This includes present and expected salary, perks, other fringe benefits, etc.

(vi) *References*: This is a common practice followed by organizations worldwide. This includes the letters of recommendations from the previous employers, departmental head and teachers who have personal experience dealing with the candidate.

Some firms are now attempting to analyze the relationship between data items on application and the extent of job success. This kind of application blanks are known as weighted application blanks.

4. **Psychological tests:** These are the most carefully designed instruments. These tests provide a systematic criteria/ base for selecting the candidates and try to eliminate any bias on the part of the employer. Such tests, designed to measure mental alertness, special aptitude, achievement, physical dexterity, etc. are used by an increasing number of organizations as an aid in the selection of prospective candidates.[2]

5. **Interviewing:** Interviewing is probably the oldest method of selection. If given an option of a single tool for selection, perhaps every organization will choose

interviewing. This is basically a subjective process and therefore sometimes proves unreliable. However, this problem can be solved by use of structures formats with standardised or similar questions for all applicants.

6. **Checking references:** Checking references and investigating background information is important in selection procedures. Opinions of previous employers, departmental heads, and university/college professors are generally asked for in order to get a clear picture of candidate's potential performance in a particular job. For checking references, organization may seek letters of references or contact them through telephone or mail.
7. **Selection decision:** Once a candidate has passed the preceding steps successfully, the critical decision is of finally picking the candidate. The HR manager has to make the final decision of hiring or rejecting an applicant on the basis of his interview, tests and reference checks. The most suitable candidates from the available pool of applicants will be chosen.
8. **Physical examination:** Generally, organizations require that a candidate goes through a physical examination before he can be finally accepted for the job. There are some jobs which require unusual strength, stamina or tolerance of hard working conditions (Defence, Police, fire-fighters, etc.) and there are some others where people with particular problems cannot be employed (for example, a person with breathing problem cannot work in a sawdust mill). Therefore, physical examination is mandatory in such cases. Physical examination also helps the organization to prevent communicable diseases from entering the organization. Also it safeguards the interest of the hiring company against payment of claims under compensation law. Generally, a physical test includes measurement of height, weight etc. and examination of vital organs like eyes, ears, heart, lungs, etc.

9. **Job offer:** Job offer is made through appointment letter to those candidates who have passed all the earlier barriers. It means a person has successfully cleared all written tests, interviews, approved by supervisors, stands good in various inquiries, and is medically declared fit. After all this, appointment letter is formally given to the candidate. This will indicate the time and place of reporting. Usually, sufficient time is provided for reporting. If the candidate was already in job, he should bring relieving certificate from the previous organization.
10. **Contract of employment:** Once an organization made a job offer and the candidate accepts the offer, then there is need to prepare and execute a contract of employment. Generally, this includes the following items:
    (i) Job title.
    (ii) Duties in detail.
    (iii) Date when continuous employment starts.
    (iv) Remuneration and method of payment.
    (v) Working hours, overtime, lunch and tea break, etc.
    (vi) Details of holidays.
    (vii) Sickness rules.
    (viii) Length of notice due to and from the employee.
    (ix) Grievance handling system.
    (x) Disciplinary procedure.
    (xi) Work rules.
    (xii) Conditions of termination of employment.
    (xiii) Terms of union memberships.
    (xiv) Employer's right to vary terms and conditions of contract subject to proper notification being given.

    Proper care should be taken while drafting the contracts. Big organizations may take the help of law firms/agencies for drafting and finalising the contracts.

11. **Evaluation of selection procedure:** Finally, there should be an assessment of the selection process followed by the organization. Success of a good selection process can be measured by the availability of competent, qualified and committed personnel in the organization. Organizations must conduct a periodic audit by people who work independently of the HR department.

Barriers to Effective Selection

1. **Pressure to hire:** There might be pressure upon selectors from superiors, politicians, family, peers, etc. to hire particular applicants.
2. **Fairness:** This demands that there should be no discrimination on the basis of religion, caste, gender or race. But in practice certain segments of the society are normally discriminated against.
3. **Perception:** The selectors due to his limited perceptual ability may make a wrong decision about a candidate's suitability.
4. **Reliability:** It refers to degree of consistency. Sometimes, even a reliable selection test fails to accurately predict job performance.
5. **Validity:** It refers to the extent to which a selection test measures what it intends to measure. It just raises the possibility of success but sometimes it does not predict success accurately.

QUESTIONS

1. Define recruitment. What are the features of a good recruitment policy?
2. What are the various internal sources of recruitment? What are its advantages?
3. Discuss the external sources of recruitment. In what ways are external sources better than internal ones?
4. What are the steps in the selection process?
5. Write a note on the barriers to effective selection.

NOTES

1. Thomas H. Stone. *Understanding Personality.* CBS College Publishing, 1989, p. 173.
2. National Industrial Conference Board, Inc. "The Use of Tests in Employment and Promotion", *Studies in Personnel Policies.* New York, p. 14.

Chapter 7

Psychological Tests and Interviews

An employment test is an instrument designed to measure selected psychological factors like capacity for learning, personality, specific attitudes and temperament, etc. A test of a particular ability does not measure that particular ability alone but also a class or group of abilities. For example, in a test of numerical ability, the candidate has not only to grasp the relation between various data presented and to deduce something new to reach an answer, but he should also be able to read and comprehend the question. All tests, therefore, are first psychological and then tests of specific abilities.[1]

Principles of Psychological Testing

The important principles of psychological testing are the following:

1. **Job analysis basis:** Job analysis is the basic parameter which determines psychological tests. The tests should be designed to measure those requirements which have been suggested under job specifications so that the qualities of the candidate can be matched with those required by the job.
2. **Standardisation:** Standardisation refers to the consistency or uniformity of the conditions and procedures for administering a psychological test. In order to make test results comparable, tests should be standardised.

3. **Objectivity:** The tests should be objective in nature and be free of subjective judgements on the part of the scorer. All applicants taking the test should be given equal opportunities and not discriminated on the basis of sex, religion, region, etc.
4. **Reliability:** Reliability refers to the degree of consistency of results obtained. In other words, it means stability of response on a test. A test is reliable if it yields the same result even if a person is tested for the second or third time provided the test and situation remain the same. A slight variation in test scores when a test is retaken at a later time is common; however, if the fluctuation is high, then the test is not reliable. There are three methods to determine the reliability of a test. These are the following:
   (i) *Test-retest (repetition) method*: This is the simplest method of determining reliability of a test. In this, a test is administered twice to the same group of people and the two sets of scores are correlated. In other words, a test is given and repeated on the same group and the correlation computed between the first and second set of scores. Closer the correlation/ reliability coefficient, the more reliable the test is considered to be.
   (ii) *Alternate / parallel / equivalent-form method*: This method also uses a test-retest approach, but instead of using the same test for the second time, an alternate/similar form of the test is administered. However, it is costly and difficult to develop two separate and equivalent tests.
   (iii) *Split-halves method*: In this method, the test is divided into two equivalent halves and the correlation found for these halves-tests. Generally, there is odd-even split. This is less time-consuming as only one administration of the test is required.
5. **Validity:** It refers to the extent to which a test measures what it is designed to measure. There may be three types of validity. These are given below:

(i) *Criterion-related validity*: This is concerned with the relationship between test scores and the subsequent job performance. If a person scores high on test, he also does well on the job, and *vice versa*.

(ii) *Rational validity*: This is the type of validity that relates to the nature, properties and content of a test, independent of its relationship to job performance measures.[2] There are following two approaches to establish the rational validity of a test:

(a) Content validity, which means how well the contents/items of the test, as a sample, represent all the situations that could have been included.

(b) Construct validity, which refers to the extent the test measures the psychological characteristics such as intelligence, motivation, emotional stability, etc.

(iii) *Face validity*: Face validity is not a statistical measure but a subjective expression of how well the test items seem to be related to the job in question.[3] There are certain test norms: In order to interpret the results of a test, a point of comparison must be established. This is necessary so that the performance of one person can be compared with the performance of others. This is accomplished by means of the test norms, the distribution of scores of a large group of people similar in nature to the job applicants being tested.[4] The most widely used psychological tests have sets of norms for men and women, for different age groups, for various racial and ethnic groups and for varying levels of education.

Types of Tests

The main types of tests used in selection can be classified into five categories which are given below:

1. **Intelligence tests:** These tests are designed to measure an applicant's ability to think and reason. Intelligence tests seek to measure the general level of intelligence of

the applicant. Intelligence is a highly complex concept and generally there is difficulty in deciding about what constitutes intelligence.

2. **Aptitude tests:** Specific abilities like mechanical aptitude, numerical aptitude, clerical aptitude and dexterity are measured by such tests. These are job-specific tests that are used to predict the potential an individual has to perform tasks within a job. These are also known as potential ability tests.
3. **Personality tests:** Personality is the combination of qualities and traits that form an individual's distinctive character. Personality tests attempt to measure the basic characteristics of an individual. These tests measure emotional stability, extroversion/introversion, agreeableness, conscientiousness (hard working and reliable), openness to experience, integrity, self-confidence, etc. For example Thematic Appreciation Test (TAT), Bell Adjustment Inventory, etc.
4. **Interest tests:** These tests attempt to measure interests and preferences of people. These are mainly used in career counselling. These tests assess a person's field of interest and identify the kind of work that will suit him. In a sense, interest tests evaluate the likes and dislikes of people. For example Strong's Vocational Interest Blank and the Occupational Interest Survey.
5. **Achievement tests:** These tests measure applicant's abilities that have already been acquainted by training or experience. Typing tests, content writing tests, etc. measure the proficiency of a candidate in performing certain tasks. These tests are also known as attainment tests and proficiency tests.

Criteria for the Use of Tests in a Selection Process

The six criteria for the use of psychological tests are mentioned below:

(i) Everyone responsible for the application of tests including evaluation, interpretation and feedback should be trained.

(ii) Potential test users should satisfy themselves that it is appropriate to use tests at all before incorporating tests into decision-making processes.

(iii) Users must satisfy themselves that any tests they decide to use actively measure factors which are directly relevant to the employment situation.

(iv) Users must satisfy themselves that all tests they use should have been rigorously developed and that claims about their reliability, validity and effectiveness are supported by statistical evidence.

(v) Care must be taken to provide equality of opportunity among all individuals required to take tests.

(vi) The results of single tests should not be used as the sole basis for decision-making. This is particularly relevant with regard to personality tests.[5]

Interviews

An interview is a face-to-face interaction between an employer and a potential employee. The employer evaluates the candidate on the basis of this conversation to determine his suitability for the position applied. Although application blanks and selection tests produce evidence of a candidate's abilities, an interview is required to further supplement this data with more detailed information about personal characteristics and experience which can be obtained only in a face-to-face meeting. An interview is a selection procedure designed to predict future job performance on the basis of applicant's oral responses to oral inquires.[6] The main aim of the selection interview is to assess information about a candidate which will enable a valid prediction of his future job performance. The interview makes three unique contributions to the selection process. First, it is the only way to see an applicant in action—how he looks like, his manners, his behaviour. Second, it is the only way to witness how he interacts and how he responds, his way of thinking, how his personality will affect others. Third, it is the best way to learn about a candidate's performance-motivation, initiative, stability, perseverance, work habits and judgements.

Types of Interviews

I. According to the Purpose of the Interview

1. *Appraisal interview*: An appraisal interview is a discussion, following the performance appraisal, in which supervisor and employee discuss the employee's rating and possible remedial action.
2. *Exit interview*: This is conducted when an employee leaves the organization. The aim of the exit interview is to elicit information about the job, supervisor or other related matters. Information obtained through exit interview may give the employer some insight into what is wrong or right about the organization.
3. *Selection/employment interview*: Here the interviews are used as a key selection device. The candidates are interviewed regarding their appropriateness to the organization.
4. *Grievance interview*: The general purpose of a grievance interview is resolution of the controversy to the satisfaction of both the employee and the company.[7]

II. According to the Structure/Pattern

1. *Structured or directive interview*: In this type of interview, a set sequence of questions is followed. These are well planned to a higher degree of precision and accuracy. The questions and acceptable responses are specified in advance and responses are related for appropriateness of content,[8] for example, in McMurray's patterned interview. There are certain benefits associated with structured interviews. As all applicants are asked same set of questions, these are more reliable and valid. Standardising the administration of the interview also increases consistency across candidates, enhances job relatedness, reduces overall subjectivity and may enhance the ability to withstand legal challenges.[9]

2. *Unstructured or non-directive interview*: Contrary to structured interview, in an unstructured interview, no set format of questions is followed. In this, the format and questions to be asked are left to the discretion of the interviewer. No advance planning is required. The main weakness of unstructured interview is that it lacks consistency in assessing candidates.

III. **According to the contents of interview**

1. *Situational interview*: This is a very accurate form of interviewing for predicting a candidate's behaviour in job situations. The interviewer asks the candidate how he would behave in a certain situation. Competence based questions are asked to judge the specific behaviour and presence of mind of the candidate.
2. *Behavioural interview*: These interviews ask interviewees to describe how they reacted to actual job situations in the past. Interviewees may be required to explain how they managed a stressful scenario or dealt with a difficult co-worker.
3. *Job-related interview*: In this interview, a number of job-related questions are asked that just focus on relevant past job-related behaviour.
4. *Stress interview*: The aim of this interview is to identify sensitive candidates and those with low or high stress tolerance. The interviewee is made uncomfortable by asking a number of rude questions. The interviewer adopts a hostile approach and deliberately frustrates and embarrasses the candidate. This is generally for the jobs where emotional balance is required.

IV. **According to the administration of interview**

1. *One-to-one interview*: In such type of interview, there is one interviewer who interacts with a single interviewee. Most job interviews are on a one-to-one basis.

2. *Sequential interview*: In this, several persons interview the candidate in sequence before a final decision is made. In an unstructured sequential interview, each interviewer may ask different questions and form an independent opinion, whereas in a structured sequential interview, each interviewer rates the candidate on a standard evaluation form.[10]
3. *Panel interview*: In this type of interview, a panel (or group) of interviewers ask questions to the candidate. The panel members may ask questions in random or turn wise on the concerned topic.
4. *Mass interview*: In this, a panel interviews several candidates simultaneously. The panel poses a problem and then sits back and watches to see which candidate takes the lead in formulating an answer.[11]

Principles of Interviewing

1. **Preparation:** The interviewer should do considerable amount of planning required for interviews well in advance. This may include the following:
   (i) *Determining the main objectives of the interview*: First of all, the objectives of the interview should be clearly spelled out. Objectives of appraisal interview will be different from those of grievance interview.
   (ii) *Determining the method*: At this stage, the method to accomplish interviewing objectives should be decided. For example, whether there is a need of stress interview or structured interview or unstructured interview, etc. to fill the objectives.
   (iii) *Information regarding the applicant*: The interviewer should acquaint himself with knowledge about the candidate. For example in an employment interview, the interviewer can study the application blank.
2. **Setting:** This involves two kinds of settings:
   (i) *Physical setting*: The physical setting should be such that it is comfortable for the interviewee and puts him at ease.

(ii) *Mental setting*: This refers to the rapport between the interviewer and interviewee and the atmosphere prevailing within the physical setting.

3. **Conduct of the interview:** This is the stage of action where desired information is obtained and facts are provided to the interviewee, if he requests so. Here, the main principles are:
   (i) The interviewer should possess and demonstrate a basic liking and respect for people.
   (ii) Questions should be asked in way that the interviewee is encouraged to answer.
   (iii) Interviewer should listen with full attention.
4. **Closing the interview:** This last step is equally important as the beginning. To begin, conduct and close the interview smoothly is an art. The main principles here are:
   (i) At the end of the interview, the interviewer should make some overt sign to indicate the end such as lay down a pen, stand up, push the chair back, say thanks, etc.
   (ii) The interviewee should be informed about how he will be contacted about the interview results.
5. **Evaluation:** When the interviewee leaves the room, the interviewer should immediately note down the strengths and weaknesses of the candidate. Finally, the interviewer should also do self-evaluation. Interviewing is largely an art, the application of which can be improved with practice.

Limitations of Interview

1. **First impression:** Interviewers tend to jump to conclusion within a few minutes of the interview. In many cases, the interviewers make up their minds before the actual interview begins, based on the first impression from the candidate's personal appearance or from the application forms.

2. **Halo effect:** Halo effect is a subjective bias about a person's one outstanding trait extending to influence the total judgement of that person. For example, a candidate's fluency in English, his 'foreign returned' status, physical appearance, etc.
3. **Contrast/candidate-order effect:** Candidates are not only evaluated on an absolute basis or on their merit alone, but are also judged relative to the other candidates interviewed during the same period.
4. **Pressure to hire:** If the HR manager is in an urgency to hire, he would judge the candidates more favourably as compared to a manager who has enough time for taking hiring decisions.
5. **Interviewers' prejudices:** Interviewers' personal likes and dislikes (regarding gender, region, etc.) affect their judgement. For example, female interviewers may be reluctant to consider men for teaching or nursing jobs. On the other hand, male interviewers may hesitate to hire women in traditional male jobs.
6. **Prior information:** The interviewers have prior information about the applicant, for example, through application blanks, psychological test results, etc. The nature of that prior information can predispose an interviewer to have favourable or unfavourable attitude towards an applicant before he or she even shows up for the interview.[12]
7. **Stereotyping:** This type of error arises when the interviewers have already formed some associations between a particular trait, origin and particular type of personality. For example, the interviewer may form the opinion that people from metro cities are more competitive and competent.
8. **Projection:** This type of error arises when an interviewer expects his own values, qualities and skills to be present in the candidate. So, he may select a candidate who just resembles him in appearance, manner, thoughts, age and background.

9. **Leniency:** This error refers to tendency to give high scores. Generally, it is associated with lack of confidence and interest in the rating.
10. **Non-verbal behaviour:** Applicant's non-verbal behaviour also has a great impact on his or her rating. The way an applicant conducts himself, makes eye contact, his body language, firmness of handshake, etc. influence the interviewer's hiring decision.

QUESTIONS

1. What are the principles of psychological testing?
2. Write notes on intelligence test and aptitude test?
3. Enumerate the criteria for the use of tests in a selection process.
4. What is an interview? Write a note on structured vs. unstructured interviews.
5. Categorise the various types of interviews.
6. Job interviews are prone to bias. Comment.
7. What do you mean by halo effect? How does it affect the interviewer's hiring decisions?

NOTES

1. Monappa and M. Saiyadin. *Personnel Management*. Tata McGraw-Hill, New Delhi, 1979, p. 114.
2. D. Schultz and S.E. Schultz. *Psychology and Work Today*. Pearson Education, Delhi, 2004, p. 99.
3. *Ibid.*, p. 103.
4. *Ibid.*, p. 100.
5. IPD. *Key Facts on Psychological Testing*. London, 1997.
6. Michael McDaniel et al. "The Validity of Employment Interviews: A Comprehensive Review and Meta-Analysis." *Journal of Applied Psychology*, 1994. 79, No. 4, p. 599.
7. Edwin B. Flippo. *Personnel Management*, Sixth ed. McGraw-Hill, New York, 1984, p. 157.

8. Michael McDaniel et al. "The Validity of Employment Interviews: A Comprehensive Review and Meta-Analysis." *Journal of Applied Psychology*, 1994. 79, No. 4, p. 602.
9. L.G. Williamson et al. "Employment Interview on Trial: Linking Interview Structure with Litigation Outcomes." *Journal of Applied Psychology*, 1996. 82, No. 6, p. 900.
10. Gary Dessler. *Human Resource Management*. Pearson Education, Ninth ed., Delhi, 2004, p. 166.
11. *Ibid.*, p. 167.
12. D. Schultz and S.E. Schultz. *Psychology and Work Today*. Pearson Education, Delhi, 2004, p. 99.

Chapter 8

Placement and Induction

Once a candidate has been selected then the final stage in the procurement is the placement of the individual on the new job and introducing him to the job and the organization. Placement refers to the determination of the job to which an accepted candidate is to be allocated and his assignment to that job. The job requirements are matched with the qualities of the candidates to place them on the most suitable job. Generally, candidates are hired for a specific position in a company. In case the number of candidates hired for the same position is large, then there may arise the problem of placement, i.e. who should be placed under which supervisor. In these cases placement decision is made by assigning the candidate to the position where he or she is considered to be best qualified. Every care should be taken for introducing candidates to the job and the organization through effective induction arrangements. Induction or orientation is concerned with the introduction of a new employee to the organization. In other words, induction is the process of receiving and welcoming employees when they first join a company, and giving them the basic information they need to settle down quickly and happily and start work.[1]

Although during the process of recruitment and selection, the interviewer imparts sufficient information regarding the history, policies and products of the organization that develops confidence and interest in the worker, yet through formal induction the organization ensures that the new employee is imparted all the necessary information that will make him more confident, interested and a capable hand. Proper orientation can help the organization to reduce employee turnover within first few months of joining.

Objectives of Induction

1. To smoothen the earlier stages where everything is strange and unfamiliar to new employee.
2. To acquaint the newcomer with the requirements of the job.
3. To explain to employee the terms and conditions of the job.
4. To establish a favourable attitude regarding the company in the mind of employee.
5. To bring about integration between the personal goals and organizational goals.
6. To provide information to the employee regarding organization's policies and procedures.
7. To get effective output from the employee.
8. To develop enthusiasm for the organization in the mind of newcomer so that he or she is more likely to stay.
9. To reduce the employees' chances of leaving the organization quickly.
10. To acquaint the new employee with his immediate supervisor and fellow workers with whom he has to work.
11. To promote the feeling of belongingness to the organization.

Importance/Benefits of Induction Programme

1. Turnover among the new employees is higher than the other workers. Employees are far more likely to resign during their first months after joining the organization.[2] Thus, the organizations should induct an employee properly.

2. An organization always needs committed employees. The first step in achieving commitment is to present the organization as one that is worth working for and to ensure that this first impression is reinforced during the first weeks of employment.
3. New employees are great learners and the organization should help them in this direction. Although the length of the learning curve and rates of learning vary, yet it is important to provide for it to take place in a planned and systematic manner from the first day to maximize individual contributions as quickly as possible.
4. For most people, social aspects of the job are very important such as relationship with fellow workers, etc. New employees are likely to settle in more quickly and enjoy working for the organization if the process of socialization takes place smoothly.[3]
5. With the help of induction programmes, the organization can easily inform the new employees regarding what is expected from them in terms of behavioural norms, values and attitudes.

Induction Procedure

There is no model induction procedure as such. Every organization has its own induction procedure according to its needs. Generally, the following steps are undertaken:

1. Properly receive the new employee: This first step just ensures that new employee receives a warm welcome. The employees already working in the organization should be informed about the new arrival. The new employee should be given correct instructions about the opening time of the office and the reception staff should be friendly and helpful towards the new entrant.
2. The administrative work which includes informing the employee regarding probationary period, vacations, leaves, etc. should be completed as soon as possible.
3. The new employee should be introduced to the department, departmental functions, etc. He should be

acquainted with his new boss and the physical layout of his work place.

4. A follow-up interview should be conducted a few weeks later to see how much the employee is satisfied with his job and whether his supervisor is satisfied with the employee's performance.

Contents of Induction

These include information regarding:

1. Organization's history, core values, mission and philosophy.
2. Organization's products/services.
3. Department's location.
4. Personnel policies and procedures.
5. Conditions of services like holidays, hours, leave, medical leave, etc.
6. Remuneration and other benefits.
7. Health and safety measures.
8. Career advancement schemes.
9. Trade unions and memberships.
10. Grievance handling system.

Methods of Providing Information

Generally, the following methods are used for providing information to the new employee:

1. Lectures
2. Motion pictures
3. Slide shows
4. Printed material
5. Trips to the department and the plant
6. Notice boards
7. Models of finished products
8. Charts and drawings.

Problems Associated with Induction

The main barriers in the successful conduct of induction programme of an organization are the following:

1. The supervisor who is in charge of the job of induction is not well trained or he is too bossy.
2. The new employee is overloaded with the forms to fill.
3. The new employee is overwhelmed with so much information in a short time.
4. The new employee is thrown into action so soon.
5. The new employee may develop wrong perceptions because of faulty process of induction.
6. The new employee may be asked to perform challenging tasks initially where chances of failure are high. This might discourage job involvement, interest and commitment.

QUESTIONS

1. What is induction? Why is the induction process important?
2. What is the correct procedure for induction? What are the consequences if the induction process is not conducted properly?
3. What are the methods of providing induction?
4. Explain the problems associated with the induction process.

NOTES

1. Michael Armstrong. *A Handbook of Human Resource Management Practice*. Ninth ed. Kogan Page, London, 2005, p. 453.
2. A. Fowler. *Induction*. IPD, 1996, London.
3. *Ibid*., p. 455.

Chapter 9

Training and Development

The HR manager recruits, selects and places the employees on the right job after careful considerations. Since human resources are the most vital assets of the organization, should take the utmost care in developing them to their full potential. No employee is fully capable of performing his job responsibilities properly at the time of procurement. Therefore, some training is essential to enable him to gain knowledge and learn job skills so that he becomes a productive addition to the workforce. Organizations view training and development programmes as an investment in employees and not as an expense because of the long-term benefits such programmes provide. Training is the act of increasing the knowledge and skill of an employee for doing a particular job.[1] Employees are imparted specific skills to perform the job better and to overcome their shortcomings. On the other hand, development is an effort to provide employees with the abilities the organization will need in the future.[2]

Difference between training and development

	Training	Development
Focus	Current job	Current and future job
Scope	Individual employees	Work group or organization
Time Frame	Immediate	Long-term
Goal	Prepare for current job	Prepare for future work

Importance of Training and Development

1. **Optimum utilization of human resources:** Human resources need to be polished and trained to enhance their potential. Training and development of employees helps to make the best use of the employee's overall worth to the organization.
2. **Creating a highly skilled, motivated and enthusiastic workforce:** The existing workforce is trained to increase their productivity, and motivated to contribute their best towards the organization. The employees will be more confident about themselves and enthusiastic about their job. They will adapt to technological changes and innovations more readily.
3. **Increase productivity:** Knowledge about usage of sophisticated machinery and new technology is imparted to employees which will enable them to use the equipment more efficiently and thereby increase productivity.
4. **Build team spirit:** Training often takes place in groups where the trainees are encouraged to interact with each other and discuss organizational issues. This helps to create team spirit among the employees.
5. **Healthy work environment:** Training and development programmes help to modify the thought and behaviour process of the employees in such a way that is conducive to building a healthy work environment.
6. **Personal growth of employees:** Development programmes provide opportunities to the employees to enhance their skills and knowledge and help them to achieve better career growth.
7. **Promote learning culture:** The employees are encouraged to continuously learn new concepts and update their talents. This helps to promote a learning culture within the organization which would greatly help in its future sustenance and growth.
8. **Improve employee morale:** When employees are trained to become better performers, they feel a sense of

accomplishment. They realize that they are effectively contributing towards organizational goals and thus get a morale boost.

9. **Better managerial skills:** Training and development programmes inspire the employees to think, plan, solve problems and take important decisions. This hones up their managerial skills.
10. **Reduce employee turnover:** A well trained employee will take more interest in his job and will be a more efficient worker. He will get more job satisfaction. People who love their jobs are more loyal towards the organization.

Identifying Training and Development Needs

Before designing a suitable training programme for enhancing the skills of the employees, it is necessary to identify their training and development needs. A performance appraisal should be conducted to analyze the current level of knowledge and skills of the employee and train them according to their requirements. Steps in identifying training and developmental needs:

(i) **Performance appraisal:** The manager should review the performance of different employees in each field of work and identify those areas where the performance is not up to the mark. The difficulty level of each job and the skills required to perform that job should be analyzed to understand why the employees had been unsuccessful in performing it.

(ii) **Identify and discuss weaknesses:** After the performance review, the manager should identify those areas where their performance has been poor. He should study the weaknesses of the employees and focus on how these could be overcome.

(iii) **Determine work assignments:** The kinds of projects or assignments that could be used to strengthen the worker's knowledge and skills should be determined. Some skills are developed gradually through work experience while some others can be developed through methods like job rotation, coaching, mentoring, etc.

(iv) **Decision regarding on-the-job training:** Many employees have lower productivity because they do not have proper knowledge about the work processes. In such cases, on-the-job training with an experienced co-worker can help the trainees to grasp important aspects of the job.

(v) **Training programmes:** The HR department should design relevant training programmes that would benefit the employees. The methods of training should be chosen carefully according to the strengths, weaknesses and requirements of the employees. Time and dates for such programmes should be informed to various departments so that interested employees can participate.

(vi) **Create an action plan:** The duration of the training programmes should be specified. Standards should be set so that the actual outcomes can be compared with the desired ones after completion of the programme. The programmes should be followed up from time to time for updating knowledge of the workers.

Designing Training Programmes

1. **Objectives of training:** The training objectives are the outcomes that are desired from the training programme. If the training is to make the staff acquainted with particular software, then the objective is to make the employee easily utilize this software.
2. **Blueprint of the training programme:** The framework of the training programme includes details about the methods to be used, mode of instruction, delivery style, programme contents, etc.
3. **Budget:** The budget for the training programme would depend on a number of factors like size of the intended audience, tools and equipment required, payment to the trainer, cost of assessing training needs, cost of developing training programmes, etc.

4. **Determine method and contents:** An outline of the programme should be made so that the appropriate methods can be decided. The method of training, i.e. job rotation, coaching, case study, conference, lectures, etc. is to be chosen. The content of the programme will be determined by an expert in collaboration with the HR manager. The instructor who will be delivering the training will also be finalized.
5. **Evaluation standards:** The variables for evaluating the success of the programme should be determined, so that the effectiveness of the training can be measured. The programmes should be reviewed from time to time, preferably annually, so that the contents can be updated according to changing organizational needs.

Training and Development (T&D) Methods

There are several T&D methods available. The use of a particular method depends on which method accomplishes the training needs and objectives. Training methods can be classified into two categories:

I. **On-the-Job methods:** This refers to the methods of training in which a person learns a job by actually doing/performing it. A person works on a job and learns and develops expertize at the same time.

   1. *Understudy*: In it, the employee is trained by his supervisor. The trainee is attached with his senior and called an understudy or assistant. For example, a future manager might spend a few months as assistant to the present manager.
   2. *Job rotation*: This refers to shifting/movement of an employee from one job to another in regular intervals.
   3. *Special projects*: The trainees may be asked to work on special projects related to departmental objectives. By this, the trainees will acquire the knowledge of the assigned work and also learn how to work with others.

4. *Experience*: It refers to learning by doing. This is one of the oldest methods of on-the-job training. Although this is a very effective method, yet it is also very time-consuming and wasteful.
5. *Committee assignment*: In it, the trainees become members of a committee. The committee is assigned a problem to discuss and make recommendations.
6. *Coaching*: In it, the supervisor or the superior acts as a guide and instructor of the trainee. This involves extensive demonstration and continuous critical evaluation and correction.

II. **Off-the-job methods:** These methods require trainees to leave their workplace and concentrate their entire time towards the training objectives. In off-the-job methods, the development of trainees is the primary task while everything else is secondary. Following are the main off-the-job training methods:

1. *Special courses and lectures*: This is the most traditional method of developing personnel. Special courses and lectures are either designed by the company itself or by the management/professional schools. Companies then sponsor their trainees to attend these courses or lectures. These are the quickest and simplest ways to provide knowledge to a large group of trainees.
2. *Conferences and seminars*: By attending conferences and seminars, trainees try to look at a problem from different angles as the participants are normally from different fields and sectors. The participants pool their thoughts, ideas, viewpoints, suggestions and recommendations while participating in such conferences.
3. *Selected reading*: This is a self-improvement training technique. The persons acquire knowledge and awareness by reading various trade journals and magazines. Most of the companies have their own libraries. The employees become the members of the

professional associations to keep abreast of latest developments in their respective fields.

4. *Case study method*: This technique was developed by Harvard Business School, U.S.A. It is used as a supplement to lecture method. A case is a written record of a real business situation/problem faced by a company. The case is provided to the trainees for discussion and analysis. Identification and diagnosis of the problem is the aim in case study method. Alternative courses of action are suggested from participants.
5. *Programmed instruction/learning*: This is step-by-step self-learning method where the medium used may be a textbook, computer or the internet. This is a systematic method for teaching job skills involving presentation of questions or facts, allowing the person to respond and giving the learner immediate feedback on the accuracy of his or her answers.[3]
6. Brainstorming: This is creativity-training technique; it helps people to solve problems in a new and different way. In this technique, the trainees are given the opportunity to generate ideas openly and without any fear of judgement. Criticism of any idea is not allowed so as to reduce inhibiting forces. Once a lot of ideas are generated then they are evaluated for their cost and feasibility.
7. *Role-playing*: In this method, the trainees are assigned a role, which they have to play in an artificially created situation. For example, a trainee is asked to play the role of a trade union leader and another trainee is required to perform the role of an HR manager. This technique results in better understanding of each other's situation by putting one's foot in other's shoes.
8. *Apprenticeship training*: This training approach began in the Middle Ages when those who wanted to learn trade skill bound themselves to a master

craftsman and worked under his guidance. Apprenticeship training is a structured process by which people become skilled workers through a combination of classroom instruction and on-the-job training.

9. *In-basket exercise*: In this technique, the trainees are provided background information on a simulated firm and its products, and key personnel. After this, the trainees are provided with an in-basket of memos, letters, reports, requests and other documents related with the firm. The trainee must make sense out of this mass of paperwork and prepare memos, make notes and delegate tasks within a limited time period.[4]
10. *Business games*: Business games involve teams of trainees. The teams discuss and analyze the problems and arrive at decisions. Generally, issues related with inventories, sales, R&D, production process, etc. are taken up for consideration.
11. *Behaviour modelling*: This is a structured approach to teach specific supervisory skill. It is based on the social learning theory in which the trainee is provided with a specific model of behaviour and is informed in advance of the consequences of engaging in that type of behaviour.
12. *Sensitivity (T-group) training*: In this type of training, a small group of trainees consisting of 10 to 12 persons is formed which meets in an unstructured situation. There is no set agenda, schedule or plan. The main objectives are, more openness with each other, increased listening skills, trust, support, tolerance and concern for others, etc. The trainers serve a catalytic role. The group meets in isolation without any formal agenda. There is great focus on inter-personal behaviour. The trainer provides honest but supportive feedback to members on how they interacted with one another.

13. *Multiple management*: This technique of training was first introduced by McCormick, President of McCormick & Co. of Baltimore in 1932. He gave the idea of establishing a junior board of directors. Authority is given to the junior board members to discuss any problem that could be discussed in senior board and give recommendations to the senior board. Innovative and productive ideas became available for the senior board.

Role Specific Training

In role based training, training modules are aligned to specific job roles of employees. A role is defined as an individual's job that includes a number of functional activities. Many organizations implement general training modules for all its employees. This may help the employees in gaining some skills but it does not help the organization to develop the workers to their full potential. In role based training, the course contents and methods are designed for particular training needs of specific roles. This approach takes into account many factors and elements that are unique to a particular role. The training module is modelled in the context of the role and the factors required performing that role. The different employees have to follow numerous processes using different tools and equipment. Therefore, the benefits derived from a common training programme would be limited. Role based training attempts to develop the employee according to his job requirements and moulds him into a more productive and efficient worker. Specialized training is provided to employees so that they are able to gain expertise in their particular work area. They learn how to utilize the machines and equipment in the most productive way, how to minimise wastages and how to perform their tasks to ensure smooth functioning of their work processes. The role based training is often followed by mentoring or coaching to further reinforce whatever the employees have learnt during the training programme. An organization can enjoy many benefits if it adopts this method, but many managers are reluctant to adopt this strategy because of high costs. Role based training is costlier than general training but it is also more advantageous in the long run.

Advantages

(i) It gives higher quality results than generic training as it focuses on a specific role.

(ii) Training material specific to the role is provided to the employees for future reference.

(iii) Employees learn how to utilize tools and equipment in the most economical and productive manner.

(iv) Employees gain specialized knowledge and skills most relevant to their jobs.

(v) It helps to save valuable time and cost in the long run.

Competency Based Training (CBT)

Competency Based Training (CBT) focuses on what a person can or is expected to do in the workplace after completing a training programme. It emphasizes increasing the competencies of the employee as compared to only theoretical knowledge. Competencies are a combination of awareness, skills, knowledge and attitude that enables an individual to perform a job successfully. CBT stresses not just the skills required for the existing jobs in the workplace, but also the ability to transfer the skills and knowledge to new situations and work environment. CBT programmes are comprised of different segments, known as learning outcomes. Standards are set for each segment and participants are assessed based on this. A CBT programme is not time based. When the participants complete the requirements of one segment, they can move on to others. The time taken to complete the programme would depend on the learning and grasping power of the trainees. Thus, the participants would themselves know when they are ready for an assessment of competence. While evaluating the employees, the assessor ensures that the participant has acquired the competence that meets the required standards. CBT programmes use on-the-job or outside-the-job elements.

Even though most CBTs are not based on time, still some programmes may be required to be completed within a fixed time frame.

Four aspects of competencies:

(i) **Task skills:** The skills required for performing individual tasks.

(ii) **Task management skills:** Skills required for managing a variety of tasks within the job.

(iii) **Contingency management skills:** Skills required for responding to disturbances and breakdowns in routine work.

(iv) **Job environment skills:** Skills required for dealing with the responsibilities and expectations of the work environment, including working with others.[5]

Characteristics of CBT

(i) The competencies to be developed are carefully selected after an analysis of jobs requirements, work environment and performance appraisal of employees.

(ii) It is more practical in nature though it may be supplemented with theoretical training.

(iii) It is a flexible training approach.

(iv) CBT is not based on time; the learning of employees is self-paced.

(v) A person's prior knowledge and experience is considered in this type of training.

(vi) Detailed training material and equipment are used to support the acquisition of knowledge and skills by the employees.

(vii) A number of media including print, audio-visual and simulations are used in the process.

(viii) The whole CBT programme is divided into segments and the programme is completed when employees achieve the specific competencies in all the segments.

Benefits of Competency Based Training

For employers:

(i) Increased confidence, competence and morale of employees.

(ii) Development of specialized skill sets in workforce.

(iii) CBT uses more on-the-job training which results in more productivity.

(iv) Creation of a pool of well trained and efficient employees within the organization.

For employees:

(i) Employees become more qualified within a shorter period of time.

(ii) The time period of training depends upon the calibre of the employee and thus people having prior experience can complete their training quickly.

(iii) Employees gain those competencies that they can use in their current jobs or transfer to other jobs in future.

(iv) It is a good option for older employees to update their knowledge and skills in a short time.

(v) Employees gain more self-reliance and job satisfaction.

(vi) CBT emphasizes more on actual performance than on theoretical knowledge.

Limitations

(i) If the trainers are not properly trained to provide CBT, then the process may not be effective.

(ii) CBT will be unsuccessful if the competencies required for performing the jobs are not properly identified.

(iii) The training would not give the expected results if the proper procedure, materials and approaches are not used.

Assessment of Competency Based Training

The employees are not evaluated in the traditional method after undergoing competency based training. In competency based assessment, evidence or information is collected to make judgement about whether the competencies have been acquired or not.

Evidence may include:

Direct demonstration/ observation	Performance of a task, or range of tasks, either in the workplace or in a simulated work environment, witnessed directly by an assessor.
Indirect demonstration	Use of photographs, videos, etc. showing performance of a task when the assessor cannot be present.
Products	Models, items, objects that have been made, fixed or repaired by the candidate.
Workplace documents	Rosters, budgets, reports, standard operating procedures, etc. developed by the candidate.
Questions—written and oral	Asking the candidate about real or hypothetical situations to check understanding, task management and contingency management skills. May be short answer, discussion, multiple choice, etc.
Assignments	Projects, reports, essays, etc. relevant to the requirements of the competency.
Third party reports	Documented and verified reports from supervisor, colleague, subject expert, trainer or others.
Self-assessment	A candidate's personal statement on their performance (not generally sufficient in isolation).
Simulation	Simulated activity to accommodate difficult to demonstrate criteria e.g. emergencies, contingencies, difficult behaviour, etc.
Portfolios	Collections of evidence compiled by the candidate.

Source: Adapted from *Training Package Assessment Materials Kit*, 2001. Department of Education, Training & Youth Affairs

If sufficient evidence about the participant's competencies has been gathered, then he can be appraised on its basis. The assessment process should be valid, reliable, and fair and have a degree of flexibility. Competency based assessment can yield two outcomes about the employee—competent or not yet competent. An unsuccessful assessment is not a failure, but rather a way to identify additional weaknesses and learning needs. The participants should be given another opportunity to overcome their weaknesses and develop their competencies.

Training Evaluation

The process of examining training programmes to check whether the training has had the desired effect is known as training evaluation. Once the training programme has been completed, the organization evaluates the programmes to check the effectiveness of the training efforts. This is done to check whether the training programme has accomplished specific training objectives or not; and whether the candidates are able to implement their learning in their respective jobs or not. Also, the conduct of training programme is costly; this includes needs assessment costs, salaries of the training department staff, purchase of equipment, programme development cost, evaluation costs, trainer's costs, rental facilities and trainees wage during the training period.[6] Thus it is important to assess the costs and benefits associated with the training programme, in order to convince the top management that the benefits outplay costs.

Purposes of Training Evaluation

1. **Feedback:** The HR manager can give feedback to the employees by comparing the desired results with the actual training outcomes.
2. **Control:** It helps in overcoming the problems and re-designing the training programmes in case the training process is ineffective.
3. **Research:** The manager can study the link between the training programme, the changes in the employees'

behaviour and knowledge, and the changes in the quality of work performed.

4. **Measuring success:** Training evaluation helps the manager to compare the actual outcome with the desired results and check whether the programme was successful or not.

What to Measure

While evaluating training programme, the experts should collect data on the following categories:

1. **Reaction of trainees:** Reaction of trainees towards the training programme, i.e. what they felt about the training.
2. **Learning:** Whether the trainees have learnt the desired principles and skills.
3. **Behaviour:** Whether the trainees' on-the-job behaviour improved.
4. **Results:** The results of the training programme are compared against the set objectives.

How to Evaluate

There are several methods of evaluation. One is the use of experimental and control group. Both of these groups are randomly selected, one group receives training (experimental group) and other does not receive training (control group). A few indicators of success are identified (e.g. number of units produced per hour) and measures are taken from both the groups. A training programme is considered successful if the experimental group shows better performance than the control group. Another way to evaluate training programme is to take interviewees of trainees regarding programme's worth or make them fill a questionnaire to know their opinion.

Various methods of training evaluation are[7]:

- Observation
- Questionnaire
- Interview

- Self-diaries
- Self-recording of specific incidents.

QUESTIONS

1. Differentiate the terms training and development with suitable examples.
2. How can the HR manager identify the training and development needs of his subordinates?
3. List various training and development methods? What do you mean by on-the-job method?
4. Write a note on Role Specific Training. What are its advantages?
5. What is competency based training? How is competency assessment different from regular assessment?
6. How can the HR manager evaluate the success of a training programme?

NOTES

1. Edwin B. Flippo. *Personnel Management*. McGraw-Hill, Kogakusha Ltd., Tokyo, 1976, p. 209.
2. Luis R. Gomez-Mejia, David B. Balkin and Robert L. Cardy. *Managing Human Resources*. Third Ed. Pearson Education, Delhi, 2003, p. 260.
3. Gary Dessler. *Human Resource Management*. Pearson Education, Ninth Ed. 2004, p. 195.
4. Edwin B. Flippo. *Personnel Management*, Sixth ed. McGraw-Hill, New York, 1984, p. 206.
5. http://www.managementfoundations.net/html/ competency_based_training.html
6. J.H. Bernardin and J.E.A. Russell. *Human Resource Management—An Experimental Approach*. McGraw-Hill, New York, p. 315.
7. http://traininganddevelopment.naukrihub.com/training-evaluation.html

Chapter 10

Management Development

Management development is a systematic process by which managers develop and improve their skills and abilities not only to benefit themselves, but also their organization. Managers learn a lot informally during the course of their work and also by participation in formal courses of instruction. Management development improves the performances of managers by giving them opportunities for growth and development. The significance of management development lies in the fact that the actions of the managers at different levels impact the working of their departments or maybe, the organization. Management development includes structured informal training, formal training courses and executive education. It is the responsibility of the company to establish development programmes for its managers. According to Dale S. Beach, "Management development is a systematic process of training and growth by which individuals gain and apply knowledge, skills, insights and attitudes to manage orientation effectively." The managers should be exposed to lectures, case studies, management games, role playing, etc. to enhance their managerial capabilities.

Skills of the Manager

While analyzing the skills of a manager, R.L. Katz speaks of following three types:[1]

1. **Technical skills:** These enable a manager to use techniques, methods, processes and equipment

effectively in performing specific jobs. These skills are developed through experience and education. These are most important for operating managers.

2. **Human skills:** These refer to the ability to work effectively with others on a person-to-person basis, and to build up cooperative group relations to accomplish the organizational goals. These include the ability to communicate, motivate and lead. These are also called human relations abilities, which enable a manager to handle human resources in such a way that personal satisfaction is achieved and organizational goals are attained.
3. **Conceptual skills:** These enable a manager to consider an enterprise as a whole and evaluate the relationships which exist between various parts or functions of a business. In long-range planning, top managers need these skills. The higher one rises in the management hierarchy, the greater the need of conceptual skills. For example, members of the Board of Directors have to rely heavily on their conceptual abilities in making decisions.

To sum up, while human skills are important at all levels of management, conceptual skill is essentially critical in top executive positions, and technical skill is an essential ingredient in low-level management.

Management development must take place in the following crucial areas considered as output variables:[2]

(i) Knowledge change;
(ii) Attitude change;
(iii) Behaviour change;
(iv) Performance change; and
(v) End-operational results (the last two changes being the result of the first three changes).

The effective success of development effort depends upon the following inputs:

(i) Trainee's personal characteristics, his intelligence and motivation to learn.

(ii) His actual learning efforts.

Both output and input variables influenced by the formal organization, leadership climate and cultural factors, such as attitudes and norms of the small group of which an individual is a member.

Objectives of Management Development

The level-wise objectives of management development are as follows:

1. **Top management**
   - (i) To improve thought processes and analytical ability in order to uncover and examine problems and take decisions in the best interests of the company.
   - (ii) To broaden the outlook of the executive in regard to his role, position and responsibilities in the organization and outside.
   - (iii) To think through problems which may confront the organization now or in the future.
   - (iv) To understand economic, technical and institutional forces in order to solve business problems.
   - (v) To acquire knowledge about the problems of human relations.
2. **Middle line management**
   - (i) To establish a clear picture of executive functions and responsibilities.
   - (ii) To bring about an awareness of the broad aspects of management problems, and an acquaintance with, and appreciation of, inter-departmental relations.
   - (iii) To develop the ability to analyze problems and to take appropriate action.
   - (iv) To develop familiarity with the managerial uses of financial accounting, psychology, business law and business statistics.

(v) To inculcate knowledge of human motivation and human relationships, and

(vi) To develop responsible leadership.

3. **Middle functional executive and specialists**

(i) To increase knowledge of business functions and operations in specified fields in marketing, production, finance and personnel management.

(ii) To increase proficiency in management techniques (e.g. work study, inventory control, operations research, and quality control).

(iii) To stimulate creative thinking in order to improve methods and procedures.

(iv) To understand the functions performed in a company.

(v) To understand human relations problems.

(vi) To develop the ability to analyze problems in one's areas of functions.

Importance of Management Development

1. **Enhanced skills:** Management development training helps the managers to increase their skill sets and knowledge. This will help them to work better in the organization and improve their productivity. A well trained team of managers can work more efficiently and achieve synergy in operations. Enrichment in knowledge and skills results in more profitability.
2. **Improves employee morale and confidence:** Development programmes are aimed towards improving employee morale and boosting their confidence. Such programmes make them feel as a valued member of the organization, and thus they are more motivated towards giving their best to their job. High morale creates a positive atmosphere of work where each member cooperates for achievement of organizational goals.

3. **Increased productivity:** The major purpose of any training and development activity is to increase the productivity of the workforce. Employees gain knowledge, skills and get to hone their talents through management development programmes. They also gain self-confidence and their morale gets a boost through such practices. All these factors help to increase the productivity of the managers.

Techniques of Management Development Programmes

I. On-The-Job Techniques

This method of training and education has its own value where the object of managers' development in improving on-the-job behaviour. It is inexpensive and saves productive hours. But on the other hand, neither the trainer nor the trainee is free from the daily chores and the pressure of their respective routine jobs even during the training period.

Most popular techniques under this type are:

1. **The coaching method:** The objective of coaching is not only to teach and guide a subordinate in the performance of his immediate assignments but also to provide him with diversified work so that he may grow and progress. It is used in developing managerial thinking processes as well as operative skills. In this method, the superior plays the role of the guide and the instructor. The coach sets some mutually agreed upon goals and tells the trainee what he wants him to do, suggest how it may be done, follows up with suggestions, and corrects errors. He helps the trainee live up to those goals through periodic reviews of the trainee's progress and suggests modifications in his behaviour where needed.

Advantages

(i) It requires the least centralized staff-coordination as every executive can coach his men even if no management development programme exists.

(ii) Periodic feedback and evaluation are also a part of coaching, which yield immediate benefits to an organization, to the coach and to the subordinate. It is learning by doing.

Disadvantages

(i) The coaching technique is authoritarian, for an executive tends to familiarise his subordinates with his own work habits and beliefs, even though these may be faulty.

(ii) It heavily relies on the coach's ability to be good teacher, which he may not necessarily be.

(iii) The training atmosphere, free from worries of the daily duties, is not available.

2. **Job rotation or channel method of development:** It is an excellent method for broadening the vision of the manager or potential manager, for turning specialists into generalists. Job rotation is often designed for beginning level managers while planned progression is more likely to occur at higher managerial levels.[3] Such rotation may continue for a period ranging from 6 months to 24 months. Under this method, the trainees are rotated over various routine jobs in a department, division or unit before they are due for promotion as managers, so that they get an overall knowledge and familiarity with different sectional jobs (such as billing, issuing challans, preparing inspection notes, setting railway claims, handling customer accounts, etc. in the sales department) before they are posted as Managers in the department.

Advantages

(i) It breaks down departmental provincialism for everyone is moved from one department to another. It rather develops inter-departmental cooperation.

(ii) Boredom and monotony are reduced. People are prepared to assume greater responsibility, especially at the upper echelons.

(iii) It injects new ideas into the older departmental personnel who may otherwise fall in a rut. New concepts are infused into them and they are diffused throughout an enterprise.

(iv) A man does not end up in just one place, but gets a chance to step into a higher position. Thus, an organization gains management strength.

(v) It ensures the avoidance of the problem which arises when a newly promoted manager is required to supervise his former peers.

(vi) Through it the management compares one man with another, and gives everyone an equal chance for advancement.

(vii) It does not develop "specialists" but produces "generalists", men whose chief ability is to handle people and make decisions.

(viii) Through awareness of what is happening elsewhere and familiarity with other task-centres it provides a balanced and informed attitude to enterprise goals and activities.

(ix) Each manager's abilities and talents are best tested in a variety of jobs, so the enterprise can secure his best utilization in the ultimate assignment.

Disadvantages

(i) It undermines organizational morale and efficiency since executives may have little inducement to sink their teeth deeply into an assignment.

(ii) Established operations are disturbed and the manager is prone to errors in a new seat.

(iii) It becomes difficult for a subordinate to adjust himself to his new bosses. Interpersonal relationship takes time for adjustment, and therefore employees with frequent moves are apt to feel insecure.

(iv) The new incumbent is likely to bring in a zeal for change; while sound changes are good, ill-conceived and hasty innovations may lead to costly experimentations.

(v) It may demotivate intelligent and aggressive trainees who seek specific responsibility in their chosen speciality.

(vi) It develops sharp cleavages, friction, jealousy and other non-cooperative and dysfunctional forms of human behaviour.

(vii) It sometimes leads to subtle class distinctions. Men who are not rotated tend to develop defensive reactions. This leads to misunderstanding and poor communication.

(viii) It may easily become over-centralized, inflexible and "closed".

In order to have an effective rotation those moved to different positions should be helped to understand the new task thoroughly, view the change as an opportunity for a genuine learning experience and identify themselves with the new position that they may exercise full responsibility over to achieve results and job improvement.

3. **The multiple-management technique:** In this method, juniors are assigned to Board or Committees, and asked to participate in their deliberations. In these sessions, their actual problems are discussed, different views are debated and decisions are taken. The juniors get an opportunity to know about managerial decision-making, learn by watching others and then delve into specific organizational problems.

Advantages

(i) It gives Board members an opportunity to gain knowledge on various issues.

(ii) It helps identify those who have executive talent. Multiple judgements are obtained on each individual through the Board rating system.

(iii) The members gain practical experience of group decision-making and team-work.

(iv) It is a relatively inexpensive method of development.

(v) It permits a considerable number of managers to participate in certain activities within a reasonable period of time.

Disadvantages

(i) It is only suitable for middle and senior level managers.

(ii) It does not permit any specific attention to training needs of the manager.

(iii) The debates in these committees often tend to be discursive lacking purposiveness or authority.

II. Off-The-Job Techniques

1. **The case study:** This is a method where an actual business situation is described, in writing, in a comprehensive manner. The trainees are asked to know and analyze the problem-situation and suggest solutions. The actual decision taken in the subject case is known only to the executive.

   It is disclosed at the end of the session when it is compared with various solutions offered by the group.

Advantages

(i) Case study can provide stimulating discussions among participants as well as excellent opportunities for individuals to defend their analytical and judgemental abilities.

(ii) It is an effective method for improving decision-making abilities within the constraints of limited information.

2. **Incident method:** This method was developed by Paul Pigors. In this method, group members address questions regarding a certain incident to the discussion leader. The general trend of questioning is to find out about the 'what, when, where and how' of the situation in which the incident developed, and who was present there at that time. Clues are also tracked down if they seem to offer reliable insight into the 'why' of behaviour. After the collection of data, it is necessary to

isolate the most important items for decision-making. According to Paul Pigors, "The central aim of this method is to stimulate self-development in a blend of understanding that is essential for productive interaction. This blend combines intellectual ability (power to think clearly, incisively and reasonably about specific facts and also about abstractions); practical judgement (capacity to modify conclusions arrived at intellectually, so that they meet the test of common sense); and social awareness (being able to appreciate the force of other people's feelings and willing to adjust or implement a decision so that it can be more acceptable to persons who are affected by it)."[4]

3. **Role playing:** It involves creating a more realistic situation, usually one involving human problems and conflicts, and then acting out the various parts. The role assuming takes place in a situation fairly similar to a real situation and affords the participants the incidental experiences that enhance their sensitivity, growth and development.
4. **In-basket method:** In it, each team of the trainees is given a file of correspondence relating to a functional area of management. Each individual studies the file and makes his own recommendations on the situation. Later, the observations of each individual member are compared and conclusions on different functional areas reached. These are put down in the form of a report.
5. **Business or management game:** Business games are classroom simulation exercises designed to be representative of real life conditions, in which teams of individuals compete against one another or against an environment in order to achieve a given objective. An atmosphere is created in which the participants play a dynamic role, and enrich their skills through involvement and simulated experience. Most business games are expressed in the form of a mathematical model controlled and manipulated by a computer, while

others can be played manually. The interacting types of games are like a game of tennis: the decisions of one team influence or affect the performance of the other teams. In the non-interacting types of games, each team is independent, and its performance entirely depends upon its own competence; the decisions of one team do not affect others.[5] Business games are intended to teach trainees how to take management decisions in an integrated manner. The participants learn by analyzing problems and by making trial-and-error decisions. Such games illustrate the existence of various group processes, including communication, the resolution of conflicts, the emergence of leadership, and the development of ties of friendship.

6. **Sensitivity training:** This is an off-the-job training technique, also known as T-group training or laboratory training. It mainly deals with developing or changing the behaviour pattern of the trainees. In these training sessions, the participants discuss their real problems, learn more about themselves, particularly their weaknesses and emotions and develop insights into how others react to their behaviour and how they themselves react to those of others. The trainees are divided into groups and these groups do not have any set agenda and work mainly in an unstructured way. The participants learn mainly by analyzing and understanding one's own or other's emotions and also through mutual interactions. They try to sort out their inter-personal problems. Supporters of sensitivity training claim great success in improving the behaviour and attitudes of the managers through this technique. The critiques, on the other hand, are equally emphatic about its dangers and limitations. They maintain that in several cases, the sensitivity training sessions have caused tremendous emotional problems for individual participants. In some cases, interpersonal relations between the peers or between supervisors and subordinates have been more embittered following the in-company sensitivity

training sessions. However, in spite of the controversy, it has to be accepted that this method is a very interesting technique for attempting a change in the behavioural patterns, although it must be handled carefully and be guided only by experts trained in this.

There are various management development techniques, both on-the job and off-the-job methods that can be used by an organization to hone the skills and improve the capabilities of its managerial staff. The company may use a combination of lectures, coaching, conferences, case studies, job rotation, role playing, etc. to design a programme that most effectively channelises the efforts of the employees towards the organizational goals. Management development plays a very significant role in improving the quality of the workforce, boosting their morale, increasing their knowledge and ultimately converting the managerial staff into invaluable assets of the company.

QUESTIONS

1. Define management development. What are the skills required by a manager to perform his duties efficiently?
2. What are the various objectives at different levels of management development?
3. Why is management development important? What role does it play in the long-term success of a concern?
4. How are management development programmes different from regular training and development programmes?
5. Write short notes on the following:
   (i) Role playing
   (ii) Sensitivity training
   (iii) In-basket method.

NOTES

1. R.L. Katz. "Skill of an Effective Administrator," *Harvard Business Review*, Vol. 33, No. 1, Jan.-Feb. 1955, pp. 33-41.

2. G.P. Asthana. "Teaching Methods in Management Development", in *Management Education and Training in India*, V.M.N.I.C.M., pp. 162-63.
3. H. Bedrosian. "Selecting Supervisors for Training, What Motivates the Boss", *Personnel*, Vol. 48, No. 1, 197, pp. 44-47.
4. Paul Pigors. "Case Method", in *Training and Development Handbook*, pp. 180-81.
5. N.S. Ramaswamy. "Management Games," in V.M.N.I.C.M. Report, p. 185.

Chapter 11

Career Development and Employee Empowerment

As a component of organizational development, career development refers to how organizations structure the career growth and progress of their employees. It is also an important element of succession planning within some organizations. Once an employee is hired, trained, and appraised, it seems that the development function comes to an end. However, neither organization's requirements nor individual's abilities are ever constant. So, people's long-term career planning and development should be an integral part of an organization's comprehensive employee development programme. A career can be defined as a sequence of separate but related work activities that provides continuity, order and meaning in a person's life.[1] Earlier, organizations did not give importance to an individual's career development. But now-a-days, many organizations view career development as a way of preventing job burnout, improving the quantity of employees' work lives and reducing employee turnover. An organization should give opportunities to its employees to grow and develop within the organization so that the workforce keeps pace with the demands of the ever changing business environment. Career planning and development is a deliberate process through which a person becomes aware of personal career-related attributes and lifelong series of stages that contribute to his career fulfillment.[2] Career planning and development is not a one-shot training programme. It has a longer time frame and wider focus. It is an ongoing organized and formalized effort that recognizes people as a vital organizational resource.

Responsibility of Career Planning and Development

I. Employee Responsibility

In today's competitive world of business, employees must play an active role in planning their career and implementing their own personal development. Employees are responsible for updating their skills, abilities and knowledge. Some organizations provide employee empowerment approach to development where employees can create their own developmental programmes. However, giving employees total responsibility for managing their own careers can create problem in today's flat organizations, where opportunities to move through the hierarchy are far fewer than in traditional bureaucratic organizations.[3]

The primary responsibility of an employee's career development lies with the employee himself. Following are few suggestions for the employees in this regard:

1. Set your own mission statement—what you want to achieve in job and life?
2. Identify your strengths and weaknesses.
3. Take full responsibility for your own growth and development.
4. Manage your image inside and outside the organization. Show your achievements.
5. Always update yourself with current knowledge, skills and abilities.
6. Build your own network by attending conferences, seminars and social gatherings.
7. Try to be a team member. Provide solutions and do not point out the problems.
8. Hope for the best but be prepared for the worst. Always have different options available with you. Develop contingency plans for yourself, in case of situations like lay-offs, retrenchment, downsizing, mergers and acquisitions, closure, etc.

II. Organization's Responsibility

An organization and its managers can play a very influential role in a person's career development. A manager should provide developmental assignments to an employee and also provide him constructive and timely performance feedback. The employer can provide career-oriented training and development opportunities, offer career management programmes and establish career-oriented performance appraisal and job-posting policies. The essence of a progressive career development programme is built on providing support for employees to continually add to their skills, abilities and knowledge and for this the logical sequence of steps includes the following:[4]

1. Clearly communicating organization's goals and future strategies to its people so that they know what is the target of organization and how they can develop themselves to achieve this.
2. Creating growth opportunities to provide employees good openings for new, interesting and challenging tasks.
3. Offering financial assistance for learning—may be in the form of tuition reimbursement so that they update their knowledge.
4. Providing the time for each employee to learn, such as paid time off from work for off-the-job training and development.

   For instance, a college or university or UGC supports a teacher/lecturer in his career development by providing him paid study leave to go for higher degrees like Ph.D. and financial support for research projects, payment for attending conferences and seminars (nationally), refresher courses, etc.

III. Steps for Encouraging Employee Career Development

1. **Realistic job previews:** Providing realistic job previews before actually hiring a person is very important. Realistic job previews can help prospective employees more accurately gauge whether the job is indeed for

them and particularly whether a job's demands are a good fit with a candidate's skills and interests.[5] This is especially important for a fresh candidate whose confidence is yet to build up. By providing interesting and challenging job to a fresh candidate an employer can prevent reality shock. Reality shock is considered as a phenomenon that occurs when the new employee's high job expectations meet/confront with reality of a boring, uninteresting and unchallenging job.

2. **Career-oriented appraisals:** In career-oriented appraisals the well-trained and experienced supervisor or manager not only appraises the employee performance but also aligns that performance with the feasible career path and finds out where training and development is required.
3. **Planned job rotation:** This refers to well-planned movement of an employee from one position to another so as to enhance his role with the organization.
4. **Mentoring:** A mentor is an older and respected manager or professional who counsels and listens to feelings as well as facts and stimulates people through ideas and information.[6] Mentoring is a developmentally oriented relationship between senior and junior colleagues or peers that involves advising, role modelling, sharing contacts and giving general support.[7] Mentoring can be voluntary and informal or involuntary and formal. Informal mentoring is generally more effective than mentoring done solely as a formal responsibility.
5. **Job-posting:** This refers to the announcement of job openings in the company either posting on bulletin board, or in a company's newsletter. Job-posting systems have the advantage of reinforcing the notion that the organization promotes from within.
6. **Coaching:** It refers to meetings and discussions between a manager and employee regarding the latter's career development. Coaching involves setting of a congenial environment, actively listening to the employee, asking questions and providing useful feedback.

IV. Life Cycle of a Career

A typical career goes through the following phases:

1. **Exploratory stage:** This is the first stage of an employee's career where he explores various options. If he has chosen to enter a particular organization, the organization should understand its responsibility towards the newcomer and try to make the job challenging and interesting for him. He should be given proper guidance and training so that he fits the job position perfectly. The employee will stay with the organization only if he is satisfied with the circumstances. Otherwise he will start exploring options outside of the organization.
2. **Establishment stage:** At this stage, the employee has chosen some specific direction and has begun to settle down in his career. He looks for growth and development. For an employee's successful career development programme an organization is required to give him feedback and progress information. The first performance appraisal, first promotion, first completed project, etc. are extremely important occasions in a young person's career.
3. **Maintenance stage:** This is the stage when an employee attempts to retain what he or she has established in the career. In today's competitive and dynamic business environment, this requires continued learning and updating in order to maintain their continuity with the organization. This is the stage where an employee faces mid-career crisis. In some cases, people try to switch over to an entirely different job. For example, an employee may leave his office job for the teaching profession.
4. **Decline:** This is the stage when the employee reaches retirement age. This is a difficult time for many employees as retirement signals the end of their productive years. The organization should provide suitable retirement benefits to the employee and ensure a smooth separation. Some private organizations may re-employ retired personnel in a different job position.

Employee Empowerment

Employee empowerment is the philosophy of enabling employees to make important decisions related to their work and take more responsibility for their jobs. The logic behind employee empowerment is to foster accountability, build employee morale and confidence, and create a sense of belongingness in the employees. If employee empowerment is undertaken in an efficient way, it results in heightened productivity, better quality of work and more job satisfaction. The process of empowerment differs from organization to organization depending upon work culture and organizational structures. By delegating work to employees at all levels, the top management can direct its energy towards important work. Human resources, in spite of being the most valuable factor of production, are often underutilized. Employee empowerment helps to utilize the skills and capabilities of the workers in the best possible manner. Proper training and resources should be provided to the employees to make them capable of taking good decisions by themselves. If employees are unable to take proper decisions, then the very purpose of empowerment is defeated. Employee empowerment requires the organization to be restructured by reducing levels of hierarchy. A flat organizational structure supports empowerment. The role of the manager also changes from that of a figure of top authority to a more supportive role. An environment of mutual trust, commitment and dedication should be maintained for successful implementation of employee empowerment.

Methods of Employee Empowerment

1. **Job enlargement:** It is a type of horizontal expansion which entails taking charge of more duties and responsibilities at the same level. Job enlargement increases the scope of the job and reduces level of specialization. Its aim is to reduce the monotony and repetition associated with a particular job by introducing newer tasks. It helps to create flexible workforces who are capable of performing a variety of jobs. One negative aspect of job enlargement is that

employees may be required to do more work at the same pay scale. For example, a waiter at a small restaurant may be required to chop vegetables or do the dishes along with his regular duty of taking orders and serving customers.

2. **Job enrichment:** Job enrichment entails increasing the depth of the job to include responsibilities that are carried out at higher levels of the organization. It is vertical expansion of a job. Job enrichment gives more control over the jobs by increasing the employees' level of responsibility. They are required to do more planning and organizing work. They are given more authority and autonomy over their jobs. Job enrichment is also known as job enhancement. It requires a higher level of knowledge, skills and challenging work. It motivates the employees and gives opportunities for personal growth. Job enrichment enhances the quality of work and provides a meaningful job experience. Workers experience more job satisfaction as job enrichment brings more scope for achievement, recognition, development and growth. If the responsibilities of a proofreader in a publication are increased to include some level of editorial work, it would be an example of job enrichment.

Benefits of Employee Empowerment

1. **Increased productivity:** A lot of time is saved when employees can take their own decisions and do not have to wait for approval from senior levels. Workflow is not disturbed due to unnecessary hassles, and delays are avoided. The increased sense of responsibility motivates employees to try out innovative methods of doing work. Employees derive more satisfaction from their work as their contribution towards the organizational goals is increased. Higher job satisfaction coupled with saving of precious time results in higher productivity.

2. **Reduced costs:** By taking their own decisions, employees save the time and efforts of top management. Since there is a high level of decentralization in an organization where employees are empowered, the need for middle level managers is considerably lower. Properly trained employees are also less likely to waste resources or have an accident. All these benefits collectively reduce the unnecessary expenditures of the organization.
3. **Improved quality:** Employee empowerment requires that the employees are properly trained in order to take good managerial decisions. Adequate resources are also provided to them to enable them to tackle day-to-day affairs in an efficient manner. The senior managers delegate much of their work to other employees so that they can concentrate on more important tasks. Better efficiency in operations is achieved as a result of employee empowerment which leads to improved quality.
4. **Competitive edge:** Empowering employees can help a firm to gain a competitive edge over its competitors. Competitive, motivated and loyal employees can be created as a result of empowerment. It helps to utilize manpower in the best possible way. Employees get a chance to exercise their managerial and decision-making abilities while performing their job duties. A dedicated, loyal and empowered workforce helps to place the company ahead of its competitors.
5. **Better job satisfaction and retention of employees:** Employee turnover is a big problem faced by many organizations in the modern world. Employee empowerment helps in curbing this problem by improving job satisfaction of the employees. Employees get to perform a variety of jobs at different levels requiring different skills and abilities. This creates a challenging and dynamic work environment where employees actually enjoy their jobs.

Challenges to Employee Empowerment

1. **Confusion:** Employees are encouraged to think on their own and take their own decisions. But this may cause confusion and chaos in organizations where employees are traditionally trained to take orders from superiors. This can also give rise to disagreements among co-workers if they are unable to take a unanimous decision.
2. **Improper training:** To enable employees to become accountable for themselves and take the best decisions it is vital that they are given proper training. Each individual should be trained intensively to develop his skills and talents so that he becomes a more productive and capable worker. But in case employees are not properly trained, they would not be able to judge the situations well and wont be able to take good decisions for the company's benefit.
3. **Resistance to change:** The people working in an organization can be resistant to changes and innovations in the work place. Some managers may feel that their employees are not competent enough to take their own decisions and be accountable for their work, while some employees themselves may not want additional responsibility. Empowering employees would also require some changes to be made in management style. The managers would no longer be the ultimate authority. Thus, employees and managers may be resistant to adopt changes.
4. **Breakdown of organizational structure:** Employee empowerment can be conducted more successfully in a decentralized organization with lesser hierarchical levels. This would require breaking down the existing structure and eliminating redundant levels. This is not an easy process. Also it would make it more difficult for the managers to control the employees once they have become used to their autonomy.

QUESTIONS

1. Define career development. Why is it important?
2. Career development of an employee is his own responsibility. Do you agree?
3. How can the organization help in the growth and development of an employee's career?
4. Discuss the various stages in the life cycle of a career.
5. What do you mean by employee empowerment? What is its significance?
6. Describe the various methods of employee empowerment.

NOTES

1. Edwin B. Flippo. *Personnel Management*. Sixth ed. McGraw-Hill, New York, 1984, p. 248.
2. Gary Dessler. *Human Resource Management*. Pearson Education, Ninth ed. Delhi, 2004, p. 274.
3. Luis R. Gomez-Mejia, David B. Balkin and Robert L. Cardy. *Managing Human Resources*. Third ed. Pearson Education, Delhi, 2003, p. 296.
4. Stephen P. Robbins. *Organizational Behaviour*. Tenth ed. Pearson Education, Delhi, 2004, p. 497.
5. Gary Dessler. *Human Resource Management*. Pearson Education, Ninth ed. Delhi, 2004, p. 275.
6. Edwin B. Flippo. *Personnel Management*. Sixth ed. McGraw-Hill, New York, 1984, p. 261.
7. Luis R. Gomez-Mejia, David B. Balkin and Robert L. Cardy. *Managing Human Resources*. Third ed. Pearson Education, Delhi, 2003, p. 309.

Chapter 12

Succession Planning

Succession planning is the process by which an organization identifies and develops potential successors for key leadership positions in the company through a systematic evaluation process and training. Capable senior employees are identified and are prepared for advancement into more challenging roles through intensive development of their knowledge, skills and abilities. Within the organization, succession planning increases the available pool of talented and capable employees who are groomed to take up highly responsible roles as and when they arise in future. It ensures that the key roles can be filled from within the organization. To develop employees for succession planning, they should be provided a wide range of internal and external training and developmental opportunities and assigned to special projects where they can hone their decision- making and leadership skills. Succession planning is also a good technique for retaining superior employees within the organization. In the modern business world, competitors often lure away an organization's capable employees by offering them lucrative salary packages and growth opportunities. By investing time and efforts in the employees and by providing them the chance to grow within the organization, the company can prevent its valuable employees from joining the competitor. The career path and professional growth of the employees should be integrated with the long-term objectives of the organization so that the employees understand the responsibilities associated with the roles they are being developed to fill.

Many corporations prefer to fill the top positions internally instead of looking for talent outside the company. One of the most well-known examples is that of U.S.–based General Electric Company (GE), a leading business conglomerate. GE has been committed to succession planning from the past many decades and some of its very successful CEOs (both past and present), like Reginald H. Jones, Jack Welch and Jeffrey R. Immelt were promoted to the position after long years of grooming and development.[1] The selection of Cyrus Mistry who succeeded Ratan Tata as the Chairman of Tata Sons Ltd. in December 2012 is also an example of succession planning. Cyrus Mistry has been on the board of Tata Sons Ltd. from 2006 and has served as a director of Tata Power and Tata Elxsi. He worked as a deputy chairman under the guidance of Ratan Tata for about one year before taking on the responsibilities of the chairman in 2012.[2]

Fundamental Principles of Successful Succession Planning

1. The basis of succession planning is a strong HR management system which includes effective training, development and performance appraisal programmes.
2. Succession planning is about effectively re-filling a certain job position with an employee most suitable for the role; it is not about replacing a specific person.
3. The succession process should be carefully planned out and thoroughly implemented to ensure that the right employees are being prepared to fill the top positions in the years to come.
4. Succession planning is the responsibility of management, and it can be implemented only with the wholehearted support of top management.
5. It is a future-oriented process and the organization needs to identify what types of employees would be needed to fill future positions arising after 5 or 10 years.

6. Personnel policies should be updated from time to time in order to ensure that fair and equitable employment practices are adopted that allow the appointment of the most talented employees.
7. A systematic approach for identifying and selecting potential successors should be established so that unsuitable employees are not chosen for succeeding outgoing leaders.
8. Efforts should be continuously made to identify high performers and eligible employees through performance evaluation and potential appraisal.
9. The skills and knowledge that are required to serve in the top positions should be identified and these qualities should be cultivated in those employees who are being developed for succession.
10. The training and development needs of the potential successors should be determined and suitable programmes should be designed to hone their skills and competencies.
11. The top management should periodically review and monitor the candidate's performance and progress.
12. Open communication should be encouraged between the management and the successors, and the successors should be provided feedback on their development.
13. The succession planning programme can be successful only if the successors are chosen keeping in mind the overall strategic goals of the organization.[3]

Succession Planning Process

1. **Planning:** The first step is to develop a strategic plan that will provide a blueprint of how the succession plan is to be implemented. The long-term vision and goals of the organization are identified and the current personnel policies and procedures are studied. For a succession plan to be successful, it is vital to integrate the plan with the interests and aspirations of the senior employees who are being groomed for succession.

2. **Analysis:** In this step, the various challenges the company is likely to face in the future and the skills and competencies the CEO would need to meet them are analyzed. The future CEO would need a variety of managerial and technical skills to be able to fulfil his responsibilities effectively. The current supply of manpower in the organization should be studied in relation to the anticipated demand. Efforts should be made to determine the knowledge, talents, skills and capabilities that would be required in the organization in the future. It is necessary to identify the overall long term talent needs of the company and not just of a particular position.
3. **Identification of talent pools:** The competencies and skill levels of the current workers need to be assessed in order to identify the available pool of talent. These may be measured by the use of performance evaluation tools like 360° Feedback, critical incident methods and rating scales. It is also necessary to evaluate the employee's capacity to perform in more responsible jobs in future through potential appraisal techniques and psychological appraisal. Factors like the employee's educational background, time spent with the company, his behaviour and attitude should also be taken into account. The skill sets of the employees should be compared with the skills needed for the key leadership roles and any gaps between the two should be identified.
4. **Development planning:** After the gaps have been identified, the next step involves creating development plans. The development plan includes the formal development procedures, coaching and mentoring, special job assignments, learning projects, etc. which will help the employees to gain the necessary skills and experiences. The employee's progress will be monitored against the plan. The duration of the development plan would depend upon the succession plan strategy of the organization.

5. **Implementing the succession plan:** The succession plan should be linked to the HR processes like compensation, recruitment, performance planning, workforce planning, etc. It is a long-term plan, and sometimes the succession planning process is started from the time a brilliantly outstanding employee begins his career (Jack Welch, the highly successful former CEO of GE was being groomed for senior positions from the time he started his career as a junior chemical engineer in the same company). Implementing the succession plan includes the retention strategies like retention bonuses, promotions, challenging work, etc. It is essential to compare the progress of the succession plan with the upcoming personnel requirements of the organization so that a capable employee is available to fill a prestigious post should it fall vacant either expectedly (due to planned retirement), or unexpectedly (due to death, disability, illness, etc. of the position holder).

Advantages of Succession Planning

1. Succession planning helps the organization to minimise risks and survive challenging events arising in case of unforeseen departure of the key leader.
2. It ensures availability of well trained, experienced and capable employees who can readily fill key positions when the need arises.
3. Investing efforts and time in developing existing employees motivates them and creates a greater sense of belonging to the organization.
4. Internal promotion policies ensure better employee morale and encourage employees to continually improve their performance.
5. Filling of key positions internally is more beneficial and less risky than hiring an outsider for a top position.
6. There is retention of superior employees within the organization by providing them opportunities for professional growth and progress.

7. Employees promoted through succession planning are more committed towards the organizational goals as they are aware that their personal success is integrated with the success of the company.
8. It enables the organization to quickly stabilize its operations should the top position fall vacant unexpectedly due to any unforeseen event such as death or disability of the position holder.
9. Regular training and development programmes for the employees in order to prepare them for future roles results in a superior quality of workforce which can easily handle more responsibilities.
10. A company which is committed to succession planning has a well-defined recruitment and selection policy which helps the company to select the best among the available pool of candidates.[4]

Hurdles in Succession Planning

1. Lack of sufficient talent and skills in the existing staff.
2. A narrow approach because outside talent is not considered.
3. Ineffective HR practices which are not conducive to successful implementation of succession planning.
4. Biasness/favouritism towards certain employees by top management.
5. Inability to retain key employees and unplanned departure during plan implementation.
6. Wrong choice of potential successors.
7. Ambiguous definition of career paths.
8. Lack of top management interest in succession planning.
9. Succession plans may become outdated with time if not reviewed regularly.

Succession planning is an important component of strategic HR planning. Certain challenges may crop up in the way of successful implementation of succession planning, but there are a number of strategies that can be adopted to manage these.

If there is a lack of suitable talent at a particular level, the organization may consider looking further down the organizational hierarchy for potential leaders. First, good HR practices should be adopted so that the organization culture supports succession planning. Emphasis should be laid on motivating the talented employees with financial and non-financial incentives so as to retain them. The potential successors should be chosen strictly on the basis of their individual merit; favouritism in the selection process should be avoided. The top management should engage itself in the periodic review of the succession plan and the progress of the candidates to ensure that things are proceeding according to plans. It is very necessary to align the succession plan with the future HR requirements of the organization in the light of changing market environment. If implemented properly, succession plan facilitates the long-term sustenance and development of the organization by creating a pool of loyal and dedicated workforce who can readily take on added responsibility as and when needed.

QUESTIONS

1. Succession planning is a concept new to India. Comment.
2. What are the principles of successful succession planning? How can potential leaders be identified?
3. Explain various steps in succession planning with suitable examples.
4. Write a note on succession planning in Indian companies.
5. Why do many companies prefer to develop talent from within for holding future leadership positions rather than selecting from outside talent?
6. What are the numerous challenges to succession planning?

NOTES

1. http://www.ge.com/company/history/ past_leaders.html
2. http://www.forbes.com/sites/naazneenkarmali/2011/11/23/ratan-tata-anoints-billionaire-pallonji-mistrys-son-cyrus-as-successor/s
3. http://www.ameinfo.com/59276.html
4. http://www.businessknowhow.com/manage/ successplan.html

Chapter 13

Morale and Productivity

Morale is a vital ingredient of organizational success for it reflects the attitudes and sentiments an individual or group has towards the organizational objectives. Morale can be defined as "the state of the spirits of a person or group as exhibited by confidence, cheerfulness, discipline, and willingness to perform assigned tasks."[1] Morale hugely affects the productivity and job satisfaction of individuals. When people are enthusiastic in their work environment, they are said to be having high morale. Morale is an employee's zest for working or the lack of it. A person with a high morale feels his work is worth doing well and derives satisfaction from accomplishing his tasks. A high morale also enables a worker to ignore minor irritants and work under pressure without blowing up.

Factors Affecting Morale

The factors which affect employee morale can be categorised into two groups.

1. **External factors:** These are the factors external to the organization. These are comprised of the personality of the individual employee, his psychological make-up, level of intelligence, physical health, family background and relations with social groups and friends. Every human has his unique characteristics that influence his perceptions, attitudes, etc. that in turn affect his morale. Since these factors are outside the control of managers,

they can do little to change, control or influence them. But these factors have a huge impact on the employee morale.

2. **Internal factors:** These factors are under the domain of control of management. These include:
   (i) *Organizational goals*: One of the biggest factors that can have profound influence on the morale of employees is the organizational objectives. If the employee feels that the goals set by the management are worthwhile, valid and useful, then he develops a positive feeling towards the job and the organization. Allowing workers to participate in setting goals enhances the morale of the employee to a larger extent.
   (ii) *Organizational structure*: Structure is another influential factor of morale. In a sound structure where lines of authority are clearly specified and responsibility is precisely defined and where there is candid communication among the people, morale tends to be high. Normally high morale prevails in a decentralized structure.
   (iii) *Nature of work*: The nature of work the employee does is the biggest factor that affects his morale. Dull, monotonous and repetitive jobs make an employee feel depressed and adversely affect his morale. On the other hand, challenging tasks may motivate him to do well and boost his morale. The nature of the job should match with the skills, competence and willingness of the individual to perform it.
   (iv) *Management philosophies*: The treatment of subordinates by their leader can have an effect on the morale of the employees. Further, the style of leadership also affects morale. It is generally felt that a participative style will enhance morale and an authoritarian style will have a negative impact.
   (v) *Working conditions*: Morale is also a direct function of the conditions in the place of work. Morale will

be generally high when employees are placed in a clean, safe, comfortable and pleasant environment. Conversely, workers will feel suffocated if they are made to work in a congested environment.

(vi) *Compensation*: The remuneration workers receive for their work is the main factor which motivates them to work. If the employees are satisfied that they are being compensated properly, then they will have a high morale. Inadequate compensation leads to low morale, lower job satisfaction and may result in low productivity.

(vii) *Work groups*: Each individual has his unique perceptions, attitudes, and beliefs about the work environment, organization and people. Social forces and work groups also exert strong influence on his individual perceptions and attitudes and to this extent the morale of individual employees will also be affected.

Morale and Productivity

It is usually assumed that high morale and high productivity go hand in hand. However, research studies do not unanimously support this assumption. Katz and his associates found that morale had four dimensions—job satisfaction, identification with company, satisfaction with wages and promotion opportunities and pride in work group. They found out that only the last dimension, i.e. pride in work group, was significantly correlated with productivity. Herzberg analyzed the results of nearly two dozen studies on the effects of morale on productivity. In 54 per cent of the studies, high morale was related to high productivity; in 35 per cent, morale and productivity were not related; and in 11 per cent, high morale was related to low productivity. It seems that the relationship between morale and productivity is not absolute, and nor is it simple. Sometimes employees in an organization may be enthusiastic and in high spirits but their actual productive contribution might be less. While in certain other cases, employees may have resentment towards their job even though they may be highly productive. Therefore, no concrete conclusion can be taken about the relationship between morale and productivity.[2]

Indices of Low Morale

There are several indicators of low morale prevailing within the organization, the major ones being absenteeism and tardiness, employee turnover, grievances, fatigue and monotony, etc.

1. **Employee unrest:** Unrest may appear in different forms and influence both the individual and the group. It may be in 'inarticulate' form where the worker does not recognize that he is restless and dissatisfied. However, he may indulge in daydreams, be late for work, be absent or change jobs frequently and thus present a disciplinary problem. The unrest may be in 'articulate' form where the worker tends to express his unrest openly and enter formal grievances. This individual form of unrest may take the group form and cause collective action which has been termed as 'crowd behaviour'. Such situations may lead to strikes, work stoppages, and allied group activities. Although these activities are temporary, they may sometimes continue longer and result in permanent unrest called 'mass movements'. A great deal of unrest results from the workers' feelings of inadequacy and insecurity.
2. **Absenteeism and tardiness:** When employees of an organization suffer from low morale, they tend to express their dissatisfaction by being absent and tardy. This poses problems to production schedules, especially where line and group production methods are involved. A great deal of absenteeism is caused by non-occupational illness. Mental health problems also contribute markedly towards total absences. Absenteeism among manufacturing workers, shop workers and nightshift workers is higher than among non-manufacturing workers, office workers and dayshift workers respectively. Job satisfaction is found to be negatively related to absenteeism and *vice versa*.

3. **Employee turnover:** The biggest indication of low morale in a company is a high rate of employee turnover. Workers may respond to severe unrest, discontentment and morale problems by deserting their jobs. Employee turnover up to a certain level is normal for any organization, but an exceptionally high rate of turnover indicates low morale and job dissatisfaction among workers. The primary concern in turnover from a morale standpoint relates to workers who leave voluntarily for avoidable reasons. Employees may leave their jobs due to improper supervision, stressful relationship with co-workers, personnel policies, dissatisfaction with compensation, poor working conditions, insecurity, etc.
4. **Grievances:** Grievances lead to lower levels of morale and may cause severe forms of unrest through social contagion. Grievances may be real or imaginary and may result from numerous reasons. Both management and labour may have grievances, and unrest on any side can lower the morale. Typical examples are increase in demand for wages, complaints against a particular boss, objections regarding not getting a promotion, protests against implementation of certain rules and regulations, etc. The grievances may reveal more deep-rooted difficulties and problems than what appears on the surface.
5. **Need for more discipline:** If there is a need to impose more discipline than is normally required, it could point towards issues of low morale. Under ideal conditions, workers would understand the rationale of rules and regulations; discipline should be self-imposed. If the management feels a need to impose discipline, it points towards poor morale. The need for discipline may be related to different fields such as attendance, punctuality, smoking, tardiness, etc. The major kinds of disciplinary actions include correction, oral reprimand, written reprimand, fines or discharge in case of severe indiscipline.

6. **Fatigue and monotony:** Fatigue has been defined as a reduction in ability to do work because of the pace of the preceding work. The rates of fatigue vary with the intensity of the motivation. Fatigue is not merely physical. Variables involved in this respect are length of work, speed of work and the extent of physical labour. Repetition and lack of variety in a job make it monotonous and routine. Monotony depends upon an individual rather than on the job. One individual may find a job interesting while other may find it monotonous. If a person is placed on an unsuitable job that fails to interest him, it gives rise to monotony.

Benefits of High Employee Morale

1. **Encourages teamwork:** Employees having high morale work better as a team. They are committed to their jobs, feel belongingness towards the organization and are enthusiastic about achieving the organizational goals by cooperating with each other within a work team.
2. **Builds harmonious relations among employees:** When employee morale is high, the individual employee adopts a more positive attitude towards his co-workers. The overall behaviour of the employees is cordial as each one is happy with his own job. There is less scope for aggressiveness or negativity and as such a friendly atmosphere prevails.
3. **Retaining valuable employees:** Employee turnover is one of the biggest problems that organizations face today. Companies with high morale are more successful in retaining their talented employees. Employees in such organizations have higher level of job satisfaction and more loyalty towards the organization. They feel motivated and appreciated for their work and are therefore likely to stay with the same enterprise.
4. **Better employer-employee relations:** Mutual respect and understanding are common features of organizations having high morale. When employees are treated with respect and are made to feel as valuable members of the

organizations, they tend to carry forward this behaviour with their own subordinates and customers. Thus, good relations are maintained between all the parties involved.

Suggestions to Improve Morale

1. **Recognition:** Employees feel good if their efforts are being recognized and appreciated by the management. Good performance should always be appreciated; otherwise employees will feel that their efforts are being ignored. Often, simple words of encouragement can uplift the morale of those who have been working to achieve the organizational objectives.
2. **Open communication:** There should be open two-sided communication between the management and the workers. The employees should be given a platform to voice their concerns and grievances. Employee grievances should be listened to and addressed in a timely manner.
3. **Effective leadership:** An efficient leader is one who is able to encourage and motivate employees to give their best. Employees develop a high level of morale under good leaders and *vice versa*.
4. **Employee feedback:** The employees should be encouraged to provide regular feedback and suggestions. Morale of employees will receive a boost when their views are given value. This will make them feel that their opinions are important to the organization.
5. **Attitude of the management:** Morale is highly contagious. If the management has a positive attitude towards work and organization, then the employees will also adopt a similar attitude.
6. **Trips/outdoor activities:** The organization can invest in trips, picnics, group activities, etc. to forge a closer bond between the employees. Such activities encourage informal networking and friendships among the employees and also foster better relations at the work place.

7. **Flexible working hours:** Some organizations give their employees the option of choosing flexible work hours as may suit them. In Western countries, people with small children or old parents to take care of are offered this option.
8. **Work-life balance:** The employees are also human beings having a personal life separate from the workplace. Organizations should be understanding enough to ensure that employees are able to achieve an optimum balance between their personal and professional life. People will be dissatisfied if they are unable to fulfil their duties towards their families.
9. **Monetary rewards:** The main reason for which people work is the monetary reward. Enough financial incentives in form of pay hikes, bonuses, rewards, etc. should be provided to the employees to sustain and increase their enthusiasm towards their job.[3]

QUESTIONS

1. Define morale. What are the internal factors that affect employee morale?
2. How are morale and productivity interlinked? Is there any direct relationship between the two?
3. What do employee unrest and a high rate of employee turnover convey about the level of morale in an organization?
4. Why is the maintenance of a high rate of morale significant to the company's well-being?
5. What steps can be taken to improve morale of employees?

NOTES

1. http://www.thefreedictionary.com/morale
2. http://www.freemba.in/articlesread.php?artcode=2568&stcode=2&substcode=109
3. http://www.wikihow.com/Improve-Employee-Morale

Chapter 14

Performance Appraisal

Performance appraisal is the periodic, formal evaluation of employee performance for the purpose of making career decisions.[1] Though with the help of training and development programmes, employees acquire new knowledge and skills and hence, become more capable and competent, yet there is need to systematically appraise them and provide them information regarding their performance. This enables employees to know how they are performing in comparison with set standards. Performance appraisal is a formal, structured system of measuring and evaluating an employee's job-related behaviours and outcomes to discover how and why the employee is presently performing on the job and how the employee can perform more effectively in the future so that the employee, organization and society all benefit.[2] Measurement of the employee performance is the basis of the appraisal system. The performance appraisal process evaluates the performance to judge the capability of the employee. A good performance appraisal scheme should be future oriented. The managers should give the employees proper feedback and guide them to higher levels of performance in future.

Objectives of Performance Appraisal

(i) To provide feedback to the employees so that they know where they stand and improve their performance.

(ii) Increase motivation to perform better in future.

(iii) Help to formulate performance linked compensation plans.

(iv) Facilitate decisions regarding promotions and transfers of employees.

(v) To identify the strengths and weaknesses of the employees in order to plan career development programmes.

(vi) To assess the potential capabilities of the employees.

(vii) To design relevant training and development programmes.

(viii) To test the effectiveness of the recruitment, selection and placement policies.

(ix) To collect information for research about effectiveness of HR department policies.

(x) To improve the communication and understanding between superiors and subordinates.

(xi) To confirm or reject the employment of probationary staff on completion of their probation period.

Process of Performance Appraisal

The logical sequence of steps in a performance appraisal process are the following:

1. **Set the objectives of performance appraisal:** Generally, a performance appraisal serves three purposes:
    (i) *Administrative*: For the use of personnel decisions like promotions, transfers, pay increase, etc.
    (ii) *Research*: For validating selection instruments.
    (iii) *Developmental*: To identify the training needs of employees.

So, objectives of performance appraisal are set depending upon the needs of the organization.

2. **Establish standards of performance:** The next step is to set the standards of employee performance. These standards act as a base, yardstick or benchmark for evaluating the performance. The set standards will inform the employee what is expected from him on the job.

3. **Communicating the performance standards to employees:** The set performance standards are communicated to the employees. The employees should be informed about what is desired from them on the job. It is important that any confusion or misunderstanding is clarified at the earliest.
4. **Measure actual performance:** Measuring the actual performance accurately is very important. The performance can be measured by personal observation, written reports, ratings by supervisors, etc.
5. **Compare actual performance with the standard performance:** After measuring the actual performance, it is to be compared with the standard set earlier. Deviations, if any, from the set standards are noted and the reasons behind the deviations are analyzed.
6. **Discuss the reports with employees:** The assessment reports are discussed with the employees and they are given feedback about their performances.
7. **Take corrective action, if any:** The last step is to take corrective action if need arises. This may include advising, counselling, warning, motivating, coaching and training the employees. These are useful ways to correct the defects and improve employee's performance in future.

Techniques of Performance Appraisal

Different methods of performance appraisal are used for evaluating the performance of the employees. Some of these are traditional and have been used for years, while some others have come into use recently.

I. **Casual, Unsystematic and Haphazard Appraisal Methods**

This is an ancient performance appraisal approach, which is very common in all organizations. In this approach, more emphasis is placed on the evaluation of the employee's worth as a person. But this approach does not evaluate all performances in the same manner.

Moreover, there is a greater scope for human bias and prejudice.

II. **Traditional Methods**

1. *Ranking*: This is one of the simplest and oldest methods of performance appraisal. In this method one person is compared with all other employees for the purpose of placing them in a simple rank order of worth. All the employees are placed in order of their relative worth. This method separates the efficient from the inefficient but it suffers from following defects:[3]

   (i) It does not appear to be desirable to compare one person with another because different persons have different traits and qualities.

   (ii) It simply tells us who is better than the other but it does not indicate how much better he is than the other.

   (iii) This method may be used only in case of small organizations. If a company employs a large number of employees then it may not be possible to rank all of them in order of their worth.

   (iv) This system is based on snap judgement and does not have any systematic procedure to determine the relative worth of an employee.

2. *Paired-comparison*: This method was developed to overcome the defects of ranking method. It compares the performance of each worker with that of every other worker in the group or section. At one time, comparisons are made between two people and a decision is made about which pair is superior. Suppose there are four employees in a firm. Employee A's performance is compared with B's and a judgement is made regarding who is better performer. Then A is compared with C and D in the same manner. Similarly, the approach is used for other personnel.

3. *Person-to-person comparison*: In this method, certain factors like initiative, faithfulness, leadership, dependability, creativity, etc. are selected for the purpose of analysis. After this, a scale is designed for each factor. Now, instead of defining varying degrees of each factor like leadership, dependability, etc. particular employees are used to represent these degrees. For each factor the most efficient and least efficient person are selected. These two persons represent the two ends of the scale. Then an average person is selected to represent the medium point. After this, two points are marked one above and one below the average. In this way a scale of five points is ascertained. Thus, a scale of persons for each factor is created. Now, instead of comparing whole people to whole people, personnel are compared to key persons, one factor at a time. The main limitation of this method is that the preparation of scales for each factor is largely complicated and difficult.
4. *Grading*: In this method certain categories of worth are established well in advance. For example categories are defined as extraordinary, satisfactory, average, unsatisfactory, etc. After this, employee performance is compared with these grades and the person is allocated the suitable grade, i.e. the grade that best represents his performance.
5. *Forced distribution*: This is the modification of the grading system. In this system, certain percentages are established for each grade and the evaluator has to rate the subordinates according to the specified distribution. A standard distribution looks like the following:

Grade	Percentage
Best/Superior	10%
Good	20%
Average	40%
Bad	20%
Poor	10%

This means that if there are 10 employees in the department, 1 will be graded as superior, 2 as good, 4 as average, 2 as bad and 1 as poor.

The main disadvantage of this technique is that it forces the rater to use predetermined rating categories that might not fairly represent that particular group of employees.

6. **Graphic rating scales:** This approach is similar to person-to-person comparison but the difference is that the degrees on the factor scales are represented by definitions rather than by key people. These are the most commonly used methods of performance appraisal. The rater is asked to rate the employees on the basis of certain factors on a scale. Generally two types of factors are considered, these are:
   (i) Job-related characteristics such as dependability, cooperation, judgement, attendance, initiative, etc.
   (ii) Contributions such as quality and quantity of work. The rater evaluates the performance on the basis of these traits on a continuous scale.

   The advantages of the graphic rating scale are that they are easy to construct and use and also they attempt to reduce the personal bias.

7. **Checklists:** This method is used to reduce the burden on the evaluator. Instead of evaluating employee performance the rater merely reports it. A checklist is prepared in which several questions in relation to a particular job are included. The rater has to simply mark the tick against the column of yes or no. The questions may be weighted but the rater is not aware of the specific values attached to different questions. The main disadvantage of the checklist system is that it is difficult to assemble and weigh a number of statements (in question forms) about a person's contribution and characteristics. Moreover, each department needs separate checklist due to difference in the nature of duties and responsibilities of different work.

8. **Forced-choice distribution:** The main objective of this method is to reduce or eliminate the possibility of rater bias by forcing the rater to choose between descriptive statements of seemingly equal worth. The rater has to select one statement out of the pair that best describes an employee or is least applicable to that employee. The statements within each pair are designed to appear equally positive or equally negative. For example, the rater may be asked to select one statement out of the following pair that best describes the worker:

   (i) He is reliable.

   (ii) He is agreeable.

   Then, the rater may be asked to choose one statement out of the following pair that least describes the worker:

   (i) He is uncooperative.

   (ii) He is not interested in doing well.

   One statement out of each pair is correct in identifying the better performance and this scoring key is kept secret and is not known to the rater. It is difficult for the rater to distinguish the items that represent desirable or undesirable characteristics. Thus, the chances of deliberately assigning favourable or unfavourable ratings are reduced very much.

9. **Critical incidents:** Critical incidents refer to certain key acts of behaviour that make the difference between success and failure on a job. The supervisor keeps the record of positive and negative acts/events of a subordinate's work-related behaviour. All these acts are critical incidents. After a fixed time interval like six months or so, the supervisor and the subordinate meet to discuss the latter's performance on the basis of the critical incidents. For example, incidents in a purchasing agent's job might be the following[4]:

   (i) Treated a salesperson in a markedly discourteous manner.

   (ii) Rejected a bid that was excessively overpriced.

(iii) Persuaded a local vendor to stock an important item.

(iv) Failed to return an important phone call.

The main advantage of this method is that by keeping systematic record helps in backing up personnel decisions when challenged by the trade union, workers, courts, etc. as these are hard evidence.

10. **Field review:** In this method, the evaluator, usually HR specialist, interviews supervisors and asks questions about their subordinates. The evaluator gets the opinions of the supervisor regarding the subordinate's work progress, performance, strengths, weakness, etc. and records it for future reference.

11. **Confidential report:** This is one of the traditional and most common methods of performance appraisal in most of the government organizations. An annual confidential report (ACR) of each subordinate is prepared by the immediate supervisor. This is descriptive in nature and is usually prepared at the end of every year. An ACR highlights the strengths, weaknesses, performance, character, ability, etc. of the subordinate. The main disadvantage of this method is that it involves a lot of subjectivity. Also, no feedback is provided to the employee being appraised. So, its credibility is low.

12. **Free essay method:** In this method, the evaluator, usually supervisor writes a report about employees' performance. The supervisor considers the following factors about an employee while preparing the essay:

(i) Job knowledge.

(ii) Relations with co-workers and superiors.

(iii) Attitudes and perceptions.

(iv) Understanding of organizational plans and policies.

(v) Training and development needs.

(vi) Strengths and weaknesses.

This is a non-quantitative technique of performance appraisal. However, the disadvantage of this method is that it is highly subjective.

13. **Behaviourally anchored rating scales (BARS):** It attempts to evaluate job performance in terms of key/specific behaviours that are important to success or failure on the job. The critical-incident approach has been merged with the graphic rating concept to produce behaviourally anchored rating scales.[5] In this method, the evaluator rates the critical employee behaviours. There are two types of scales:
    (i) Behaviour Expectation Scales (BES), where anchors are illustrations that help the rater to define as superior, average or below average the behaviour of the employee.
    (ii) Behaviour Observation Scales (BOS), where the rater reports the frequency with which the employee engages in the behaviour specified in the anchor.

III. **Modern Methods**

These methods are the improvements over the traditional methods. They attempt to remove the defects of the earlier methods.

1. **Management by objectives (MBO):** There is one thing common in all the traditional methods of performance appraisal that the superior sits in the chair of a judge for his or her employees' performance. He evaluates and gives his judgement. However, this philosophy of performance appraisal has attracted a lot of criticism. To overcome this problem, a new concept of performance appraisal known by management by objectives (MBO) was given by Peter F. Drucker in 1954.

   MBO refers to joint setting of specific measurable goals and periodical review of the progress made. MBO tends to emphasize a participative but joint determination of objectives followed by a participative but joint evaluation of success in periodic appraisal interviews.[6] The major steps involved in an MBO programme are the following:

(i) *Establish the objectives/goals*: The first step is the meeting of superior and subordinates with the aim to reach an agreement upon the key goals to be achieved by the subordinate. It is better if there are a limited number of goals.

(ii) *Performance reviews*: The second step is to compare each employee's actual and targeted performance. Each employee's achievement is compared with the agreed goals.

(iii) *Provide the feedback*: Finally, the superior discusses with the subordinate his progress towards the earlier set goals. The atmosphere of the discussion is of mutual respect and is supportive. Here, the superior does not sit in the capacity of a judge to pass judgement. Here, the approach is of two persons working on joint problems with joint goals.

However, there are few limitations of this method. Firstly, problems are encountered in the individual goal setting process. As all the activities in an organization are interdependent and interrelated, clear-cut setting of individual objectives is a complex task. Secondly, this is a time-consuming process. Lot of time is taken in meeting, joint setting of objectives, measuring progress and conveying to the employee. Thirdly, it is not applicable to all jobs in a firm. There is difficulty in applying this approach to non-managerial positions such as assembly-line work where there is very little or no flexibility to set performance standards as these are already determined. Moreover, comparative assessment of so many employees in an organization is a very difficult task to do.

2. **360° feedback:** This method of performance appraisal is also known as multi-source assessment or multi-rater feedback. 360° feedback can be

defined as the systematic collection and feedback of performance data on an individual or group derived from a number of the stakeholders on their performance.[7] The stakeholders are immediate supervisors, peers, team members, customers (internal and external) and self. The main objective of 360° appraisal method is that each employee gets his performance report/feedback from all angles in an organization (i.e. supervisor, peers, customers, etc.) and this makes him understand how effective he is as an employee, team member, co-worker, etc. This provides an employee a broader perspective about his performance. This method of performance appraisal is mostly concentrated on the senior level employees, for example, managers, directors, senior executives, etc. The main advantages of this method are the following:[8]

(i) A broader perspective to the individual of how they are perceived by others.

(ii) Increased awareness of and relevance of competencies.

(iii) Increased awareness by senior management that they too have development needs.

(iv) More reliable feedback to senior managers about their performance.

(v) Gaining acceptance of the principle of multiple stakeholders as a measure of performance.

(vi) Encouraging more open feedback—new insights.

(vii) Reinforcing the desired competencies of the business.

(viii) Provides a clear picture to senior management of individual's real worth.

The main drawbacks of this system are the following:

(i) It is difficult to receive and organize feedback from different sources.

(ii) Employees remain under stress and there is threatening environment while receiving or giving feedback.

(iii) It is time-consuming. Lot of time is spent upon selection of raters, designing questionnaires, sending and receiving them, analyzing the data and providing feedback.

(iv) Sometimes, personal differences or biases come in the way of honest rating.

Development and Implementation of 360° Feedback: The main steps involved are the following:[9]

(i) *Define objectives*: Spell out clearly what 360° feedback is expected to achieve.

(ii) *Decide on recipients*: Who will be at the receiving end of feedback.

(iii) *Decide on who will give the feedback*: Means supervisor, peers, customers, etc. the stakeholders in the performance.

(iv) *Areas of work*: Decide on the areas of work and behaviour on which feedback will be given.

(v) *Collecting the data*: Decide on the method of collecting the data— questionnaire, etc.

(vi) *Data analysis*: Decide on data analysis and presentation—develop or purchase software.

(vii) *Plan implementation programme*: It is desirable to pilot the process, preferably at the top level or with all the managers in a function or department.

(viii) *Outcomes*: Analyze outcome of pilot scheme.

(ix) *Plan and implement full programme*: This should include briefing, communicating, training and support from HR and, possibly, the external consultants.

(x) *Monitor and evaluate*: This process can cause anxiety and stress or produce little practical gain in terms of development and improved performance for a lot of effort.

3. **Psychological appraisals:** Psychological appraisals are conducted to assess the future potential of the

employees. In this method, the past and actual performance is not assessed. The focus is on the future potential. Big organizations generally employ full-time industrial psychologists for the purpose. Usually, the appraisals consist of psychological tests, in-department interviews and discussions with the immediate supervisors. The areas covered about an employee are his or her emotional stability, reasoning abilities, sociability, intellectual abilities, ability to foresee the future and analytical abilities. The psychologist prepares his report on the above-said characteristics of employees. The report may suggest or predict the employee's future performance. This will help in taking decisions regarding employee's career planning and development, training, placement, etc.

4. **Assessment centre:** This is a widely used technique of selecting and appraising the candidates. Earlier, it was called situational testing. It was developed by the German army in 1920s to select officer candidates of higher quality. Generally, an assessment centre involves 6 to 12 candidates at a time. These candidates will be evaluated with the help of a series of exercises over next several days (1 to 3 days). These tests do not assess actual job behaviour but a variety of activities that are likely to encounter on the job. The candidates or managers participate in simulated job tasks such as in-basket tests, role-playing, leaderless group discussion, computer simulations, group problem solving, management or business games, interviewing, etc. The raters, who are the trained observers, record the observations of participants and, later on, discuss these observations and finally give their decision regarding the performance of each participant.
5. **Human resource accounting (HRA):** According to American Accounting Association, "HRA is

the process of identifying and measuring data about human resources and communicating this information to interested parties." HRA aims to quantify the economic value of people to the organization in order to provide input for managerial and financial decisions.[10] HRA evaluates the cost and contributions of human resources to the organization. Cost of human resources refers to all expenses incurred on human resource planning, recruitment, selection, induction, placement, training and development, salaries, benefits, etc. Contribution refers to revenue from employee services to the organization. It provides information about the values of human capital to the organization. It facilitates the effective and efficient management of human resources by providing information about utility of cost reduction and budgeting control.

Problems Associated with Performance Appraisal

Certain barriers work against the effectiveness of the appraisal system. Most employers still depend on graphic-type rating scales to appraise performance but these scales are especially susceptible to several problems: unclear standards, halo effect, central tendency, leniency or strictness, and bias.[11]

1. **Unclear standards:** In some rating scales, the traits and degrees of merit are ambiguous. For example, different raters have different definitions of terms 'good', 'bad', 'fair', 'creativity', 'dependability', etc.
2. **Halo effect:** This occurs when the rater is influenced by a particular quality (good or bad) of a specific employee and he evaluates the entire performance accordingly.
3. **Central tendency:** This problem occurs when the rater evaluates all employees the same way, generally rating them all average.
4. **Leniency or strictness:** This problem occurs when the rater is too lenient and rates all employees very high or is very strict and rates everyone low on a scale.

5. **Bias:** The evaluator can be prejudiced against a particular employee or may discriminate on basis of sex, religion, caste, etc.
6. **Psychological blocks:** There are certain psychological barriers due to which the raters may not evaluate the employees impartially and subjectively. For instance, considering appraisal as extra burden, supervisor's feeling of insecurity, disliking resentment by subordinates, disliking conveying poor performance to subordinates, etc.
7. **Faulty assumptions:** There are some faulty assumptions of both the parties—superior and the subordinates, about the appraisal system, because of which it does not work properly. These are the following:
   (i) The assumption that managers naturally wish to make fair and accurate appraisal of subordinates is not practical.
   (ii) Another faulty assumption is that managers take a particular appraisal system as perfect and feel that once they have launched a programme it would continue forever.
   (iii) Managers sometimes assume that personal opinion is better than appraisal and they find little use of systematic appraisal and review procedures.
   (iv) Managers' assumptions that employees want to know frankly where they stand and what their supervisors think about them. These assumptions are not valid as employees resist to be appraised.

QUESTIONS

1. What is performance appraisal? What are objectives of performance appraisal?
2. What are the steps in the process of performance appraisal?
3. Differentiate between paired-comparison method and person-to-person comparison?

4. Explain the 360° feedback technique.
5. What are the problems associated with performance appraisal?

NOTES

1. D. Schultz and S.E. Schultz. *Psychology and Work Today*, Pearson Education, Delhi, 2004, p. 127.
2. R.S. Schuler. *Personnel and Human Resource Msanagement*, West Publishing, New York, 1981, p. 221.
3. D.C. Sharma and R.C. Sharma. *Personnel Management & Industrial Relations*, First Edition, S.J. Publications, Meerut, p. 191.
4. Richard D. Scott. "Taking Subjectivity Out of Performance Appraisal", *Personnel*, Vol. 50, No. 4, July-August, 1973, pp. 45-49.
5. Edwin B. Flippo. *Personnel Management*, Sixth Edition, McGraw-Hill, New York, 1984, p. 234.
6. *Ibid.*, p. 241.
7. P. Ward. "A 360° Turn for the Better", *People Management*, 1995, February, pp. 20-22.
8. Michael Armstrong. *A Handbook of Human Resource Management Practice*, Ninth Edition, Kogan Page, London, 2005, p. 519.
9. *Ibid.*, p. 518.
10. S. Sackmann, E. Flamholtz and M. Bullen. "Human Asset Accounting", *Journal of Accounting Literature*, 1989, 5, pp. 235-64.
11. Gary Dessler. *Human Resource Management*, Pearson Education, 9th edition, Delhi, 2004, p. 253.

Chapter 15

Potential Appraisal and Employee Counselling

Potential Appraisal

Potential appraisal refers to the identification of hidden skills, talents and abilities in a person which even he may be unaware of. It is a future oriented concept and is a powerful tool for employee advancement.1 The latent skills of a person are tracked and his true potential is evaluated. An employee with high potential is a good candidate for assuming more responsibilities in future. In western countries, many organizations use potential appraisal as a part of performance appraisal process. However, in India, not many managers are aware of this term though informally every organization makes potential assessments. Higher officials often determine whether a particular employee has the potential to take added responsibilities in future. Potential appraisals help in deciding a career plan for the employees. It also helps to evaluate candidates for promotions and developing a suitable employee base for succession planning. This method is based on the aptitude of the employee, his willingness to take additional responsibility and his motivation for accomplishing tasks.

Parameters of Potential Appraisal

The future potentials of an employee can be measured using certain performance and behavioural parameters.

Performance parameters

(i) Targets accomplished in the current appraisal period.
(ii) Particular areas where superior performance is shown.
(iii) Overall performance rating.
(iv) Skills, knowledge and talents which have scope for development.
(v) Steps taken by the employee for improving his performance and furthering his career development.
(vi) Knowledge of the employee regarding his job and related fields.

Behavioural parameters

(i) Level of independence and autonomy.
(ii) Decision-making capabilities.
(iii) How the employee handles stress and work pressure.
(iv) Degree of confidence.
(v) Communication and interpersonal skills.
(vi) Leadership and motivation.
(vii) How he handles and diffuses conflicts at work place.

Requirements of Potential Appraisal System

The following requirements are to be followed while introducing a potential appraisal system in the organization.

(i) Role description: The roles and functions associated with different jobs should be defined clearly. The tasks and processes involved in the performance of each job in the organization should be extensively described.
(ii) Qualities required: There should be a detailed list of qualities that a person should possess in order to perform a particular job. These qualities may be broadly divided into the following categories:
   - Technical knowledge and skills.
   - Managerial capabilities.
   - Behavioural qualities.
   - Conceptual capabilities.

(iii) Indicators of qualities: A good potential appraisal system should have a mechanism for judging the various qualities in a given employee. Some of these tools are:
- Self-appraisal.
- Ratings by superiors and peers.
- Psychological tests.
- Performance appraisal records.
- Simulation games.

Uses of Potential Appraisal

- Helps in designing a career plan for the employees based on his potential skills.
- Provides career development guidance and exploration of future prospects of employees.
- Identifies the areas where employees need additional training.
- Motivates employees to further develop their skills and capabilities.

Potential appraisal identifies the hidden potential of the employees and helps the organization to take appropriate steps for converting the latent potential into actual performance. It helps the company build a base of highly productive and motivated employees for meeting future manpower requirements. Potential assessment should be undertaken as a part of performance appraisal so that employees can be developed to achieve their highest potential and contribute towards organizational goals.

Employee Counselling

An employee counselling session is a meeting between the supervisor and the employee which may focus on a specific incident, a particular aspect of an employee's performance which the supervisor has identified as needing improvement, or the employee's overall performance or conduct.[2] The aim of counselling is to provide help and support to the employee during the difficult times of their lives to enable them to face problems and challenges successfully. It is generally conducted as a private face-to-face meeting between the employee and the counsellor where the counsellor attempts to understand the employee's problems and give him suggestions.

Employees may face problems in their personal or professional life which may start affecting their performance and work place behaviour. When a person faces some difficulties, his stress level would increase and start having a negative influence on his work performance. Therefore, the need for employee counselling arises. The counsellor counsels, guides, and advises the employee at times of need and help the employee to manage his issues effectively. The problems of the employee if not dealt with at the earliest may escalate into bigger disciplinary issues. Thus, it is vital to address the behavioural problems and conflicts between the employees as soon as they are detected and control the issues at the very beginning. With the increasing incidence of stress in the modern employee's life more and more organizations are adopting counselling to retain their best employees and improve quality of their work life. Employees may become frustrated and stressed due to personal or family problems, office politics, deadlines, targets, etc. This reduces their productivity greatly and also affects their team spirit and the overall work environment. Now-a-days, organizations have realized the importance of having a motivated and stress-free workforce. Many companies have therefore made counselling a part of their corporate culture. In smaller organizations the manager may play the role of a counsellor himself, while in bigger companies services of professional experts may be taken.

Reasons for Employee Stress

(i) High workloads, unrealistic deadlines and targets, etc.

(ii) Poor work relationships with co-workers.

(iii) Insufficient workload making employee feel worthless.

(iv) Unsuitability of job.

(v) Pressure to work without proper training.

(vi) Difficulty adjusting with a new job environment.

(vii) Problems in personal life/family life.

(viii) Insecurities about job stability, salary, career growth.

(ix) Harassment by boss or colleagues.

(x) Poor working environment.

(xi) Problems in top management.

Basic Requisites of Employee Counselling

1. The counsellor should be an experienced and sensitive person who is able to win the trust and confidence of employees.
2. Counsellor should encourage the employees to talk openly without any inhibitions. Time should never be a constraint for counselling sessions.
3. The counsellor should be a patient listener and try to see the situation from the employee's perspective. He should be open-minded and flexible in approach.
4. The counsellor should study the situation from different angles and identify the underlying causes behind the problem. He should be able to provide proper advice for dealing with it.
5. The aim of the counselling should be to boost the employee's morale, regain his confidence and help him deal with his issues in a positive manner.

Types of Counselling

1. **Performance counselling:** If the performance of an employee starts declining at the workplace, the need for performance counselling arises. The counsellor should try to identify the underlying causes behind the employee's poor performance. The reasons could be office stress, unachievable deadlines, problems in interpersonal relations with other employees, etc. After recognizing the problem, the counsellor can advise about how to deal with it.
2. **Disciplinary counselling:** This type of counselling takes place when an employee's behaviour falls short of the

standards expected. An employee may suddenly start picking up fights, become irritable, be absent from work for long, etc. The counsellor should interview the employee and confront him about his behavioural problems. He should try to analyze all the reasons that could be causing the behavioural lapses. An employee may be frustrated because of personal problems; high absenteeism may be due to bullying by co-workers in the office. The counsellor may give tips on how to face the situation and improve his behaviour.

3. **Personal counselling:** Workplace problems are not the only problems that employees face; personal and family problems also affect their performance. Families and friends are integral parts of any human being's life; tension in a worker's personal life affects his work performance adversely. Personal problems could include sickness of a family member, marital conflicts, dysfunctional family life, problem with children, family feuds, etc. The counsellor should lend a sympathetic ear to the employee's personal problems and support them in resolving them so that the employee is able to concentrate on his job wholeheartedly.
4. **Stress management in workplace:** Working in the modern job environment is very stressful with so many deadlines to meet and targets to achieve. Employees may become anxious and tense due to their high pressure workload. This not only affects their productivity on the job, but also their mental health. It is the duty of the organization to take care of the employees' well-being and provide them guidelines for dealing with stress. Bigger organizations may engage experts for providing psychiatric counselling to employees as part of employee welfare programmes.3

Benefits of Counselling

(i) Helps the employee to understand his problem from a wider angle.

(ii) Boosts employee confidence and morale.

(iii) Helps the employee in arriving at solutions for his problems.

(iv) Employee is better equipped to deal with stress after counselling.

(v) Behavioural problems are dealt with before they become full-blown disciplinary issues.

(vi) Provides much needed support to the employee during difficult situations.

(vii) Helps to tackle workplace relationships between co-workers.

(viii) The employee understands that the company is concerned about his well-being.

Challenges to Effective Employee Counselling

(i) Employees are not comfortable sharing their problems with manager/counsellor.

(ii) Lack of trust in counselling procedure.

(iii) Providing counselling to employees is a time-consuming and costly process.

(iv) The very purpose of counselling is defeated if the counsellor is ineffective.

Employee counselling can go a long way in helping employees face their day-to-day problems more effectively and deal with stress in a better manner. It helps them to take increased control over their job and life and maintain a healthy balance between work and personal life. Counselling helps the organization to identify the problem areas at the earliest and handle them before they blow out of proportion. Workplace stress and anxiety can affect the mental health, productivity and behaviour of the employees. Counselling is necessary to manage the stress so that the productivity and efficiency of the employees is maintained. Counselling also addresses the psychological and behavioural issues of the employees, thereby helping them to become better human beings who are more loyal and enthusiastic about their workplace commitments.

QUESTIONS

1. Potential appraisal is a powerful tool for employee advancement. Explain.
2. Explain in detail various parameters of potential appraisal.
3. Why do employees need counselling? What are the factors triggering employee stress?
4. What could be the possible challenges to effective employee counselling?
5. Write a note on performance counselling vs. personal counselling.
6. Under what circumstances does disciplinary counselling become necessary?

NOTES

1. http://appraisals.naukrihub.com/potential-appraisal.html
2. http://www.stonybrook.edu/lrweb/counseling/
3. http://www.direct.gov.uk/en/Employment/Resolving Workplace Disputes/DG_10028138

Chapter 16

Job Changes

A job change refers to a change in the job title and responsibilities currently held by an employee in the organization. Promotions and transfers are two of the most common methods of job change within an organization. An organization makes adjustments in its workforce in order to meet the changing business situations. Such changes may be due to changes in the organization structure, expansion or growth of the organization, changes in product lines, market innovations, etc. All these necessitate workforce readjustment according to new situation.

Promotion

Promotion means advancement in terms of job designation, salary and benefits. The employee progresses to a better job with increased responsibility, more prestige and status. Promotion involves the following ingredients:

(i) Improves job, status and prestige.

(ii) Gives more responsibility.

(iii) Brings increase in pay and perks.

Purposes of Promotions

The main purposes of promotion in organizations are the following:

1. To recognize and reward the efforts of an employee.
2. To attract and retain the competent personnel.

3. To inculcate enthusiasm in employees to acquire knowledge, skills and jobs in the organization.
4. To develop a competitive spirit in the workforce.
5. To motivate employee for higher productivity.
6. To develop a ready internal pool of competent personnel within the organization who can take higher level of challenging jobs.
7. To promote a sense of belongingness in the employees.
8. To boost the morale in the workforce.
9. To increase an employee's effectiveness.
10. To place a worker in a position where he or she is more valuable to the organization.
11. To fill vacancies from within the organization.
12. To reduce discontent and labour unrest.
13. To promote interest in training and development programmes.
14. To increase job satisfaction.

Principles of Promotion Policy

Promotion is a very critical subject in human resource management. It should be handled very carefully. It may prove to be a source of satisfaction, if handled well or it may attract lot of criticism from employees in case of mishandling. It is the duty of an HR manager to design a sound promotion policy in the organization and also ensure its full implementation. A sound promotion policy means a policy, which is fair, impartial and enjoys consistency. It should state management's intention regarding filling of vacancies from within the organization (i.e. by promotions) or recruiting from outside or from both. In most cases, the superior/higher vacancies in an organization are filled through external recruitment, while the lower level vacancies are filled by promotions. A promotion policy should provide a well-defined and clear-cut promotion chart. Management should state clearly the base of promotion, i.e. whether seniority is considered or merit, or both. Seniority means the length of service and is counted from the date of employee's appointment in the organization. Merit refers to a person's qualifications and his competence. There has always been a great controversy with regard to the question whether promotions should be based on seniority or merit, or both. Each base has its own advantages/merits and disadvantages/demerits.

Seniority-based Promotion

Seniority is the oldest and widely used basis of promotion, especially in government owned organizations, unionised industrial establishments and educational institutes.

Advantages

(i) It is easy to measure the length of service and judge the seniority.

(ii) It brings objectivity in distinguishing personnel, and so there is less scope for subjectivity or favouritism.

(iii) It is simple to understand and easy to administer.

(iv) Trade unions provide full support to this system.

(v) This ensures that a more experienced person takes higher position first.

(vi) It creates a sense of security.

(vii) It helps to reward loyal workers.

(viii) There is less scope of grievances and conflicts.

(ix) Employees are willing to work under an older and experienced person.

(x) It is economical.

(xi) It reduces labour turnover, as employees will not be willing to lose their seniority by quitting.

Disadvantages

(i) Employees with longest service need not necessarily be the more competent.

(ii) Young, ambitious and able persons with less years of service may get frustrated and leave the organization.

(iii) Seniority fails to differentiate between efficient and inefficient workers.

(iv) It kills the enthusiasm to do better as everyone will be promoted as his turn comes.

(v) It acts as a hurdle in attracting capable persons.

(vi) It is not a valid assumption that employees learn more with length of service. Up to a certain age employees learn and beyond that learning capabilities may diminish.

Merit-based Promotion

When a promotion is given to an employee on the basis of his qualification, ability, competence or performance while not considering his seniority in the organization, then the promotion is known to be on the basis of merit. It is just like a reward or incentive for hard work, dedication and excellent performance. Management favours promotions on the basis of merit.

Advantages

(i) It encourages, recognizes and rewards extra knowledge, competence and efficiency of employees.

(ii) It motivates the competent persons to work hard.

(iii) It helps to retain the capable persons.

(iv) It increases productivity.

(v) It increases efficiency and profitability of the organization.

(vi) It encourages employees to keep on learning, adding knowledge and skills, which enhances their personal growth also.

(vii) It results in maximum utilisation of employees.

Disadvantages

(i) Accurate measurement of merit is highly difficult.

(ii) There is scope for subjectivity and favouritism.

(iii) Trade unions distrust management's integrity in judging merit.

(iv) Loyal senior persons are not rewarded.

(v) There is a feeling of discontent among senior employees.

So, whether it is seniority or merit as the basis for promotion, each has its own merits and demerits. Managements mostly prefer merit base for promotions as it increases the productivity and profitability of organization. Moreover, it rewards those who deserve it. But trade unions prefer seniority as the sole basis for promotion in order to protect the interests of their workers. A combination of both seniority and merit can be considered as the basis for promotion. In other words, a balance should be struck between the two and a new basis of promotion should be developed which will satisfy all the concerned parties. A sound promotion policy should ensure that whenever there are two employees of equal seniority, then ability or competence should be the deciding factor in a promotion. And, on the other hand, where two persons of almost equal competence are available, then seniority should be the deciding factor.

Types of Promotion

Promotions may be of following types:

1. **Horizontal promotion:** This type of promotion includes an increase in responsibilities, pay and a change in designation. However, the employee doesn't shift the job classification. For example, an assistant manager in HR department may be transferred to production department.[1]
2. **Vertical promotion:** In this type of promotion, an employee is moved to higher level in the hierarchy. This involves increase in pay, status and responsibilities.
3. **Dry promotion:** This type of promotion involves increase in responsibilities and status without any increase in pay.

Transfers

A transfer refers to a movement of an employee from one job to another with no change in salary, status and responsibilities. In other words, a transfer is a change in job where the new job is substantially equal to the old in terms of pay, status and responsibilities. The main objective of transfer is to make adjustment in the work, place and the employee. Employees seek transfers for many reasons, including personal enrichment, more interesting jobs, greater convenience, better hours, location of work and so on—or to jobs offering greater advancement possibilities.[2] On the other hand, employers may transfer a worker to vacate a position where he is no longer needed, or more generally to find a better fit for the employee within the firm.

Purposes of Transfers

The main purposes behind the transfers in any organization are the following:

1. **To meet the organizational requirements:** Transfer may be due to changes in the volume of production, change in technology, changes in product mix, market fluctuations, production schedules, etc. Because of these factors there may be surplus labour in one department or plant and there may be shortage of labour in another department or plant. So, employees are transferred in order to stabilise the situation.
2. **To meet employees request:** Employee also make request for transfer to work under a friendly boss, to work on interesting jobs where advancement chances are bright, to work in the branch nearest to their home town, to work on a job of flexible working hours, etc.
3. **To utilize employee's service properly:** An employee may be transferred to another place where the management can utilize his or her capacities better.
4. **To increase the productivity of an individual:** Transfer from one job to another breaks the monotony associated with the earlier job.
5. **To correct the faulty initial placement of an employee:** If an employee has been faultily placed on the wrong job, he may be transferred to a more suitable one.
6. **To suit the health and age of an employee:** An employee may request a transfer to a more convenient city or office location because of old age or health reasons. For example a heart patient who cannot tolerate cold weather might request to be transferred to a warmer place.

7. **To maintain a tenure system:** When employee holds a certain job for a fixed tenure, he is made to move to the next place.

Principles of Transfer Policy

Every organization should have a clear, unambiguous and sound transfer policy. It must be based on the following principles:

(i) It should clearly indicate the types and circumstances under which a transfer will be made.

(ii) It should state the frequency of transfers and minimum time period between the transfers.

(iii) It should tell who will be responsible for initiating and approving the transfers.

(iv) It should indicate the criteria or the basis of transfer and follow it strictly.

(v) It should point out the effect of transfer on the pay and seniority of the transferred employee.

(vi) It should indicate whether this transfer is temporary or permanent.

(vii) It should make a provision for timely communicating the transfer decision.

(viii) It should specify the area of the organization over which the transfers can be made.

Types of Transfers

1. **Production transfers:** These are transfers made from one department or plant to the other department or plant where there are labour surpluses or shortage. It is not desirable that in one part of the organization there is condition of surplus labour or lay-offs and in another part of the organization there is need/requirement of labour. So, production transfer helps to stabilise the employment in the organization.

2. **Replacement transfers:** These are similar to production transfers as these are also intended to avoid lay-offs, especially of senior employees. A new employee may be

replaced by a senior employee to avoid laying off the senior employee.

3. **Remedial transfers:** Transfers made to remedy the situation are known as remedial transfers. These take place if the initial placement of the employee has been faulty, or the employee cannot get along with his supervisor or with other workers in the department. Then his transfer to a more appropriate job or under a more agreeable supervisor might result in better performance.
4. **Versatility transfers:** These are made to make an employee more competent and versatile by shifting him from one job to another. In this way, an employee learns more skills and gets varied and broader job experience. These also help the employee for future advancement.
5. **Shift transfers:** When the industrial establishments are operating in more than one shift then shift transfers are made. An employee is shifted from one shift to another on the same work. These transfers are made on rotation basis.

QUESTIONS

1. Explain the principles of promotion? What purposes does a promotion serve?
2. Compare seniority based promotion vs. merit based promotion. Which one is better according to you, and way?
3. What is a transfer? Why are transfers necessary for an organization?
4. What are various types of transfers? In what cases do companies adopt remedial transfers?
5. Why do some employees detest transfers?

NOTES

1. Edwin B. Flippo. *Personnel Management*. Sixth Ed. McGraw-Hill, New York, 1984, p. 266.
2. Richard Chanick. "Career Growth for Baby Boomers", *Personnel Journal*, 1991, Vol. 71, pp. 40-46.

Chapter 17

Voluntary Retirement Scheme and Lay-offs

A voluntary retirement scheme (VRS) package is offered to employees as an incentive to retire earlier than their normal retirement age. The VRS package usually contains generous retirement benefits for certain employees.[1] Such schemes are normally offered to those employees who are closer to retiring age or have been with the organization for a long period of time. It is an alternative to lay-offs and retrenchment. It is the most humane method of reducing the number of excess employees in an organization. The Golden Handshake, a concept similar to VRS is also followed in the western countries where companies pay huge severance package to the employee when their employment is terminated. The main objective of VRS is to reduce the number of employees, especially those who have been with the organization for long. It is a method of removing the excess manpower from the organization, and thus the vacancies created by VRS are not filled with new employees. Certain employees who are near retirement age and do not have any dependents prefer to take VRS because they get substantial retirement benefits. But this may not be suitable for employees who have dependents and require a fixed income every month. In order to reduce workforce, a few organizations try to force employees to take VRS though it is a wrong practice to do so. The term VRS itself implies that the scheme has to be accepted by the employee voluntarily.

Situations where VRS Scheme may be Adopted

(i) When business is not running profitably.

(ii) A need for reducing workforce arises due to market conditions.

(iii) At times of mergers and acquisitions.

(iv) When the product or technology of the organization becomes obsolete.

Different companies can form their own schemes for voluntary retirement for different classes of their employees, though these rules have to conform to the guidelines prescribed in section 10 (10C) of the rule 2BA of the Income Tax rules. The guidelines provide that the scheme of voluntary retirement framed by a company should be in accordance with the following requirements:

1. It applies to an employee of the company who has completed ten years of service or completed 40 years of age.
2. It applies to all employees (called by whatever name), including workers and executives of the company excepting Directors of the company.
3. The scheme of voluntary retirement has been drawn to result in overall reduction in the existing strength of the employees of the company.
4. The vacancy caused by voluntary retirement is not to be filled up, nor is the retiring employee to be employed in another company or concern belonging to the same management.
5. The amount receivable on account of voluntary retirement of the employees does not exceed the amount equivalent to one and one-half months' salary for each completed year of service or monthly emoluments at the time of retirement multiplied by the balance months of service left before the date of his retirement on superannuation.
6. The employee has not availed in the past the benefit of any other voluntary retirement scheme.

Attractive packages are offered to employees opting for VRS. Some companies may also provide counselling to the employees handling their concerns about their future, management of funds, rehabilitation plans, etc.[2]

Benefits of VRS

1. **Help to reduce costs:** The seniormost employees are often paid the most. Thus, by encouraging them to retire the company saves a lot in salary expenses.
2. **Better morale:** VRS is the preferred method of reducing number of employees in the organization. Since employees voluntarily take up this scheme, their morale and confidence does not suffer.
3. **Alternative to lay-offs:** There are a lot of problems associated with lay-off of workers—low morale, fall in image, insecurity among surviving workers, etc. VRS is a much better option for companies which want to reduce workforce, but do not want to hurt their morale.

Lay-off (Downsizing)

Lay-off or downsizing refers to suspension or termination of employment (with or without notice) by the employer or management. Lay-offs are not caused by any fault of the employees but by reasons such as lack of work, cash, or material.[3] Lay-offs are basically temporary in nature and the company may call back all or some of the laid off workers when situations improve. Permanent lay-offs are called redundancy. According to Section 2 (kkk) of the Industrial Disputes Act, 1947, lay-offs mean the failure, refusal or inability of an employer to give employment to a worker whose name is borne on the muster rolls of his industrial establishment and who has not been retrenched. The reasons for lay-offs may be the following:

(i) Shortage of raw material (coal, power, etc.).
(ii) Excessive accumulated stocks.
(iii) Organizational restructuring.
(iv) Breakdown of machinery.

(v) Termination of a particular project in which many employees were engaged.

(vi) Natural calamity like earthquake, flood, etc.

(vii) Inability of the employees to move to a new location to where the factory has shifted.

(viii) The company is incurring losses and cannot afford to have too many employees.

(ix) Lack of funds.

(x) Elimination of job positions where the particular job has been completely outsourced to a different company.

Lay-offs result in immediate unemployment, although temporary in nature. But the laid off workers have no idea about when they would be called back. Also it affects the morale and confidence of the workers who survived the lay-off. When the employer initiates lay-offs, employees have to be paid compensation for the period of lay-off. According to section 25 of Industrial Disputes Act, 1947, a workman is entitled to lay-off compensation at the rate equal to fifty per cent of the total of the basic wage and dearness allowance for the period of his lay-off except for weekly holidays, which may intervene. Compensation can normally be claimed for not more than forty-five days during any period of twelve months.

Lay-offs hurt the image of the company. It is a decision which has powerful impact not only on the laid off workers, but also on the remaining workers and the stakeholders. Companies may face difficulties in attracting talented workforce in the future, the value of its shares may go down in the market and future investors will be discouraged to invest in such companies. Thus, the management should be very cautious while taking lay-off decision. The basis for lay-off should be decided, whether it would be based on seniority or merit. If it is based on merit, then the employees who are not performing well would be laid off first. The merit of the employees would be based on performance appraisal. But this method is opposed by labour unions. Therefore many companies adopt seniority basis, i.e. junior most employees will leave first.

Lay-offs have become common now-a-days due to restructuring and business process re-engineering. Thousands of employees were laid off worldwide due to the economic recession of 2008-09. Even though sometimes it might be a necessity for a company to lay-off its employees, there are other instances where a company adopts lay-offs just to reduce its expenses. In such a case, the morale, faith and confidence of all its employees—the ones laid off and the ones who survive—are affected. Therefore, organizations should go for lay-offs only as the last resort. They may explore some alternatives to lay-off to counter the problems of low demand or lack of funds.

Some alternatives available to lay-offs are:

1. The company may freeze its hiring process to prevent any addition to the workforce while maintaining the existing employees.
2. The organization may offer Voluntary Retirement Schemes (VRS) to encourage employees to leave on their own.
3. The company may divide full time jobs into a number of part time jobs and assign at least a part time job to each employee.
4. The pay packages of the employee may be reduced to cut costs.

QUESTIONS

1. What do you mean by VRS? What are the guidelines to be followed by companies while implementing VRS?
2. What are the benefits of VRS? Is it better than downsizing?
3. Why do sometimes organizations lay off their employees?
4. Lay-offs affect the morale of not just the laid off workers, but also the surviving ones. Comment.
5. Are there any alternatives that the company may adopt instead of laying off the workers?

NOTES

1. http://www.ehow.com/facts_7292055_meaning-_voluntary-retirement-scheme__.html
2. http://business.gov.in/manage_business/vrs.php
3. http://www.businessdictionary.com/ definition/ layoff.html

Chapter 18

Employee Compensation

Determination of suitable monetary compensation is one of the most difficult and complex duties of human resource manager. It is highly important to both the organization and employee. It is significant for the employee as, in most cases, it is the only means of economic survival besides determining their social status. It is important for the organization as wages and salaries constitute the highest cost of doing business. Also, employee compensation programmes play an important role for organization in attracting, motivating and retaining the competent employees. There are many options before an organization from which it has to decide most appropriate pay system. There is no exact and accurate yardstick that can determine the correct pay rate. Although systems like job evaluation play a significant role, yet lots of other factors have to be considered to arrive at the best decisions.

Employee compensation refers to all forms of pay or rewards going to employees and arising from their employment.[1] Employee compensation has three main components and the relative proposition of each component in the total compensation varies by the organization. Components of compensation are:

(i) Base compensation

(ii) Incentive payments

(iii) Benefits and services

Compensation is a comprehensive term which includes everything an employee receives in return for his work such as wages, salaries, allowances, benefits and services. Although there is no basic difference between the term 'wages' and 'salaries', generally 'salary' is used for compensation to white-collar employees while 'wages' is used to denote the payment made to blue-collar workers. Another difference is that salaries are paid on a monthly basis whereas wages may be paid on hourly or daily basis.

Objectives of Employee Compensation

The main objectives of employee compensation are the following:

1. To attract well-qualified and competent personnel.
2. To motivate them for higher levels of performance by making arrangement of incentive payments.
3. To retain the present workforce by keeping their pay levels at the competitive levels.
4. To raise the morale of workforce.
5. To establish internal as well as external equity. Internal equity refers to payment of similar wages for similar work. External equity means payment of similar wages to similar jobs in comparable firms.
6. To maintain the labour and administrative costs in line with the ability of the organization to pay.
7. To comply with wage legislation.
8. To project a good image of company.
9. To satisfy employees and to reduce the incidents of grievances, absenteeism and quitting.
10. To reward the desired behaviour such as good performance, loyalty, dedication, etc.

Compensation Policy

The compensation policy is a basic document that describes details about the compensation practices in the organization. It includes details about the individual compensation components, i.e. basic compensation, incentive payments, bonus, benefits, etc. and their role in the overall compensation scheme of the organization. Each component has to be described along with the method of its calculation, which the employee is eligible for this particular component and how it is approved. The compensation policy naturally is the most read and widely discussed policies of the organization. Each employee is interested in the components that constitute his salary and would want to know how he can maximise his monetary earnings. Therefore, he takes a keen interest in the compensation policy. The contents of the policy motivate and encourage the employees to put in their best efforts so that they earn the highest possible income. The policy should be clear and easy to understand. There should be no scope for ambiguity in the methods for calculating specific component or the conditions under which they can be approved. A transparent compensation policy would support a high performance work culture in the organization as it would be clear to the employees about what they need to do in order to be eligible for bonuses and benefits. A good compensation policy should cover all compensation components clearly and comprehensively to serve its purpose efficiently.

Factors Influencing Employee Compensation

The significant factors affecting the employee compensation can be grouped together into two broad categories, external and internal factors.

1. **External Factors**
   - (i) Demand and supply of labour in the labour market.
   - (ii) Labour union influence.
   - (iii) Government policies like Minimum Wages Act, 1948, the Equal Remuneration Act 1976, etc.
   - (iv) The prevailing rate of pay or comparable wage rates also influence the employee compensation.
   - (v) The present cost of living.
   - (vi) The state of the economy (boom, recession, depression, etc.).

(vii) Advancement of technology also influences the fixation of wage levels.

2. **Internal Factors**

These factors include the following:

(i) Ability of the organization to pay.

(ii) The performance, experience and seniority of the employee.

(iii) Requirements of the job such as physical and mental abilities.

(iv) Job evaluation helps to establish satisfactory wage differentials.

(v) Organization's strategy regarding employee compensation.

Principles of Compensation Administration

Compensation administration refers to the process of determining a cost-effective pay structure that will attract and retain competent employees, provide an incentive for them to work hard and ensure that pay levels will be perceived as fair.[2] Some basic principles of compensation administration are the following:

1. Different jobs require different kinds and levels of skills, knowledge and abilities and these vary in their value to the organization. So, efforts should be made to ensure that differences in pay are according to these variations.
2. Compensation administration should always be consistent with overall organizational plans.
3. Wage structure should be flexible enough to accommodate the changes in internal and external environment.
4. Compensation administration plans should be carefully designed and developed by considering the best interests of all the concerned parties such as management, trade unions, employees, society and government.
5. There should be equal pay for equal work.
6. Wage plans should be clearly defined and written to ensure stability and uniformity.

7. The level of wages should be in line with the prevailing rates in the labour market.
8. The employees should receive guaranteed minimum wages in order to maintain a reasonable standard of living.
9. There should not be any secrecy in the establishment of wage rates. Employees and trade unions should be well-informed regarding the procedure of setting wage rates.
10. There should be a provision of hearing and handling grievances related to wages.
11. Wages should be paid in time and wage rates revised periodically. For this a wage committee should be appointed.
12. Finally, wages should be such that they attract, motivate and retain competent personnel.

The Compensation Determination Process

Compensation is very important for the employee as his livelihood depends on it and it is his salary that determines his purchasing power. Compensation affects a person not just economically but also psychologically. Thus, compensation should be determined very systematically by following the steps mentioned below:

1. **Conduct job analysis:** It provides crucial information in designing pay systems. It describes the duties, responsibilities and other important job characteristics. Thus, it helps to determine and weigh the compensable factors (experience, skill, responsibility, effort, etc.).
2. **Rate worth of all jobs by job evaluation:** The next step is to determine the worth of jobs with the help of job evaluation. This is to achieve internal equity. For each degree of a compensable factor, some points are assigned.
3. **Create a job hierarchy:** In this stage, the points assigned to all compensable factors are aggregated. The listing

of jobs is done in the order of their importance to the organization (starting from highest point to lowest point).

4. **Conduct market survey:** After job hierarchy is created, the next step is to determine the prevailing wage rates. This is done to achieve external equity. Usually, a survey is conducted on a sample of selected key jobs and selected companies in the industry. Thus, the rates of key jobs in the labour market are determined.
5. **Establish a pay policy:** The market survey may provide a range of wage and salary rates. The organization has to decide its pay policy keeping in view this range.
6. **Pricing the jobs:** In this step, the job evaluation worth is matched with labour market worth. Then appropriate pay levels for each job are established and different pay levels are grouped into pay grades.
7. **Achieve individual equity:** Individual equity refers to fairness in pay decisions for employees holding the same job.[3] At this stage, each employee is assigned a pay rate within the range established for his job. Generally, firms use previous experience, seniority and performance appraisal ratings to determine how much an employee should be paid within that job's pay range.

Methods of Wage Payments

The important wage systems are as follows:

1. **Time wage system:** This is the oldest and popular method of wage payment. Under this system, the wages are paid on the basis of time the employee puts on the work without considering the output of the employee. The wage rates are fixed for an hour, a day, a week, a month, etc. So, the wages are calculated on the basis of attendance. Wages are calculated as follows:

   Wages = Number of days/hours worked × Rate per day/hour

Illustration

In a factory, a wage rate of ₹ 100 per day is fixed. A worker 'A' attends work for 30 days and another worker 'B' work for 20 days, respectively.

Wages of worker 'A' = 30 × 100 = ₹ 3000

Wages of worker 'B' = 20 × 100 = ₹ 2000

Advantages

(i) *Simplicity*: This is the simplest method and is very easy for the workers to understand.

(ii) *Security*: This provides a sense of security to workers as wages are paid irrespective of output.

(iii) *Better quality of work*: As there is no hurry to complete the work, the worker will handle the work with care and maintain quality.

(iv) *Trade union support*: This system has full support of trade unions, as this system does not distinguish between employees on their performance.

(v) *Economy in costs*: As the workers are not in a hurry to finish the task, so the materials, machinery and equipment are handled with care. This results in less wastage.

(vi) *No need of standardization*: This system does not create the necessity for standardization.

(vii) *Good for the beginner*: This system is beneficial for the beginners as they may not be able to reach a specific level of production in the early years of their career.

Disadvantages

The demerits of time wage system are the following:

(i) *No incentive for efficiency*: Under this system, efforts and rewards are not correlated. Thus, this system works as a disincentive to efficient workers.

(ii) *More supervision is required*: The workers do not care for time and they consume time uselessly. Thus, to make them work, there is a need for more supervision and control.

(iii) ***Low production***: As wages are not related to output, employees may be producing at slower rate.

(iv) ***Dissatisfaction among workers***: As efficient and inefficient employees get equal wages, thus efficient workers lose their enthusiasm for more efforts.

(v) ***Difficulty in measuring labour cost***: As wages are not related to output, labour cost is uncertain, thus it creates difficulty in determining labour cost per unit.

(vi) ***Piece wage system***: Under this system, the wages are paid on the basis of output without considering the time taken by the workers in performing the work. Workers are paid on the basis of quantity of work produced. Wages can be calculated as follows:

Wages = Number of units produced × Rate per unit

Illustration

If the rate per unit is ₹ 10 and if a worker produces 10 units, then the worker will get 10 × 10 = ₹ 100 as wages.

Advantages

(i) ***Increased production***: As wages are paid according to number of units produced, workers are encouraged to produce more.

(ii) ***Differentiation between efficient and inefficient employees***: Under this system, the efficient worker will work more as wages are linked to the efforts.

(iii) ***Less supervision is required***: As workers are paid on the basis of performance, less control and supervision is required.

(iv) ***Optimum utilisation of machinery***: Under this system, workers may not like to keep their machines idle, which results in the optimum utilization of machines and equipment.

(v) ***Effective cost control***: Increase in output will result in the reduction of overhead costs per unit. This alternatively results in the form of lower price of goods, which is beneficial for customers.

(vi) *Act as an incentive*: This system works as an incentive to employees to produce more. So, it maximises the output.

(vii) *Breakage is minimised*: Under this system, the worker handles the machines and equipment with great care; thus, loss of breakage is minimised. Workers know that breakage will reduce their output, which means reduced wages.

Disadvantages

(i) *No guaranteed wage*: Under this system, workers are not guaranteed minimum wages as wages are directly linked to their efforts and not to the time spent on work.

(ii) *Poor quality*: Workers are encouraged to have quantity at the cost of quality. Workers are always in a hurry to produce more and this results in sub-standard products.

(iii) *Deterioration of health of workers*: This system motivates workers to produce more and more, which affects health of workers adversely.

(iv) *Opposition of trade unions*: This system creates unhealthy competition among workers and also it does not provide any sense of security. Therefore, trade unions oppose this method of wage payment.

(v) *Determination of piece rate is difficult*: Difficulty arises in determining the piece rate and generally disputes arise between labour and management in this regard.

(vi) *Not suitable for beginners*: Due to lack of experience, the newcomers may not be able to produce more goods.

(vii) *Discontentment*: This system frustrates inefficient workers. People who get fewer wages may feel jealous of the others. This results in discontent among workers.

QUESTIONS

1. Explain the concept of employee compensation. What are the main components of compensation?
2. What are the external factors that influence employee compensation?
3. Discuss the principles of compensation administration?
4. What are the steps in the process of wage determination?
5. Explain the time wage system of wage payment with a suitable illustration.
6. Discuss the piece rate system of wage payment. How does it motivate employees to perform better?

NOTES

1. Thomas Patten Jr. *Pay: Employee Compensation and Incentive Plans*. Free Press, New York, 1977, p. 1.
2. Stephen P. Robbins and David A. Decenzo. *Fundamentals of Management*. Third Edition, Pearson Education, Delhi, 2002, p. 202.
3. Luis R. Gomez-Mejia, David B. Balkin and Robert L. Cardy. *Managing Human Resources*. Third Ed. Pearson Education, Delhi, 2003, p. 345.

Chapter 19

Job Evaluation

The process of establishing a consistent and systematic relationship among compensation rates for all jobs within the organization is known as job evaluation. Job evaluation is conducted in order to have equity in compensation. It is the systematic appraisal of each job in the organization to determine its comparative value. Job evaluation is an attempt to determine and compare demands, which the normal performance of a particular job makes on normal workers without taking into account the individual abilities or performance of the workers concerned.[1] The aim of job evaluation is to determine systematically a job's relative worth.

Importance of Job Evaluation

1. It helps in establishing a consistent wage structure in the organization and helps in obtaining internal and external consistency in wage and salaries. Internal consistency refers to the concept of relative wages within the firm whereas external consistency means the desired relativity of an organization's wage structure to that of industry and economy.
2. It helps to establish harmonious and good industrial relations on the issues of wages. Job evaluation is a systematic process; so it brings uniformity in wage rates and thus prevents industrial disputes due to wages.

3. It is a standard and factual basis for determining the relative worth of all jobs in an organization.
4. It helps to raise the morale of employees. Fair and justifiable wage payment plans and their proper administration have a great impact on the workforce. Employees feel satisfied with their salaries and their morale increases.
5. It helps to settle the wage rates of new jobs in the organization.
6. It is a logical and objective method of ranking the jobs in terms of salaries.

Prerequisites of Job Evaluation

In order to establish a job evaluation programme in an organization, there are some necessary prerequisites which are as follows:

1. Availability of job analysis information, i.e. job description and job specification.
2. Job evaluation system should be simple and easy to understand.
3. The job evaluation system should be taken as an adjustment to collective bargaining.
4. Active involvement of a trade union and employees is essential.
5. Availability of industry rates (through labour market survey) to know the prevailing salary rates.
6. Selection of groups of employees and jobs to be covered by the evaluation system.
7. Proper communication of objectives and implication of job evaluation to employees and unions to avoid any misunderstanding.
8. Involvement of outsider experts/consultants such as specialists from National Productivity Council, administrative staff college of India, etc. These people have a rich experience in job evaluation.

Principles of Job Evaluation

There are certain principles of job evaluation, which are relevant to all jobs and in all organizations. The following principles must be kept in mind before putting the job evaluation programme in actual practice:

1. Execution of job evaluation programme is a mutual cooperation of management and employees; so chosen members of committees must be agreeable to all concerned.
2. Objectives of job evaluation process should be well determined and communicated to all concerned parties.
3. The system should be transparent. Decision regarding the evaluation system (type of system, why it is chosen, and its procedure) should be communicated to concerned parties to avoid misunderstanding.
4. The level of wage rates for the selected jobs must be in conformity with the jobs prevailing in the company and in the industry.
5. It is advisable to see that all the concerned parties have an opportunity to fully engage themselves in the job evaluation process.
6. Job evaluation is concerned only with the job, i.e. its contents and not the person or job-holder.
7. Final appraisal and conclusion should not be formalised until and unless the judgements of different raters agree.
8. There should be provision for consistency checks in the operating procedure.
9. Special care should be taken in developing a grade structure following a job evaluation exercise to ensure that grade boundaries are placed appropriately and that the allocation of jobs to grades is not in itself discriminatory.[2] The system should be regularly reviewed in order to ensure that it is being properly operated and it serves its objectives.

Process of Job Evaluation

The main steps in the process of job evaluation are as follows:

1. **Need identification:** The first step is identifying the need for the job evaluation programme in the organization. For example, dissatisfaction reflected in the high turnover, work stoppages or arguments may result from applying different wage rates for similar jobs. This reveals that there is a need of systematic evaluation of jobs in order to know their worth rather than informally assigning payments to all jobs.
2. **Obtaining cooperation:** The next step is getting cooperation of employees in the evaluation. For launching job evaluation programme, close cooperation among managers, trade unions and employees is essential. The management should assure the employees that they will not be adversely affected due to job evaluation process.
3. **Constitution of an evaluation committee:** After ensuring the cooperation of the employees, a committee comprising about 5 to 8 members should be formed. The committee should include several people who are familiar with the jobs in question, each of whom may have a different perspective regarding the nature of the jobs. Generally, committee members include employees, trade union representative, HR specialists and outside specialists. Each committee member should be provided with the manuals, which will explain the job evaluation procedure and special instruction for conducting job evaluation.
4. **Identification of key jobs:** It is not practically possible to evaluate each and every job. Thus, the appointed committee identifies 10 to 15 key benchmark jobs. These jobs will be evaluated and later on, these will serve as standards against which the relative value of all other jobs can be obtained.
5. **Selection of compensable factors:** Now the committee selects the compensable factors. These are the factors

that establish how the jobs compare to one another. A compensable factor is a fundamental element of a job, such as skills, efforts, responsibility and working conditions that can be compensated for.

6. **Selection of method:** This is the most important task of a committee. At this stage, the committee chooses the most appropriate method of evaluation.
7. **Obtaining the job information:** The next step is to get detailed information about key jobs. The products of job analysis, i.e. job description and job specification can be used for obtaining job facts. Job description is a statement of duties and responsibilities and job specification is a statement of minimum human qualities needed for the job.
8. **Job rating:** The method of job evaluation so selected is used to study the job description and job specification. Then on the basis of this analysis, a relative score is assigned to each key job.
9. **Wage rate allocation:** Appropriate wage rates are to be allocated to each key job according to its worth.
10. **Job classification:** The jobs are graded and categorised on the basis of pay scale.

Job Evaluation Methods

There are many methods which are used for job evaluation. Some of these are:

1. **Simple ranking method:** In this method, the committee evaluates the job description and ranks the jobs in order of their importance. No specific factors are selected and the worth of each job is assessed on the basis of its contents or title. A simple job to job comparison is made and ranks are assigned to each job.

Array of jobs according to ranks is shown below:

Rank	*Job*	*Salary*
1	B	₹ 3,000
2	E	₹ 2,000

(Contd...)

3	C	₹ 1,500
4	A	₹ 1,200
5	D	₹ 800

Merits

(i) Simple and easy to understand.
(ii) Suitable for smaller organizations.
(iii) Easy to explain to employees and trade unions.
(iv) Inexpensive.
(v) Less time-consuming and less paperwork.

Demerits

(i) No set standards of judgement.
(ii) Jobs are simply ranked but the exact difference between different jobs cannot be determined.
(iii) Employees may resent the arbitrary job ranking.

2. **Job grading or job classification system:** In simple ranking method, there is no predetermined scale of values, but in case of job grading, grades or classes are established and different jobs are classified accordingly. There is a scale consisting of job grades or classes. The jobs and their descriptions can be compared to this scale. The process of job evaluation consists of reading the job description, reading the grade description and allocating the job to a specific grade.

Job grading description is given below:

Grade	*Description of job grading*
Unskilled/manual	No education required, no responsibility, work under supervision, routine work
Semi-skilled	At least high school passed, need some training work under supervision
Skilled	College educated, trained, need to take initiative and supervise others

Merits

(i) Improvement over simple ranking as it has a pre-determined scale of values.
(ii) Simple and inexpensive to operate.
(iii) Appropriate for small organizations.
(iv) Evaluation can be supported by job description and job grade description.
(v) Easy to understand.

Demerits

(i) Job grade descriptions are broad and vague and cannot be quantified.
(ii) Multiple systems are required for different types of jobs. For example, description of production jobs will be entirely different from office jobs.
(iii) Not appropriate for large organizations.
(iv) Difficulty in explaining to employees and convincing trade unions regarding inclusion of a particular job in a broad category.
(v) Prone to human biasness.

3. **Point system:** This method was developed by Meril Latt in 1923. It is a widely used job evaluation system. It deals with the job factors or components instead of the whole job. A job factor is a compensable factor which determines the worth of a job. These factors represent the values for which an organization provides salary. The factors can be divided into four major categories, i.e. skill, responsibility, effort and working conditions.

Specific factors in job evaluation system are given below:

Skill	*Responsibility*	*Effort*	*Working condition*
Education	Tools, machinery and equipment	Physical	Risk involved
Experience	Material or product	Mental	Work surroundings
Expertise	Safety of others		
Initiative	Accountability		

A scale or yardstick of values for each selected factor is constructed so as to measure the factor in each job, as shown below:

Factor	*Number of points*	*Percentage*
Skills	200	50
Responsibility	100	25
Effort	60	15
Working condition	40	10

The committee members carefully read the job specifications and compare that information with the values on the factor scale. The points of each factor are summed up to arrive at the total score for a job. Jobs are then grouped by total point scores.

Merits

(i) Objective and systematic.

(ii) More accurate as compared to other methods. Each major factor is divided into sub-factors.

(iii) Human bias is reduced.

(iv) Stable method which can be used for a long period.

Demerits

(i) Selection of factors and sub-factors is difficult.

(ii) Time-consuming method.

(iii) Expensive and can be used only by big organizations.

(iv) Allocation of marks to several factors and sub-factors is difficult.

4. **Factor comparison method:** This system of job evaluation was developed by Eugene J. Benge in 1962. In this method, first the compensable job factors, i.e. skill, responsibility, effort and working conditions are identified. Then the jobs are compared with each other in terms of the job factors so identified. Rather than ranking of whole jobs, the jobs are ranked by one factor

at a time. Ideally, all the jobs being measured should include all the job factors so that each job can be scored for each factor. The total scores across factors can be used to sort the jobs into different categories.

Process of factor comparison method:

(i) Key jobs (15 to 20) are selected across the organization, representing as many departments as possible. Key jobs are those which are stable, well-defined, fair and relative to other jobs.

(ii) Factors are selected in terms of which the jobs are to be evaluated (skill, responsibility, etc.).

(iii) The selected jobs are ranked under each factor independently.

(iv) Money value is assigned to each factor and the wage rates are determined for each key job. The wage rate for a job is allocated on the basis of certain factors.

(v) The other jobs are compared with the key jobs and their wage rates are determined.

Merits

(i) Most accurate system of job evaluation.

(ii) Objective, analytical and systematic method.

(iii) Reliable and valid as each key job is compared with all other jobs in terms of key factors.

(iv) As limited number of factors is used it avoids overlapping.

Demerits

(i) Expensive and complicated system.

(ii) Difficult to operate.

(iii) Cannot be easily understood by non-supervisory staff members.

(iv) Expensive method, only big organizations can afford it.

(v) Frequent changes in wage level require adjustment in the key jobs.

QUESTIONS

1. What do you mean by job evaluation? Why is it important?
2. Explain various steps in the process of job evaluation.
3. Discuss the job grading method of job evaluation. What are its merits and demerits?
4. Who developed the point system of job evaluation? What are the specific factors considered in this technique?
5. Explain the process of factor comparison method. What are its merits?

NOTES

1. ILO. *Job Evaluation—Studies and Reports*. New Series, No. 56, Geneva, 1960, p. 8.
2. Michael Armstrong. *A Handbook of Human Resource Management Practice*. Ninth Ed. Kogan Page, London, 2005, p. 640.

Chapter 20

Incentive Systems (Performance Linked Compensation)

Incentive system is related with wage payment plans which tie wages directly or indirectly to standards of productivity or to the profitability of the organization or to both criteria.[1] So, incentive plans refer to all the plans that provide extra pay for extra performance in addition to regular wages for a job. Such payments are also called payment by results.

Importance of Incentive Payments

The incentives schemes are beneficial for both the employer and the employees in the following stages:

1. **Benefits to employees**
   - (i) Due to incentives the earnings of the employees increase, as they will get besides the prescribed wages the premium also.
   - (ii) As a result of additional money, workers' standard of living goes up.
   - (iii) It results in the improvement of the work capacity of employees. To get the incentives, employees work hard to finish the job in the prescribed time or before time.
   - (iv) Employees are encouraged to become innovative in the ways of doing work.

(v) A spirit of mutual cooperation and teamwork is created among the employees.

(vi) The morale of the employees goes up when rewards are tied with the performance.

2. **Benefits to employers**

(i) It motivates the workers for higher efficiency and hence production increases rapidly.

(ii) There is reduction in production cost per unit and also the overall cost.

(iii) Minimum supervision is required.

(iv) All incentive schemes are based upon the scientific work-study. Thus, it brings improvement in work-flow, work methods, man-machine relationship, etc.

(v) It brings improvement in the overall climate of the organization. Workers become more responsible and disciplined and minimise time wastage.

(vi) It results in the adoption of good practices by the employees. For example, reduced wastage, better utilisation of wastage, reduced absenteeism and turnover, and increased output.

Limitations of Incentive Payments

The disadvantages of the incentive payments are the following:

(i) In order to maximise the output, quality of products may deteriorate until and unless a strict checking and inspection is maintained.

(ii) Incentive systems may provoke jealousy, conflict and competition while discouraging cooperation.

(iii) Workers cannot control all of the factors affecting their performance. For example, factors beyond an employee's control are the supervisor, performance of other work group members, the quality of materials the employee is working with, working conditions, the amount of support from management and environmental factors.

(iv) In some cases, employees tend to overwork and this affects their health.

(v) Employees may disregard the safety regulations in order to produce more output, thus increasing risk of accidents.

(vi) In group-incentive systems, hardworking and active employees may be dissatisfied from slow and old workers.

(vii) Difficulties arise for appraisers in measuring the performance whether at individual employee level or at group or team level. Accurate measures of performance are not easy to achieve and pay to inaccurate measures is likely to create problem.[2] Once the incentive scheme is implemented it becomes difficult to change the scheme even when the conditions call for a change due to workers' opposition.

(viii) Pay-for-performance systems may lead to greater productivity but lower job satisfaction as workers are treated like machines.

(ix) Establishment and administration of incentive plans requires additional time and cost.

Prerequisites of an Effective Incentive System

In order to be a successful incentive system, it should possess some essential characteristics. These are the following:

1. The incentive system should be simple enough to operate and easy to understand.
2. It should be installed with the cooperation of workers and trade unions.
3. There should be a climate of mutual trust and faith between employer and employee for the successful implementation of the incentive system.
4. The incentive system should be based on scientific work measurement.
5. Top management support is essential for meeting cost and time requirement.

6. There is a need for careful and detailed planning for the installation of an incentive scheme.
7. The scheme should have constant attention of competent supervisors.
8. The scheme should be economical.
9. The standards once fixed should not be frequently changed except where there are changes in methods, materials or equipment used in the production process.
10. The scheme should be comprehensive in nature. It means that the scheme should cover all the employees.
11. There should be the provision of prompt payment of incentives when they are due.
12. A minimum wage rate should be guaranteed to every employee, irrespective of security to employees.
13. Provision should be made for quick and fair redress all of grievances arising from the implementation of the scheme.

Types of Incentive Schemes

An organization may use a variety of incentive schemes. It can be designed to reward the performance of the individual, group, business plant, entire organization or any combination of these. The main incentive schemes are the following:

I. **Individual incentive systems:** These are the most +6 widely used incentive systems in industry. Here, an organization attempts to identify and reward the contribution of individual employees.

   1. **Straight piece work system:** This is the oldest and simplest method. It is also most commonly used method. In this method, the rate per unit of output is fixed and the total wages of a worker are arrived at by multiplying the total output by the rate per unit. The total output is measured in terms of unit. For example, if the rate per unit is ₹ 1 and the total output of an employee is 50 units, then his wages

will be 50 × 1 = ₹ 50. However, employee's time-rate is guaranteed here.

2. **Standard hour system:** In this system, standard time in terms of hours is fixed for the job completion. Rate per hour is determined. An employee is paid according to standard time wages. If the employee takes more than the standard time then he or she will be paid the same wages unless it is guaranteed time wages. If time wages are guaranteed, the employee is paid on the basis of time taken multiplied by the time-rate.

   For example Standard time = 8 hours

   Rate per hour = ₹ 1

   1st Case

   Time Taken = 6 hours

   Wages = 8 × 1 = ₹ 8

   2nd Case

   Time taken = 10 hour

   Wages if time wages are not guaranteed = 8 × 1 = ₹ 8.

   Wages if time wages are guaranteed = 10 × 1 = ₹ 10.

3. **Time-based systems**

   (i) **Halsey Plan:** This plan was developed by F.A. Halsey. Under Halsey plan, a standard time is fixed in advance for completing the job. An employee taking standard or more time is paid for the time taken by him. An employee completing his or her job in less than the standard time is paid for some of the time saved. In other words, if the worker completes the job in less than the standard time, he will receive a bonus payment at his time rate for a specific percentage of the time saved. This percentage may vary anywhere from 30 per cent to 70 per cent, but usually it is fixed at 50 per cent (the rest 50 per cent goes to the employer).

Wages = $(T \times R) + [(S - T)/2] \times R$

Where S = Standard time

T = Time taken

R = Hourly rate

For example,

Standard time = 12 hours

Rate per hour = ₹ 1

1st Case

Time taken = 12 hours

Wages = 12 × 1 = ₹ 12

2nd Case

Time taken = 13 hours

Wages = 13 × 1 = ₹ 13

3rd Case

Time taken = 10 hours

Wages = (10 × 1) + [(12 – 10)/2] × 1 = ₹ 11

Merits

(a) Halsey plan guarantees minimum wage to all workers, which creates a sense of security.

(b) The wages of time saved are divided between the employer and employee. Thus, this plan benefits the employer also.

(c) This plan is simple to introduce and easily understood by the workers. They can easily make their calculations.

(d) Workers can utilize their saved time in doing other jobs and earn more.

Demerits

(a) Difficulty arises in fixing standard time for completing a job.

(b) Quality of goods may suffer as workers may try to finish the work in the shortest possible time.

(c) More supervision is required to ensure that workers in their eagerness to complete the work fast do not waste materials unduly or damage the machines and tools.

(d) Workers do not receive full benefits for their efforts as usually they are paid for half of the time saved, the other half goes to the employer.

(ii) *Halsey-Weir plan*: This plan was developed by Messer's G & J Weir Ltd. of Glasgow in 1900. This plan is just another form of Halsey plan. Under this plan, a worker receives 30 per cent of the time saved (i.e. standard time-actual time taken). Similar to Halsey plan, a minimum wage is guaranteed here also.

(iii) *Rowan plan*: This plan was developed by James Rowan in 1898. In this plan also, a standard time and rate per hour are fixed. This plan differs from Halsey plan only in respect of the determination of the bonus. The bonus is calculated on the basis of the proportion which the time saved bears to the standard time.

Bonus = (Time saved/standard time) × Time taken × Hourly rate

For example,

Standard time = 12 hours

Rate per hour = ₹ 1

1st Case

Time taken = 12 hours

Wages = 12 × 1 = ₹ 12.00

2nd Case

Time taken = 13 hours

Wages = 13 × 1 = ₹ 13.00

3rd Case

Time taken = 10 hours

Wages = 10 × 1 = ₹ 10.00

Bonus = (2/12) × 10 × 1 = 1.66

Total wages = 11.66

Merits

(a) It guarantees minimum wages to workers.

(b) Increase in production reduces overhead cost per unit.

(c) It enables the employer of the share in the benefits of increased output.

Demerits

(a) This plan is more complex and expensive than the Halsey plan.

(b) This plan's incentive value is low at high production levels, thus this is unjust to efficient workers.

(iv) **Bedeaux plan:** This plan was developed by Charles E. Bedeaux in 1911. In this plan, each minute of the allowed time is called a Bedeaux point or 'B' in short. There are 60 B's in one hour. Each job has a standard number of B's and the hourly rate is also determined. In addition to hourly rate, a worker receives a bonus calculated at 75 per cent of the points earned in excess of 60 per hour, multiplied by one-sixtieth of the worker's hourly rate.

For example,

Standard time = 12 hours

Rate per hour = ₹ 1

Time taken = 10 hours

Standard B's = 60 × 12 = 720 B's

Actual B's = 60 × 10 = 600 B's

Saving in terms of B's = 120 B's

Wages = 10 × 1 = ₹ 10.00

Bonus = (75/100) × [(120 × 1)/60] = ₹ 1.50

Total wages = 10 + 1.50 = ₹ 11.50.

4. **Differential piece rate plans:** Under these plans different piece rates are set for different amounts of

outputs which may be recognized either by actual numbers or pieces or as percentage of tasks. The important ones are the following:

(i) *Taylor's differential piece-rate system*: This system was developed by F.W. Taylor in 1880. Under this plan, there are two piece rates, namely high rate and low rate for each job or task. For each job, standard output and task time are established. If the output of workers is equal to or exceeds the standard, he or she receives wages at the higher rate to enable them to get the bonus. On the other hand, if the output of the worker is less than the standard, then he or she receives wages at the lower rate. Then standard is determined on the basis of time and motion studies. This plan is basically designed to encourage the especially efficient worker with a higher rate of payment and to penalise the inefficient worker by a lower rate of payment. However, this plan is rarely used now.

Illustration

Standard output = 10 units

Rate: (i) High rate = ₹ 5 per unit

(ii) Low rate = ₹ 2 per unit

Case (i) actual output = 10 units

In case actual output equal or exceeds standard output,

Wages = 10 × 5 = ₹ 50

Case (ii) in case actual output is below the standard output (actual output = 8 units)

Wages = 8 × 2 = ₹ 16

(ii) *Merrick differential piece-rate system*: This system was developed by D.V. Merrick. This system is the modification of Taylor's system. Merrick realized that it was unreasonable and unrealistic to classify all the employees into two broad categories only, i.e. workers of high efficiency and workers of lower efficiency because there are various degrees of efficiency and there are many workers who actually put their efforts to produce more. These kind of persons need to be encouraged. This system introduces three piece rates and made the lowest piece rate equal to the ordinary rate which becomes the base piece rates. The rates introduced by Merrick are the following:

Output (percentage of task)	Piece Rate Wage
Less than 83%	Basic piece rate
From 83 % to 100%	110% of basic piece rate
Over 100%	120% of basic piece rate

For the potentially high producer, this plan is a good incentive system. This plan pays a production bonus at 10 per cent of the basic rate to the workers when they reach 83 per cent task and further 10 per cent bonus on reaching over 100 per cent.

(iii) *Gantt's task and bonus plan*: This system was developed by H.L. Gantt, a close associate of F.W. Taylor, in 1901. Gantt is considered as one of the pioneers of scientific management. He modified Taylor's plan considerably. The significant modification is the substitution of Taylor's punitive wage rate by a guaranteed basic wage. Under this plan, a worker's wage consists of two parts, which are the following:

(a) A guaranteed minimum wage on time rate, which is usually an hourly rate.

(b) A bonus, which is paid to the worker when output is equal to or more than the task. The bonus is a percentage of the guaranteed wage. Bonus varies from 20 per cent to 50 per cent of the guaranteed wage.

(iv) *Emerson efficiency plan*: This plan was developed by Harrington Emerson in 1919. Under this plan, whenever the efficiency of a worker reaches 67 per cent, he will get a bonus. Then as the efficiency increases the bonus also increases. When a worker's efficiency varies from 67 per cent to 99 per cent, he receives a bonus at different percentages of his basic wages. And when the efficiency is 100 per cent, the worker's bonus is 20 per cent of the basic wage. Further, when the efficiency is more than 100 per cent, for every 1 per cent increase in efficiency there is a 1 per cent increase in bonus. Just like other incentive plans, a minimum wage is also guaranteed in this plan. The efficiency of a worker should be determined on the basis of the monthly or at least worker's weekly output.

Merits

(a) This plan is simple and easily understood by workers.

(b) Minimum wages are guaranteed.

(c) In this plan, whenever the efficiency of a worker reaches 67 per cent he or she will get bonus. In addition, the rate of bonus increases progressively. Thus, it provides a stimulus to employees for increasing their efficiency.

Demerits

(a) Wage calculations require careful attention.

(b) Employees may not be encouraged to increase their output beyond the standard level, as rewards may be nominal.

(v) *Accelerated premium plans*: Under this system, the earnings of the employees increase with output, the rate of increase itself rising progressively with the output. The employees receive a strong reward or incentive to increase their output in order to obtain increased earnings. However, this is a complicated system and not easy to understand and administer.

II. **Group incentive systems:** Many incentive plans are for individual workers. However, in many cases the output of individual workers cannot be measured although output as a group of workers can be conveniently measured. In such situations group incentive systems are very useful. Under situations where workers are engaged in the assembly work, for example automobiles, textiles, grinding and welding, etc. group incentive schemes are followed.

Advantages of group incentive plans:

(i) It creates cooperation and team spirit among workers.

(ii) There is less need of inspection and supervision.

(iii) The calculation of wages requires less clerical work.

(iv) It raises production and reduces wastage.

(v) It reduces absenteeism.

(vi) It guarantees time wages and thus it creates a sense of security in the workers' mind.

Disadvantages of group incentive plans:

(i) It does not distinguish between efficient and inefficient workers in a group for the purpose of proper distribution of bonus.

(ii) The incentive may be insignificant to motivate the workers.

(iii) Difficulty arises in the determination of the basis of distribution of bonus.

(iv) Jealousy and rivalry among workers defeats the very purpose of teamwork and cooperation.

1. **Profit-sharing plan:** Employee profit-sharing plans constitute one of the more glamorous forms of monetary compensation used in business. In 1897, the International Cooperative Congress defined employee

profit sharing as an agreement freely entered into, by which the employees receive a share, fixed in advance of the profits. The employee profit-sharing plans are mainly of two types. These are (i) cash or current distribution and (ii) trust or deferred distribution. In the cash or current arrangement, the benefits are distributed among participants in cash at least once each year. The deferred type involves a trust fund, the benefits from which are distributed in the event of death, retirement or disability. Some managers prefer to place a part the profit share in trust and distribute the remaining part in the form of cash each year.[3]

Features of Profit-sharing

The main features of profit-sharing are the following:[4] The profit-sharing arrangement is voluntary but based on an agreement between the employer and the employee. In it, there is following arrangement:

(i) The amount to be distributed amongst the participants depend upon the profits earned by the enterprise, and

(ii) The proportion of the profits to be distributed is determined well in advance.

Objectives of Profit-sharing

(i) To secure employee cooperation and to maintain industrial harmony.

(ii) To promote employee loyalty towards organization by supplementing his or her earning.

(iii) To promote increased employee effort.

(iv) To strengthen unity of interest between the employer and the employees.

Advantages of Profit-sharing:

(i) It effects an increase in productive efficiency through reducing costs and increasing output.

(ii) This scheme is relatively easy and less expensive to adopt.

(iii) It improves employee morale.

(iv) It results in cordial relations between the employees and the employer.

(v) It reduces labour turnover.

(vi) It provides security for the employee in the event of disability, death and retirement.

(vii) It provides additional earning to the employees.

(viii) It constitutes a mechanism for employees, economic education.

(ix) It enhances team spirit among employees.

Disadvantages of Profit-sharing:

(i) This scheme does not distinguish among individuals on the basis of effort and contribution. In other words, it does not differentiate between efficient and inefficient workers.

(ii) Besides labour there are many other factors that affect profits. For example, economic and social factors, government policies, demand of the product, etc.

(iii) The employer may indulge in the manipulation of accounts.

(iv) Under this scheme, the extra compensation is not paid immediately after the employee effort is made.

(v) The main disadvantage of this scheme is its high discontinuance rate. These discontinuances are caused by such factors as employee apathy to profit-sharing appraisal, lack of profits, insufficient share, union opposition and unintelligent plan administration.[5]

2. *Employee stock ownership plans* (*ESOPs*): ESOPs reward employees with company stock; either as an outright grant or at a favourable price that may be below market value.[6] These plans are more common among major insurance companies, commercial banks, gas and electric companies and those with over half billion dollars in sales. The main objective of ESOPs is to promote a mutuality of interests. Other possible

values are the promotion of thrift and security, the creation of an added incentive to work productively and cooperatively and the creation of an additional source of investment capital.

Some salient features of ESOPs are as follows:

(i) Generally, a mechanism is adopted through which certain eligible employees may purchase the stock of the company at a reduced rate.

(ii) Usually, the eligibility is determined by the salary level or years of continuous service or both.

(iii) There is a provision for installment buying. The employee authorises a payroll deduction, and stock is periodically purchased for him in the market by the company.

(iv) Sometimes, there is also a provision of the right to purchase a certain amount of stock in future at a stated price.

(v) ESOPs are most widely used in executive compensation plans rather than with the rank and file workers.

QUESTIONS

1. What is an incentive? What are the prerequisites of an effective incentive system?
2. Discuss the Halsey plan and Rowan scheme of incentive payment.
3. What are the different types of differential piece rate plan?
4. Describe the main features of the profit sharing plan. What are its major demerits?
5. Write a note on individual incentive plan vs. group incentive plans.
6. What are the disadvantages of incentive plans?

NOTES

1. Wendell French. *The Personnel Management Process: Human Resources Administration*. 1974, p. 521.

2. Luis R. Gomez-Mejia, David B. Balkin and Robert L. Cardy. *Managing Human Resources*. Third Ed. Pearson Education, Delhi, 2003, p. 361.
3. Edwin B. Flippo. *Personnel Management*. Sixth ed., McGraw-Hill, New York, 1984, p. 320.
4. A.M. Sarma. *Understanding Wage System*. Himalaya Publishing House, Bombay, Third Ed. 1992, p. 60.
5. Edwin B. Flippo. *op. cit*., p. 322.
6. R. Edelman. "Record Amount of Stock Awards Allocated for Compensation Plans", 1996, ACA News.

Chapter 21

Employee Benefits and Services

Employee benefits or indirect compensations are group membership rewards that provide security for employees and their family members. Benefits are indirect financial and non-financial payments employees receive for continuing their employment with the company. They constitute an important part of every employee's compensation. Benefits and services are alternatively known as supplementary compensations, service programmes, non-wage payments, employee benefits and hidden payrolls. Generally, they are known as fringe benefits. In the broadest sense, such "fringes" can be constructed to include all expenditures designed to benefit employees over and above regular base pay and direct variable compensation related to output.[1] For the success of employee benefits and services programmes, the management should ensure the following:

(i) To provide employees meaningful choices of benefits that exactly matches their needs.

(ii) To keep the costs of these programmes under control.

(iii) To ensure that employees are fully informed regarding the various options of these benefits and services.

There are some basic components of employee benefits and services programme. These are the following:

1. **Cafeteria programme/system:** This is also known as flexible benefit programme. This programme is based on the principle of individual differences. This system

allows employees to choose from a variety of benefits that are most valuable to him or her. This is a flexible programme which offers a menu, or a package of different benefits and allows the employees to select from them.

2. **Co-insurance:** In it, the payments made to cover healthcare expenses. Usually, the payments are spilt between the employer's insurance company and the insured employee. For example, the company will pay 70 per cent of employee's health care costs and the employee will pay the remaining 30 per cent.
3. **Contributions:** These are payments made for the benefits coverage. Depending on the type of benefits, contributions are made from the employer, the employee, or both. For example, the premiums for health-care insurance are usually paid from both the parties, whereas vacations are an employer-provided benefit.

Importance of Benefits and Services

Employee benefits and services programmes are valuable because of the following reasons:

1. Benefits are helpful in most effective recruitment.
2. Benefits are helpful in retaining the talented and skilled employees.
3. They improve the morale and loyalty.
4. They reduce absenteeism and labour turnover.
5. They reduce the influence of trade unions.
6. They reduce the threat of government intervention.
7. They are helpful in maintaining harmony in the industry.
8. They are helpful in maintaining good public relations.
9. They protect employees against certain hazards, e.g. life insurance, pension, etc.

Features of Benefits and Services

The main features of fringe benefits are the following:

1. These are supplementary to regular wages. These are extra payment other than wages.
2. These are regularly payable, not in piecemeal.
3. These benefits are indirect compensation and are not directly related to employee performance.
4. These benefits have a direct relation to the real wages of the workers during a given period of time.
5. These benefits constitute a labour cost for the employer and are not meant directly to improve efficiency.
6. These benefits provide help in raising the standard of living of employees.
7. These benefits may be statutory or voluntary. For example, housing and educational facilities are voluntary benefits whereas gratuity and provident funds are statutory benefits.

Principles of Employee Benefits and Services Programmes

The main principles of employee benefit programme are the following:[2]

1. The employee benefit should satisfy a real need.
2. Benefits should be confined to activities in which the group is more efficient than the individual.
3. The benefit programme should be characterised by sufficient flexibility to enable adaptation to varying employee needs.
4. If the firm is to receive values from providing employee services, it must undertake an extensive and well-planned communication programme.
5. The cost of the benefit should be calculable and provision should be made for sound financing.

Types of Employee Benefits and Services (Fringe Benefits)

Various kinds of employee benefits and services offered by the organizations are the following:

1. **Legally required benefits:** This includes the following:
   (a) Social security benefits such as benefits during sickness, accident compensation, maternity benefit, old-age pension, provident fund and gratuity.
   (b) Workers' compensation.
   (c) Unemployment insurance or compensation.
   (d) Severance pay (this refers to one-time payment which an employer provides when terminating the services of an employee).

   These benefits are compulsory to be provided under legislation.
2. **Labour welfare benefits:** These includes (i) canteens, (ii) subsidised food and other supplies, (iii) subsidies to cooperative stores and fair price shops, (iv) housing facilities, (v) crèches, (vi) schools, (vii) holiday homes, (viii) recreation (parties and picnics), (ix) birth, marriage and death grants, (x) aid towards buying or constructing homes, (xi) transportation facilities, etc.
3. **Payments for time not worked:** These include: (i) vacations, (ii) leave with pay, (iii) holidays, (iv) voting time, (v) paid rest periods, (vi) clothes change time, (vii) get ready time, (viii) sick leave, (ix) jury duty, etc. These types of benefits are the most expensive benefits for an employer.
4. **Employee services:** These are tax-free or tax-preferred services that enhance the quality of employees' work or personal life. These include (i) education subsidies, (ii) travel expenses (car reimbursement, food and entertainment reimbursement), (iii) parking privileges, (iv) discounts on company products, (v) physical awareness and fitness programmes, (vi) clothing allowance, (vii) tool allowance/reimbursement, (viii) relocation expenses, (ix) emergency loans, (x) on-site health services, (xi) credit union (it is an organized group of people who pool their money

and agree to make loans to one another), and (xii) counselling services.

5. **Hazard protection:** These include payment made to maintain income of the employees during the periods of hazards such as injury, illness, disability, unemployment, etc.

Administration of Benefits and Services

Usually the HR department takes the lead in designing and administering benefit and service programmes. However, the managers provide help in communicating various options to employees and in keeping records (e.g. sick days, vacation timings, etc.) of employees. The main steps involved in the administration process are as follows:

1. **Establishment of objectives:** First of all, the management should establish clear-cut objectives of benefits and services programmes. Generally, the main objectives are:
   (i) To meet the real needs of employees.
   (ii) To meet the legal requirements.
   (iii) To show organization's social responsibility.
   (iv) To foster external competitiveness.
   (v) To attract and retain competent employees.
2. **Assessment of environment:** Both the external and internal environment factors influence the benefit and service programmes. External factors include economic factors, government policies and regulations and labour unions. Internal factors include employee preference and demographics, organizational objectives and strategies and organization's ability to pay. Employees have different benefits and services needs depending on a number of factors such as age, marital status, whether spouse works or not, presence of kids, etc.
3. **Assessment of competitiveness:** It is very essential to assess the benefits and services offered by the competitors in order to match or outplay them. Usually, this is

assessed by the market survey conducted by professional associations.

4. **Communication:** The benefit and service programmes should be communicated properly to all employees with the help of brochures, calendars, slide presentations, booklets and meetings.
5. **Evaluation and control:** The last step involves the assessment of fringe benefits. It is checked whether the organization has been able to attract and retain the competent employees or not, whether employees' earnings have been improved or not, whether labour-management relations are better or not, whether morale of employees is raised or not, whether the programmes were cost-effective or not, etc.

QUESTIONS

1. What are fringe benefits? Give suitable examples.
2. Discuss the role of fringe benefits in improving employee morale.
3. What are the principles of employee benefits and services programmes?
4. How can the HR manager successfully administer employee benefits to the workers?
5. Explain various benefits that are compulsory to be provided under legislation.

NOTES

1. Edwin B. Flippo. *Personnel Management*. Sixth Ed. McGraw-Hill, New York, 1984, p. 331.
2. *Ibid.*, p. 334.

Chapter 22

Industrial Relations

Industrial relations refer to the collective relationship between management, employees and government in any organization. It deals with the people at work. It is a comprehensive field of study, subtle as well as gross, a vast area of interactions, actions and reactions which affect not just a company or an industry, but also the economy. Industrial relations can be described as the relationship between management and employees or among employees and their organizations that characterise or grow out of employment. According to *Encyclopaedia Britannica*, "The concept of industrial relations has been extended to denote the relations of the state with employers, workers and their organizations. The subject, therefore, includes individual relations and joint consultations between employers and work people at their workplace, collective relations between employers and their organizations and trade unions and the part played by the state in regulating these relations."[1]

Objectives of Industrial Relations

(i) To promote mutual understanding and goodwill among employees and management.

(ii) To raise the productivity of labour and organization as a whole.

(iii) To establish and maintain industrial democracy through workers' participation in management, collective bargaining, etc.

(iv) To minimise all forms of industrial conflict for example, strikes, lockouts, *gheraos*, etc.

(v) To promote smooth and healthy labour management relations.

(vi) To promote mutual cooperation between the employers and the employees.

(vii) To integrate the interests of labour and management.

(viii) To minimise absenteeism and labour turnover.

(ix) To promote the welfare of the workers.

(x) To encourage and develop strong trade unions.

(xi) To bring about government control over plants and units running into losses.

(xii) To ensure that the government endeavour to bridge the gap between the unbalanced, disordered and maladjusted social order.

Participants in Industrial Relations

There are three main participants in an industrial relations system:

1. **Workers and their organizations:** The major party in the industrial relations system consists of the workers and their organization, i.e. labour unions. The workers' organizations are basically political institutions which safeguard the interests of the workers.
2. **Management:** This refers to the top management or employers who lay down the terms and conditions of employment and administer labour welfare and social security programmes. Conflict of interests between the management and workers is one of the major reasons behind industrial unrest.
3. **Government:** The government acts as a regulator. The government, both at the central and the state levels constitutes labour legislations, rules, regulations, etc. to control the employer-employee relations in industrial undertakings.

Factors Influencing Industrial Relations

1. **Institutional factors:** These factors include factors such as labour policy of the government, labour legislation, employers' and employees' organizations and their policies, collective bargaining agreements, voluntary codes, implementation machinery, etc.
2. **Social factors:** These include factors like norms, customs, beliefs, traditions, values, social status, level of education, level of awakening, etc.
3. **Economic factors:** These include factors such as system (capitalist, socialist, communist, mixed economy), economic conditions and policies, source of labour supply, nature and composition of workforce, relative status of labour market, level and structure of wages, dearness allowance, incentives, price level, nationalisation of industries, level of unemployment, etc.
4. **Psychological factors:** These include the attitudes and perceptions of workers towards management, their behaviour towards labour unions, fellow workers, their views about living and working conditions, their level of morale, motivation and boredom, etc.
5. **Technological factors:** The technology used and the work methods adopted in the factory influence the working conditions, wage levels and the employment status which have a bearing on industrial relations.
6. **Political factors:** These factors include the ideology and philosophy of the ruling party, political institutions, attitude of oppositions, etc.
7. **Organization-related factors:** These are also known as internal factors. These include industrial relations policy of the organization, working environment, prevailing management style, living conditions, organizational culture, trade unions, wages and salary administration, HR management policies, etc.

8. **Global factors:** These include international relations, international trade agreements, role of International Labour Organization (ILO), and economic and trading policies of powerful nations.

Approaches to Industrial Relations

The main approaches to industrial relations are as follows:

1. **Psychological approach:** This approach suggests that the conflicts between labour and management are deeply rooted in the perceptions and attitudes of all the participants. Differences in the perception of the parties are due to their individuality. Conflicts arise when each party negatively perceives the other's behaviour. Labour and management view and interpret the situations differently and these differences create the problems of industrial relations.
2. **Sociological approach:** Industry is a part of society. So, various sociological factors such as value system, norms, customs, traditions and status symbols affect relations among the parties. The social consequences of industrialisation like social mobility and migration generate many social evils like disintegration of family, stress and strain, delinquency, personal and social disorganization (leading to growing incidences of gambling, drinking, prostitution, drug abuse, etc.). These influence workers' efficiency and productivity which, in turn, impact industrial relations.[2]
3. **Human relations approach:** This approach focuses on human beings as a key factor of production in industry. Unlike other resources such as finance and material, human beings have emotions, sentiments, desires, perceptions, attitudes, personality, etc. For harmonious industrial relations, there is a need for proper integration of individuals' needs with the organization's requirements. Management should motivate the employees in order to raise productivity.

4. **Socio-ethical approach:** This approach to industrial relations emphasizes that besides having a sociological base, it does have some ethical ramifications. Good industrial relations can be maintained only when both the labour and management realize their moral responsibility in contributing to the said task through mutual cooperation and greatest understanding of each other's problems.[3]
5. **V.V. Giri approach:** This approach to industrial relations was given by V.V. Giri, the 4th President of India. He emphasized collective bargaining, voluntary arbitration and mutual negotiations between the employers and the employees for settlement of industrial disputes. This approach stresses internal settlement of issues rather than relying on some outside compulsion. Voluntary arbitration is preferred to compulsory arbitration.
6. **Gandhian approach:** This approach to industrial relations is based on the fundamental principles of truth, non-violence and non-possession. There is a presumption that capital and labour can co-exist peacefully. Gandhiji emphasizes that if the employers follow the principle of trusteeship then there is no scope for conflict of interest between labour and management. Gandhiji accepted the workers' right to strike, but cautioned that they should exercise this right for a just cause and in a peaceful and non-violent manner and this method should be resorted to when all other methods fail to get the employer's response.
7. **Systems approach:** A system is an organized or complex whole, an assemblage or combination of things or parts forming a complex unitary whole. The systems approach tells us that no single element or phenomenon should be dealt with without regard for its interacting consequences with other elements. This suggests that there is always an interaction between the four basic elements, i.e. input, transformation, output and feedback.

In the field of industrial relations, the systems approach to industrial relations was developed by John T. Dunlop. Dunlop described an Industrial Relations System (IRS) as consisting of three actors: workers and their organization, managers and their organization and the governmental agencies concerned with the work community. These groups interact with a specified environment which includes: technological environment, market or economic constraints and the balance of power in society. An IRS creates an ideology that regulates the relations among the participants. An ideology is a set of ideas and beliefs commonly held by the actors that helps to build or integrate the system together as an entity.

Goals of Industrial Relations

1. **Development of healthy labour-management relations:**
   (i) *Trade unions and employers associations*: Strong, well-organized, democratic and responsible trade unions and associations of employers in an industry bring about a greater sense of job security among the employees and assist in the workers' increased participation in decision-making regarding issues directly affecting them. They also try to create favourable conditions for negotiations, consultations and discussions with employers to pave the way to better labour-management relations.
   (ii) *Collective bargaining and a willingness to accept voluntary arbitration*: Collective bargaining, plant discipline and satisfactory trade union relations are the three principal items which determine the quality of industrial relations. Collective bargaining presumes an equality of status between two contending groups conflicting with each other. It prepares the ground for mutual trust and goodwill to ensure fair discussion, consultation and negotiation on matters of common interest to both industry and labour.

(iii) *The welfare work undertaken by the government, the trade unions and employers*: It creates and maintains good and healthy labour-management relations and creates an atmosphere conducive for industrial peace.

2. **Maintenance of industrial peace:** It can be established by the following:

    (i) *Machinery for the prevention and settlement of industrial disputes*: It is provided in the form of legislative enactments and administrative action, works committees and joint management councils, conciliation officers and conciliation boards, labour courts, industrial tribunals, national tribunals, courts of enquiry and voluntary arbitration.

    (ii) *Adjudicator*: The government has armed itself with appropriate powers to refer disputes to an adjudicator when the situation gets out of control and the industry is faced with economic collapse because of strikes, or when it is urgent and in the public interest to refer disputes for adjudication.

    (iii) *Maintenance of status quo*: The government has the power to maintain the status quo, and exercise it when it discovers that even after a dispute has been referred to an adjudicator, a strike or lockout continues which is likely to adversely affect the economic life of the community or create chaotic conditions in an industry.

    (iv) *Bipartite and tripartite forms of the settlement of disputes*: These operate on the basis of the code of discipline in industry, the code of conduct, the code of efficiency and welfare, and on the basis of model standing orders, grievance redressal procedure and the grant of voluntary recognition to trade unions by industrial organizations.

    (v) *Implementation and evaluation committees*: These are created and maintained for the specific purposes of ensuring the implementation of agreements, settlements and awards, and of looking into any violations of statutory provisions of the various labour laws.

3. **Industrial democracy:** It can be established by the following:
   (i) *Joint management councils*: These endeavour to improve the working and living conditions of employees, to step up their productivity, to encourage suggestions from workers, to assist in the administration of labour laws and agreements, to serve as a channel of communication between management and workers, and to create in the latter a sense of participation in the decision-making process and a sense of belonging to the organization.
   (ii) *Recognition of human rights in an industry*: The era when labour was regarded as a commodity is long by-gone. Today it is a recognized fact that human beings should be treated with respect and dignity. Workers should be recognized as valuable assets of the organization and they should be given a chance to satisfy their urge for self-expression through close association with the management.
   (iii) *Increased labour productivity*: The factors which contribute to higher productivity are improvements in the efforts and skill of the workers, the production design and the process of manufacture, in the materials and equipment used, in layout and methods of work, research and techniques of manufacture, the management methods and practices.
   (iv) *Suitable social environment*: Workers may adjust and adapt themselves according to the work environment of the organization where they are employed. The work environment has a profound influence on industrial relations. A congenial atmosphere and comfortable working conditions would stimulate the workers to perform better and improve industrial relations.

As R.A. Lester stated, the function of industrial relations is to bring about solutions of conflicts between labour and management—conflicts between objectives and values, between the profit motive and social gain, between discipline and freedom, between authority and workers, between bargaining and cooperation, and these solutions should be in the interests of the individual, the group and the community.

Pre-Requisites for a Successful Industrial Relations Programme

The necessary prerequisites for establishing good industrial relations are as follows:

1. **Top management support:** The industrial relations is basically a staff function, thus the managers in charge of industrial relations should derive authority from the line executive, i.e. president or vice-president as the case may be. For the success of industrial relations programme, support of top management is essential.
2. **Constructive attitude:** Both management and trade unions should develop constructive attitude towards each other. Mutual understanding and cooperation is necessary for the smooth conduct of industrial relations programme. On one hand, the management must recognize the union as the spokesperson of the workers' grievances and as custodian of their interests. It should accept workers as equal partners in the industry. On the other hand, the workers and their trade unions must also consider and understand the rights, authority and responsibility of the management.
3. **Developing sound policies and procedures:** The policies and procedures relating to industrial relations should be well-designed and revised timely for maintaining good industrial relations in an organization. All the policies and procedures should be clear to everybody in the organization, including union leaders.
4. **Development of effective practices:** The implementation of various policies pertaining to management selection

calls for developing effective practices so that various policies are translated into action.

5. **Good communication system:** There must be a good and prompt communication system in an organization in order to avoid any rumours, doubts and misunderstanding between both the parties. Efficient communication system removes distrust between management and union leaders. The HR manager should play a key role in bringing both the parties together.
6. **Adequate supervisory training:** To a large extent the problem of industrial relations is a human problem. So, in order to deal with the human beings in the organization and also to ensure that organizational policies and procedures are properly implemented, it is necessary that all the supervisors and foremen are provided with sufficient training. These are the people who come in direct contact with the employees and therefore they should be well trained in the techniques of human relations. Success of industrial relations programme is largely determined by the attitude and dealing of supervisors. Thus, they should be trained in motivation, communication and leadership.
7. **Development of right kind of union leadership:** On the pattern of developing good supervisors, management should also encourage the development of right type of union leadership. Although the management should not interfere with the union activities, it can create conditions which would stimulate the growth of constructive and competent union leadership.
8. **Follow-up of results:** This refers to the constant review of industrial relations so that existing practices may be evaluated and problems, if any, may be identified. Along with the regular follow-up of various industrial relations policies and procedures, special emphasis should be placed upon gathering relevant information related to absenteeism, employee turnover, morale, job satisfaction,

grievances, disputes, accident rates, wage and salary administration, etc. so that corrective action may be taken if needed.

QUESTIONS

1. Explain the concept of industrial relations. Who are the main participants in it?
2. What are various factors influencing industrial relations?
3. Write notes on: V.V. Giri approach and Gandhian approach to industrial relations.
4. What are the goals of industrial relations? Why is the concept of industrial relations important?
5. List the pre-requisites for a successful industrial relations programme.

NOTES

1. *Encyclopaedia Britannica*. Vol. 12. London, 1961, p. 297.
2. C.B. Mamoria, Satish Mamoria and S.V. Gankar. *Dynamics of Industrial Relations*. Fifteenth Ed. Himalaya Publishing House, 2005, p. 194.
3. *Ibid*., p. 196.

Chapter 23

Employee Health and Safety

For a manager, employee safety and health must be a top priority in all he does. To ensure a safe working environment is also legally mandated. Moreover, it is an obligation for any socially responsible manager. It is very important that managers understand the importance of health and safety issues and take steps to maintain a safe working environment at the workplace. An organizational culture that places a greater value on speed or saving money than on safety can result in the workplace accidents—some that involve the loss of human life.[1] Though line managers are primarily responsible for the maintenance of a safe and healthy work environment in the organization, yet the human resource managers should provide staff expertise to help them deal with these issues.

Safety involves protecting employees from injuries caused by work-related accidents. Health refers to employees' freedom from physical or emotional illness. Both health and safety programmes are concerned with protection against hazards. The achievement of the highest standards of health and safety in the workplace is important because the elimination or at least minimisation of health and safety hazards and risks is the moral as well as the legal responsibility of employers.[2] Proper attention to safety and health of employees is important as illness and injuries cause suffering and loss to individuals and their dependents. Also it damages the organization's reputation.

Accidents

An accident is an unplanned and uncontrolled event in which an action or reaction of an object, a substance, a person or a radiation results in personal injury. According to the Factories Act, 1948, an accident is an occurrence in an industrial establishment causing bodily injury to a person which makes him unfit to resume his duties in the next 48 hours.

Types of Accidents

Accidents can be of different types. An employee may fall from a height while engaged on a particular assignment, or he may be caught in a machine while working on it, or he may fall against a machine, or parts of machine having a horizontal protruding motion may strike against him, or explosive used carelessly may explode and injure an employee.[3] This injury may be internal one, e.g. a bone fracture, muscle pull, etc. or external one which shows clearly the signs of injury. Further, both these kinds of injuries may be major or minor. Minor accident may result in a cut or a scratch, which is not a serious one. Whereas a major accident may be fatal or non-fatal. In other words, the major accidents may result in death or disablement.

According to the Workmen's Compensation Act, 1923, disablement means loss of capacity to work or to move. Disablement of a workman may result in loss or reduction of his or her earning capacity. In the latter case, he or she may not be able to earn as much as he or she used to earn before his or her disablement.

Disablement may be partial or total. According to Section 2(1)(g) of the Workmen's Compensation Act, 1923, partial disablement means any disablement that reduces the earning capacity of a workman as a result of some accident. Partial disablement may be (i) permanent, or (ii) temporary. Temporary partial disablement means any disablement that reduces the earning capacity of a workman in any employment in which he was engaged at the time of accident which results in such disablement. On the other hand, permanent partial disablement is one, which reduces the earning capacity of a workman in every employment, which he was capable of undertaking at the time of injury. Finally, total disablement means such disablement, whether of a temporary or permanent nature, as incapacitates a workman for all work which he was capable of performing at the time of the accident resulting in such disablement. In other words, this refers to that condition where a workman becomes unfit for every type of work and is not able to get job anywhere due to that disablement.

Causes of Accidents

The primary causes or factors responsible for accidents are as follows:

1. **Machine factors:** These factors are also called as technical factors. Machine factors mean the faulty mechanical or physical conditions. Although they are less in number, usually they are serious in nature, i.e. they normally result in injuries of serious or fatal nature. These include the following factors:
   - (i) Improperly or inadequately guarded equipment.
   - (ii) Defective equipment.
   - (iii) Deficiencies in tools.
   - (iv) Deficiencies in plant.
   - (v) Unsafely designed tools, machines, etc.
   - (vi) Insufficient lighting, glare, etc.
   - (vii) Improper ventilation, impure air source, etc.
   - (viii) Unsafe storage, overloading, congestion, etc.
   - (ix) Poor house-keeping.
   - (x) Lack of automatic quick stoppage devices.
   - (xi) Inadequate fencing of machines.
   - (xii) Wrong and faulty plant layout, bad location, etc.
   - (xiii) Inadequate safety devices.
   - (xiv) Defective electrical fitting.

2. **Non-machine factors:** As per an estimate around 80 per cent accidents occur due to non-machine factors. These factors can be divided into two categories as follows:

   (i) *General factors*

   These include the following:

   (a) Prick of a wire nail carelessly thrown away by someone at the workplace.

   (b) Falling down from ladder or slipping off the ladder itself, especially in construction work/ repairing/ innovating/maintenance work, etc.

   (c) Loading or unloading of heavy material without taking due care or without giving proper warning.

   (d) Improper foot rests or grips.

   (e) Non-wearing of right dress while working on or near an exposed moving part of a machine.

   (f) Not-using goggles in welding.

   (g) Flying-off of hammerheads or chisels, sometimes the whole hammer itself.

   (h) Lack of inspection of machines, etc. by experts.

   (i) Defective work methods.

   (j) Inefficient supervisor/leadership.[4]

   (ii) *Personal factors*

   These factors relate to an individual's proneness to accident. There are a few individuals who get involved in more accidents than others. An individual's proneness to accidents may be due to the following personal factors:[5]

   (a) Poor eye-sight.

   (b) Poor physique.

   (c) Nervousness.

   (d) Fear complex.

   (e) Suffering from diseases such as high blood pressure, fits, epilepsy, etc.

(f) Immaturity, irresponsibility, etc.
(g) Colour-blindness.
(h) Fatigue.
(i) Depression, worry, etc.
(j) Ignoring safety instructions.
(k) Emotional instability, too much sensitiveness, etc.
(l) Addiction to drugs, liquor, etc.
(m) Day-dreaming.
(n) Absent-mindedness.
(o) Frustration.

(iii) *Other factors*

Apart from the earlier discussed causes of accidents, there are a few others, which are the following:[6]

(a) Young, untrained and new workers generally sustain injuries more frequently than older, trained and experienced employees.
(b) The way the management motivates employees affects the rate and frequency of accidents. For example, the tensions, which aggressive and negative supervisors generate among the employees, also tend to increase this rate and frequency.
(c) Unmarried employees generally have more accidents than married employees.
(d) Accidents are more frequent during night shift.
(e) Women employees have a better safety record than male counterparts.
(f) Workers who work under stress, or who feel their jobs are threatened or insecure, seem to have more accidents than those who do not.

Accident Costs

Accidents are generally costly, both to an employee and to an employer. Some losses are direct and some are indirect. Some losses are visible and some are invisible. From a worker's point of view, an accident creates pain for him and his family. From an employer's point of view, it disrupts production and also causes financial loss. From the employer's context, the accident costs can be divided into two parts:

1. **Direct costs:** These include the following:
   - (i) Payment of wages to the injured worker during his period of absence due to injury.
   - (ii) Amount of compensation to be paid on account of death, disablement, etc. The rates are decided as per the provisions of the Workmen's Compensation Act, 1923 or the Employees' State Insurance Act, 1948.
   - (iii) Cost of medical aid.
   - (iv) Cost of recruiting and training a substitute worker.
   - (v) Loss in production and quality due to lack of skill and experience of a newcomer.
   - (vi) Loss due to waste of raw materials.
2. **Indirect costs:** The indirect costs of accidents are estimated to be two to four times the direct costs. The indirect costs are the following:[7]
   - (i) Cost of lost time of injured employee.
   - (ii) Cost of time lost by other employees who stop work out of curiosity and sympathy, to assist the injured employee, etc.
   - (iii) Cost of time lost by foremen, supervisors in assisting the injured employee, investigating the cause of the accident, arranging for the injured employee's production to be continued by some other employee, recruitment, selection and training of the new employee, preparing state accident reports or attending hearings before industrial commissioner, etc.
   - (iv) Cost of time spent on the case by first-aid attendant and hospital staff when this is not covered by insurance.

(v) Cost due to damage to the machine, tools, or other property, or to the material.

(vi) Cost due to interference with production, failure to fill orders on time, loss of bonuses, payments of forfeits and other similar causes.

(vii) Cost under employee welfare and benefit systems.

(viii) Cost in continuing the wages of the injured employees in full, after his return—even though the services of the employee (who is not yet fully recovered) may for the time be worth only about half his normal value.

(ix) Cost due to the loss of profit on the injured employee's productivity and on idle machines.

(x) Cost of subsequent injuries that occurs in consequence of the excitement or weakened morale owing to the original accident.

(xi) Overhead cost—the expense of light, heat, rent, and other such items—that continues while the injured employee is a non-producer.

Prevention of Accidents

Many industrial accidents are preventable if necessary preventive steps are taken. Thus, it is essential for all concerned to take the necessary preventing steps. Following steps are taken for the prevention of accidents:

1. **The safety programme:** Once the management develops interest in promoting safety measures, then it should plan the safety programme. Any particular safety programme could be composed of one or more of the following elements:

   (i) *Support by top management*: Top management's support is essential for the conduct and success of a safety programme. Management's support was characterised by personal attendance at safety meetings, periodic personal inspections, and insistence on regular safety reports and inclusion of safety figures and achievements on the agenda of the company's board of director's meetings.[8]

(ii) *Appointing a safety director*: The next step is to appoint a safety director who shall be given the primary responsibility for the installation and maintenance of the safety programme. In case of a small organization then this job can be assigned to any responsible line manager. However, in case of a larger organization, staff safety director/safety engineer is usually appointed.

(iii) *Engineering a safe plant and operation*: A sound and forward-looking engineering is an essential requirement for a safety programme. While preparing a safety programme all possible mechanical safety devices and human engineering should be thought of for application. Factory should be kept clean, well-lit, properly ventilated and free from dust. All dangerous parts of machines and equipment should be properly fenced.

(iv) *Educating all employees to act safely*: A good safety programme should have proper provision for educating the employees to act, think and work safely. This can be done through the following:

(a) Educating the new employees at the time of induction.

(b) Giving emphasis on safety points during training periods especially during the off-the-job training.

(c) Making of special efforts by first level supervisor.

(d) Establishment of employee safety committees.

(e) Holding of employee safety meetings.

(f) Use of company periodical, if any.

(g) Use of charts, posters and displays emphasizing the need to act safely.

(v) *Record keeping*: The employer should maintain a proper record showing the number of accidents, occupational illnesses and the number of lost workdays.

(vi) *Accident analysis*: Even after taking all the preventive measures, accidents occur. They should be thoroughly investigated in terms of both costs and causes. All sorts of direct and indirect costs should be listed and the management should take a lesson from this.

(vii) *Safety contests*: Safety contests stimulate employees to think and act safely. These are a form of employee education. It has been observed that accident rate is lower in the pre-contest and during the contest period but once the period of contest is over the accident rates goes up again.

(viii) *Enforcement*: A safety programme should be enforced rigorously; only then the desired results can be obtained. Although the basic approach of a safety programme should be positive in nature, yet in some cases the negative approach by way of imposing fines, reprimands, discharge, lay-offs, etc. may also be necessary to enforce discipline in case someone deliberately violates the safety rules and instructions.

2. **Legal provisions regarding safety of workers:** The Factories Act, 1948 makes detailed provisions in regard to various matters relating to the safety of the worker. These provisions impose upon the occupiers or managers certain obligations to protect workers, who are unwary as well as negligent, from accidents. Sections 21 to 41 provide the safety provisions, which are absolute and obligatory in their character, and the occupier of every factory is bound to follow them.

(i) *Fencing of machinery* (*Sec. 21*): In every factory, all dangerous parts of each machine shall be properly fenced. Machineries include every moving part of a prime mover and every fly-wheel connected to a prime mover, the headrace and tailrace of every water-wheel and water-turbine, any part of a stock-bar which projects beyond the headstock of a lathe, every part of an electric generator, a motor or rotary converter and every part of transmission machinery.

(ii) *Work on or near machinery in motion* (*Sec. 22*): In any factory, any examination, adjustment or lubrication of any part of operating machinery shall be carried out by trained adult male worker wearing tight fitting clothing. Women and young persons are not allowed to carry the above-said task.

(iii) *Employment of young persons on dangerous machines* (*Sec. 23*): There is a restriction on young persons to work on dangerous machines.

(iv) *Striking gear and devices for cutting off power* (*Sec. 24*): Suitable striking gear to be provided, maintained and used. Also, suitable devices for cutting off power in emergencies from machinery should be provided and maintained in every workroom.

(v) *Self-acting machines* (*Sec. 25*): No traversing part of a self-acting machine in any factory and no material carried thereon shall be allowed to run on its outward or inward traverse within 45 centimetres from any fixed structure which is not part of machine.

(vi) *Casing of new machinery* (*Sec. 26*): All machinery driven by power shall be sunk, encased to guard against danger/accidents.

(vii) *Prohibition of employment of women and children near cotton-openers* (*Sec. 27*): No women or child shall be allowed in any part of the factory to press cotton when cotton-opener is at work.

(viii) *Hoists and lifts* (*Sec. 28*): Hoists and lifts should be of good mechanical construction and should be properly maintained and examined once in every six months.

(ix) *Lifting machines, chains, ropes and lifting tackles* (*Sec. 29*): Lifting machines, chains, ropes and lifting tackles should be of good construction and should be examined once in every 12 months. Also, cranes and lifting machines should not be loaded beyond safe working load.

(x) *Revolving machinery* (Sec. 30): Maximum safe working speed of grindstone or abrasive wheel, etc. should be clearly stated on a notice to be kept near machine.

(xi) *Pressure plant* (*Sec. 31*): The limit of safe working pressure should not be exceeded.

(xii) *Floors, stairs and means of access* (*Sec. 32*): All floors, steps, stairs, passages and gangways should be of sound construction and properly maintained.

(xiii) *Pits, sumps, opening in floors, etc.* (*Sec. 33*): Every pit or opening in the floor should be properly covered or fenced.

(xiv) *Excessive weights* (*Sec. 34*): No person shall be employed in any factory to lift, carry or move any load so heavy as to be likely to cause him or her injury.

(xv) *Protection of eyes* (*Sec. 35*): In every factory, screen or suitable goggles should be provided for the protection of persons who are employed in a work which involves danger or injury to the worker's eyesight.

(xvi) *Precautions against dangerous fumes* (*Sec. 36*): No person shall be allowed to enter any chamber, tank, pit, pipe, etc. in which any gas, dust or fume is likely to be present.

(xvii) *Precautions regarding the use of portable electric light* (*Sec. 36-A*): No portable electric light or any other electric appliance of voltage exceeding 24 volts shall be permitted for use inside any chamber, tank or pit unless adequate safety devices are provided.

(xviii) *Precautions against explosive or inflammable dust, gas, etc.* (*Sec. 37*): Effective measures should be taken to prevent explosion on ignition of gas, fume, etc.

(xix) *Precautions in case of fire* (*Sec. 38*): Effective measures should be taken to prevent the outbreak of fire and its spread. Workers should be made familiar well in advance with the means of escape in case of fire.

(xx) *Power to require specifications of defective parts or tests of stability* (*Sec. 39*): The inspector of the factory may ask the occupier or the manager or both to furnish drawings and specifications, which may be necessary to determine whether the buildings, ways, machinery or plant can be used with safety.

(xxi) *Safety of building and machinery* (*Sec. 40*): If any building or part of a building or machinery or plant in a factory is in such a condition that it is dangerous to human life or safety, then the inspector may serve on the occupier or the manager or both of the factory an order specifying the measures which in his opinion shall be adopted and requiring them to be carried out.

(xxii) *Maintenance of building* (*Sec. 40-A*): If it appears to the inspector that any building or any part of a building in a factory is in such a state of despair as is likely to lead to conditions detrimental to the health and welfare of the workers, then he may serve on the occupier or the manager or both of the factory an order specifying the measures which should be taken.

(xxiii) *Safety officers* (*Sec. 40-B*): In every factory, (a) wherein 1000 or more workers are employed, or (b) wherein, any manufacturing process or operation is carried on, which involves any risk of bodily injury, poisoning or disease, or any other hazard to health, to the persons employed in the factory, then the occupier shall appoint the required number of safety officers.

3. **Other voluntary steps:** In addition to adopt a safety programme and comply with the legal provisions, management can take other voluntary steps also. For example, it can ensure good working conditions with special emphasis on safety measures, pay attention to individual differences of employees, ensure proper speed of work, motivate safety attitudes, encourage safety habits, arrange strong motor tests, emotional stability tests, intelligence tests, etc.[9] Along with this, the workers and trade unions should also take voluntary steps in this regard, e.g. guiding workers on safety measures, arranging lectures, publishing periodicals/ magazines, etc.

Health

Prevention of accidents for the employee's well-being is just one part of the comprehensive safety and health programme. The employee's physical conditions can be harmed through diseases, stress and strain as well as through accidents. Thus, it is also equally important for the organization to be concerned with the general health, both physical and mental, of its employees for both economic and humanitarian reasons.

According to World Health Organization (WHO), health is a state of complete physical, mental and social well-being and not merely an absence of disease or infirmity.

Need and Importance of Industrial Health

The need and importance of industrial health is clear from the following points:

1. It improves the efficiency and productivity of the workers.
2. It reduces absenteeism and labour turnover rate.
3. It reduces indiscipline.
4. It improves motivation and morale.
5. It lessens industrial discontentment.
6. It reduces occupational diseases.

7. It enables the workers to work for longer periods of time.
8. It reduces industrial unrest.
9. It reduces spoilage and cost of operation.

Physical Health

Healthy employees are more safety conscious, more regular to work, more productive and more efficient. A healthy worker is confident, always happy and cheerful and a great asset for an organization. Realizing the significance of health generally the following measures are included under physical health programmes[10]:

1. A stated health and medical policy.
2. Pre-placement physical examination.
3. The performance of periodic physical examinations on all employees to health hazards.
4. The availability of facilities for voluntary periodic physical examinations for all employees.
5. A competent medical staff.
6. Systematic attention to sanitation, safety precautions and industrial hygiene.
7. A chief medical officer who reports to a responsible member of management.
8. A well-equipped dispensary for emergency cases and physical examination.
9. Well-qualified medical and nursing personnel.

Statutory/Legal Health Provisions

Sections 11 to 20 of the Factories Act, 1948 deal with the provisions related with the health of the workers in the factories. These provisions are the following:

1. **Cleanliness (Sec. 11):** Every factory should be kept clean and free from effluvia and dirt. Effective means of drainage should be provided.
2. **Disposal of wastes and effluents (Sec. 12):** In every factory effective arrangements should be made for the treatment

of wastes and effluents due to manufacturing process carried on therein, so as to render them innocuous, and for their disposal.

3. **Ventilation and temperature (Sec. 13):** Adequate ventilation and temperature should be maintained in every workroom of the factory.
4. **Dust and fumes (Sec. 14):** Where dust or fumes or impurity of such a nature as is likely to be injurious to the workers is given off as a result of the manufacturing process being carried on in a factory, effective measures shall be taken in the factory for prevention of inhalation or accumulation of dust and fumes in workrooms.
5. **Artificial humidification (Sec. 15):** In respect of all the factories in which the humidity of the air is artificially increased, the State Government may make rules prescribing the standards of humidification. The water used for this purpose should be taken from a public supply or other sources of drinking water.
6. **Overcrowding (Sec. 16):** There should not be overcrowding in any room of the factory so as to be injurious to the health of the workers employed. There shall be at least 9.9 cubic metres (for the factories in existence at the time of the commencement of the Act) and 14.2 cubic metres (for the factories built after the commencement of the Act) space for every worker.
7. **Lighting (Sec. 17):** There should be the provision of sufficient and suitable lighting in every part of the factory. All glazed windows and skylights used for the lighting of the workrooms should be kept clean on both the inner and outer surfaces and free from obstruction.
8. **Drinking water (Sec. 18):** There should be the provision of suitable points for wholesome drinking water. All points for supply of drinking water shall be legibly marked 'drinking water' in a language understood by a majority of the workers employed in the factory. There should be the provision of cooling of drinking water where more than 250 workers are employed.

9. **Latrines and urinals (Sec. 19):** Separate latrines and urinals for male and female workers should be provided. These should be conveniently situated and adequately lighted and ventilated.
10. **Spittoons (Sec. 20):** In every factory, sufficient number of spittoons should be provided in convenient, places and they should be maintained in a clean and hygienic condition.

Mental Health

The rationale behind the organization's mental health programme is the same as for programmes designed to maintain physical health. The aim of mental health programme is to help the employees to adjust themselves to the realities of actual life. Firstly, in modern life mental breakdown is common due to various tensions and pressures. Secondly, various types of mental difficulties are reflected in the lower productivity and lower profits of the organization. Thirdly, mental illness takes its toll through alcoholism, high accident rates, high tardiness rates, high labour turnover and poor human relationships. It has been reported that emotionally ill workers commit more safety violations, meet more number of accidents, file more grievances and are dismissed more than the sound and healthy employees. Despite its importance, mental health still ranks third behind safety and physical health. The following items can be included in a mental health programme:[11]

1. Availability of psychiatric counselling.
2. Cooperation with outside psychiatric specialists and institutions.
3. Education of company personnel concerning the nature and importance of mental health problems.
4. Development and maintenance of a proper human relations programme.

QUESTIONS

1. To ensure a safe working environment is not only legally mandated, but also the moral responsibility of the organization. Comment.
2. Accidents need not always be machine related. What are the major non-machine causes for accidents?
3. What steps can be taken by the management to prevent accidents?
4. Briefly describe the legal provisions in India regarding safety of workers.
5. What are the different organizational factors that affect the health of the workers?
6. Mental health of the workers is as important as physical health. Explain.

NOTES

1. Luis R. Gomez-Mejia, David B. Balkin and Robert L. Cardy. *Managing Human Resources*. Third Ed. Pearson Education, Delhi, 2003, p. 526.
2. Michael Armstrong. *A Handbook of Human Resource Management Practice*. Ninth Ed. Kogan Page, London, 2005, p. 828.
3. C.B. Mamoria and S.V. Gankar. *Personnel Management*. Himalaya Publishing House, Mumbai, Twenty-fifth Ed. 2005, p. 790.
4. D.C. Sharma and R.G. Sharma. *Personnel Management and Industrial Relations*. First Ed. S.J. Publications, Meerut, p. 365.
5. *Ibid*., p. 366.
6. C.B. Mamoria and S.V. Gankar. *Op. cit.*, p. 792.
7. H.W. Heinrich. *Industrial Accident Prevention*. McGraw-Hill, New York, 1959, pp. 50-52.
8. Edwin B. Flippo. *Personnel Management*. Sixth Ed. McGraw-Hill, New York, 1984, p. 523.
9. D.C. Sharma and R.G. Sharma. *Op. cit.*, p. 368.
10. Edwin B. Flippo. *Op. cit.*, p. 523.
11. *Ibid*., p. 537.

Chapter 24

Employee Welfare and Social Security

Once the employees are hired, trained and compensated, they also need to be looked after so that they serve the firm well. The aim of the welfare work is to preserve and improve physical, mental and economic conditions of the employees. Employee welfare includes both social and economic welfare. Social welfare aims at the social development through social legislation, social service, social reform and social work. The aim of economic welfare is to promote economic development by increasing production and productivity and through equitable distribution. Employee welfare can be defined as anything done for the comfort and improvement, intellectual and social, of the employees over and above the wages paid, which is not a necessity of the industry.[1] According to the Labour Investigation Committee (1944-46), employee welfare means anything done for the intellectual, physical, moral and economic betterment of the workers, whether by employers, by government or by other agencies, over and above what is laid down by law or what is normally expected as part of the contractual benefits for which the workers may have bargained.[2] Labour welfare may be understood to mean such services, facilities and amenities, which may be established outside or in the vicinity of undertakings, to enable the persons employed therein to perform their work in healthy and congenial surroundings and to provide them with the amenities conducive to good health and high morale.

Concept of Employee Welfare

Employee welfare may be viewed as a total concept, as a social concept and as a relative concept. The total concept is a desirable state of existence involving the physical, mental, moral and emotional well-being. All these four elements together constitute the structure of welfare, on which its totality is based. The social concept of welfare means the welfare of man, his family and the community. The relative concept of welfare refers to that welfare which is relative in time and place. It is a dynamic and flexible concept and hence the meaning and content differ from time to time, region to region, industry to industry, and country to country, depending upon the value system, level of education, social customs, political system, degree of industrialisation and general standard of the socio-economic development of the people.[3]

Importance of Labour Welfare Work

In India, labour welfare work assumes great importance because of the following reasons:

1. **Lack of strong trade union movement:** In the absence of strong trade unions and effective leaders, welfare work helps the workers in the industry to stand on their own feet, think properly and systematically of their interests, progress hand in hand and participate in the nation's development.
2. **Poverty:** Poverty is one of the main reasons behind the provisions of labour welfare activities. Indian workers in majority are poor, and are, therefore, unable to provide a healthy living for their families and good education for their children.
3. **Illiteracy:** In India, the number of educated workers is low. Being illiterate, they are unabile to receive advanced industrial training, understand the problems in industries, understand their own interests and those of nations.

4. **Low level of health and nutrition:** Due to poverty and illiteracy, the Indian workers remain unhealthy and ill fed. This reduces their productivity and efficiency.
5. **Lack of healthy recreation:** Due to lack of healthy recreation, the workers indulge in crime and other wrong activities. The employer should provide means of healthy recreation in order to maintain their efficiency.
6. **Lack of training:** The number of trained workers in India is very low. Thus, it is necessary to have training facilities for such a vast workforce.

Aims and Objectives of Employee Welfare Work

The main aims and objectives of employee welfare work are as follows:

1. **Economic betterment of employees:** This refers to increasing the efficiency and productivity of the workers, which raises their chances to earn more, and it aims at improving their standard of living.
2. **Humanitarian consideration:** This aims to enable workers to enjoy a fuller and richer life by providing them certain facilities and amenities.
3. **Civic consideration:** This aims to develop a sense of responsibility and dignity among the workers and thus, to make them worthy citizens of the nation.

Classification of Welfare Work

Employee welfare work may be divided into three categories as follows:

1. **Statutory welfare:** This includes all those employee welfare activities, which are undertaken by the employers because of legal requirements. The statutory welfare facilities are provided under the Factories Act, 1948; the Mines Act, 1952; the Plantations Labour Act, 1951; the Motor Transport Worker Act, 1961; the Contract Labour (Regulations and Abolition) Act, 1970; the Merchant Shipping Act, 1958; Dock Workers (Safety, Health and Welfare) Scheme, 1961; and Inter-

State Migrant Workmen (Regulation of Employment and Conditions of Service) Act, 1979.

2. **Voluntary welfare:** This includes all those welfare activities, which are undertaken by the employers at their own, e.g. provision of educational facilities, medical facilities, transport facilities, recreational facilities, housing facilities, etc.
3. **Mutual welfare:** This includes all those activities which are undertaken by the workers themselves through the platform of their trade unions, e.g. reading rooms, sports, indoor games, etc.

Agencies of Labour Welfare Activities

The main agencies engaged in labour welfare activities are as follows:

1. **Government:** The Government of India has enacted numerous laws in order to make it mandatory for employers to provide certain welfare facilities to their employees. These include the Factories Act, 1948; the Mines Act, 1952; the Plantations Labour Act, 1951; the Motor Transport Worker Act, 1961; the Contract Labour (Regulations and Abolition) Act, 1970; the Merchant Shipping Act, 1958; Dock Workers (Safety, Health and Welfare) Scheme, 1961; and Inter-State Migrant Workmen (Regulation of Employment and Conditions of Service) Act, 1979. In addition, the Central Government has constituted welfare funds for the benefits of employees. These funds are constituted in mica, coal, iron-ore, limestone and dolomite mines. These funds are meant for providing medical, housing, educational and recreational facilities.
2. **Employers:** At present, the employers have to provide the various welfare activities as per the norms set by government under various legislations. It has become obligatory on the part of employers to provide welfare facilities, e.g. canteens, dispensary, etc. Most of the employers still consider the expenditure on labour

welfare activities as a mere wastage of money rather than an investment.

3. **Trade unions:** Trade unions in India have also rendered welfare services for the benefit of their members. These welfare activities are provided out of their own resources and also administered by them. Although limited in extent and scope, certain trade unions have undertaken great interest in various social welfare programmes. Some of these programmes include adult literacy programme, leadership training programme, publication and research activities, establishment of libraries, establishment of schools and even trade union colleges. Some of the important workers' organizations are Textile Labour Association (TLA) of Ahmedabad; Mill Mazdoor Union, Indore; Rashtriya Mill Mazdoor Sangh (RMMS) of Mumbai; Mill Mazdoor Sabha of Mumbai; and Transport and Dock Workers' Unions of Mumbai. The services offered by TLA for its members are the following:
   (i) Schools for workers' children.
   (ii) Pre-natal and maternal care through a maternity home and dispensary.
   (iii) Cultural and religious centres.
   (iv) Gymnasiums, libraries and reading centres.
   (v) Legal aid in civil as well as in criminal matters.
   (vi) Vocational training like radio repairing, sewing, typewriting, etc.
   (vii) Formation of community development centres.
   (viii) Blood banks.
   (ix) Workers' cooperative banks.
   (x) Publication of a bi-weekly, *Mazdoor Sandesh*.
   (xi) Attending to civil and municipal problems.
   (xii) Hostels for students.
   (xiii) Girls' hostel for backward communities.
   (xiv) Celebration of national festivals.

4. **Other agencies:** There are various voluntary agencies which are doing good labour welfare work. These include the philanthropic, charitable and social service organizations such as Social Service League, the Maternity and Infant Welfare Association, the Seva Sadan Society and the Women's Institute of Bengal. These agencies provide educational facilities, medical aid, libraries, recreational facilities, etc.

Principles of a Welfare Programme

For the successful implementation of any welfare programme, the following principles should be kept in mind:[4] The labour welfare activities should provide the entire hierarchy of an organization. In other words, the employer should be welfare-oriented at every level.

1. The employer should not bargain labour welfare as a substitute for wages, or monetary incentives. Workers have a right to adequate wages in addition to welfare measures.
2. The employer should look after the welfare of his employees as a matter of social obligation.
3. Labour welfare must aim at assisting employees to help themselves in the long run. Self-help principle will enable them to become more responsible and efficient.
4. There should be proper coordination, harmony and integration of all labour welfare services in an undertaking.
5. The labour welfare work of an organization must be administratively viable, and essentially, development-oriented.
6. The management should ensure cooperation and active participation of unions and workers in formulating and implementing labour welfare programmes.
7. There should be periodical assessment or evaluation of welfare measures and necessary timely improvements on the basis of feedback.

Labour Welfare Officer

Realizing the importance of Labour Welfare Officer in Indian industry, the Royal Commission on Labour in 1931 recommended their appointment in order to protect the workers from the evils of jobbery and indebtedness, to act generally as a spokesman of labour and to promote amicable relations between the workers and the management. According to Section 49 of the Factories Act, 1948, in every factory wherein 500 or more workers are ordinarily employed, the occupier shall employ in the factory such number of Welfare Officers as may be prescribed. The State Government may prescribe the duties, qualifications and conditions of service of a welfare officer.

The main functions or duties of Labour Welfare Officers are the following:[5]

1. Supervision of the following:
   (i) Health, safety and welfare programmes.
   (ii) Working of joint committees.
   (iii) Redressal of workers' grievances.
2. Counselling of workers on the following:
   (i) Personal and family problems.
   (ii) Adjustment to their work environment.
   (iii) Undertaking their rights and privileges.
3. Advising management on the matters mentioned below:
   (i) Formulating labour and welfare policies.
   (ii) Apprenticeship training programmes.
   (iii) Meeting statutory obligations of workers.
   (iv) Developing fringe benefits programme.
   (v) Workers' education.
   (vi) Use of communication media.
4. Establishing liaison with workers for undermentioned purposes:
   (i) Understand various limitations under which they work.

(ii) Appreciate the need for harmonious industrial relations in the plant.

(iii) Interpret company policies clearly.

(iv) Come to a settlement in case of disputes.

5. Establishing liaison with management so that they may,

    (i) Appreciate workers' point of view on various matters in the plant.

    (ii) Maintain harmonious industrial relations in the plant.

6. Working with management and workers in order:

    (i) To maintain harmonious industrial relations in the plant.

    (ii) To arrange for the prompt redressal of all grievances and speedy settlement of disputes.

    (iii) To improve productivity and efficiency of the enterprise.

7. Working with outside public in order:

    (i) To ensure the proper enforcement of various Acts that are applicable to the plant by establishing contact with factory inspectors, medical officers and other authorities.

    (ii) To assist other agencies to help workers to make use of community services.

The above-said functions of Labour Welfare Officer highlight that he will act as a counsellor, advisor, mediator and liaison-man between the labour and the management.

Employee Social Security

Social security for employees refers to the measures which provide protection not just to the employees but also to their entire families at times of retirement, resignation, maternity, old age, unemployment, death, disablement and other similar conditions. This concept has gained much importance in today's world, especially in the more developed sector. Social security includes financial security and health care benefits provided to the employees at times of need. The aim of social security is to facilitate the long-term sustenance of the employee's family when the earning member loses his earning capacity due to retirement or disability or passes away. Social security schemes enable the employees to plan their future and ensure their family's security through insurance and other benefits. Social security schemes can be successful only if there is active support and involvement of both the employees and the employers. The employee or worker is the source of social security protection for himself and his family while the employer is responsible for providing adequate social security coverage to all his employees.

Social Security in India

In India the government bears the primary responsibility for developing a suitable system for providing protection against future uncertainties to the workers. Social security schemes are designed in such a way as to assure the individual worker and his dependents of a basic minimum income in case of contingencies. Social security is a significant part of the development process as it creates a more positive outlook towards work and the workplace.

Matters relating to Social Security in India are listed in the Directive Principles of State Policy and the subjects in the Concurrent List. The following social security issues are mentioned in the Concurrent List (List III in the Seventh Schedule of the Constitution of India):

Item No. 23: Social security and insurance, employment and unemployment.

Item No. 24: Welfare of labour including conditions of work, provident funds, employers' liability, workmen's compensation, invalidity and old age pension and maternity benefits.[6]

The Indian labour force is roughly divided into the organized and unorganized sectors, with the majority belonging to the unorganized. The organized sector basically includes those establishments which are covered by the Factories Act, 1948; the Industrial Employment Standing Orders Act, 1946; the Shops and Commercial Establishments Acts of State Governments, etc. The organized sector is properly structured and therefore social security schemes are administered to the workers under these legislations. But on the other hand, there is no labour law coverage in the unorganized sector. This sector is characterised by seasonal occupation, low bargaining power, temporary employment, high labour mobility, lack of organizational support, etc. These features make it very difficult for workers in the unorganized sector to enjoy benefits of social security schemes. These workers have to endure more socio-economic hardships. Therefore, the government has implemented special social security schemes for catering to the labour in unorganized sector.

Social Security Acts in India

1. **The Workmen's Compensation Act, 1923 (WC Act):** This Act necessitates the payment of compensation to the worker or his family in cases of disability or death resulting from employment related injuries.
2. **The Employees' State Insurance Act, 1948 (ESI Act):** All the factories and establishments with 10 or more employees are covered by this Act. It provides for comprehensive medical care to the employees and their families as well as cash benefits during sickness and maternity and monthly payments in case of death or disablement.
3. **The Employees' Provident Funds and Miscellaneous Provisions Act, 1952 (EPF and MP Act):** This applies to specific scheduled factories and establishments employing 20 or more employees and ensures terminal benefits to provident fund, superannuation pension and family pension in case of death during service. Separate laws exist for similar benefits for the workers in the coal mines and tea plantations.
4. **The Maternity Benefit Act, 1961 (MB Act):** This Act provides for payment of 12 weeks wages during maternity as well as paid leave in certain other related contingencies.

5. **The Payment of Gratuity Act, 1972 (PG Act):** It provides for 15 days wages for each year of service to employees who have worked for five years or more in establishments having a minimum of 10 workers.[7]

The government has set up a social security division under the Ministry of Labour and Employment which focuses mainly on framing social security policies for the workers of organized sector.

Recently, the government has started to make efforts for extending social security benefits to the unorganized sector too as the majority of the Indian labour force belongs to this sector.

Some of the social security acts enacted keeping the unorganized sector in mind are briefly explained below:

1. **The Mahatma Gandhi National Rural Employment Guarantee Act, 2005:** This act aims at enhancing the livelihood security of people in rural areas by guaranteeing hundred days of wage-employment in a financial year to a rural household whose adult members volunteer to do unskilled manual work.[8]
2. **Unorganized Workers' Social Security Act, 2008:** This Act aims at extending social security schemes to the workers in the unorganized sector like disability cover, health and maternity benefits, old age protection and other benefits which are currently provided to the organized sector.
3. **Domestic Workers Act, 2008:** The Domestic Workers Act, 2008 aims at regulating payment and working conditions of domestic workers and entitles every registered domestic worker to receive pension, maternity benefits and paid leave (a paid weekly off).

Social security schemes are very vital for providing the workers and their families with future security and for ensuring a monetary payment at the time of retirement, death or disability of the workers. Such measures help to build loyalty and faith in the minds of the workers and impact their productivity in a positive way. It is the moral responsibility of the organizations to secure the futures of their employees and social security schemes help them to achieve this. Another benefit of these schemes is that they facilitate better industrial relations between the management and the employees.

QUESTIONS

1. Discuss the importance of labour welfare work.
2. Explain the concepts of statutory, voluntary and mutual welfare.
3. Which are the main agencies engaged in labour welfare activities?
4. What are the main principles of labour welfare programme?
5. What are the duties and responsibilities of the labour welfare officer?
6. Write a note on employee social security in India.

NOTES

1. Arthur James Todd. *Industry and Society—A Sociological Appraisal of Modern Industrialism.* pp. 250-51.
2. Report of the Labour Investigation Committee, 1946, p. 345.
3. A.M. Sarma. *Understanding Wage System.* Himalaya Publishing House, Bombay, Third Ed. 1992: p. 3.
4. *Ibid.*, pp. 11-12.
5. Report of the Labour Welfare Committee, 1964.
6. http://labour.nic.in/ss/welcome.html
7. http://labour.nic.in/ss/overview.html
8. http://nrega.nic.in/netnrega/home.aspx

Chapter 25

Workers' Participation in Management

Workers' Participation in Management (WPM) is a complex concept. Traditionally, it refers to the participation of non-managerial employees in the decision-making process of the organization. Workers get involved mentally and emotionally in the management process. According to F.S. Walpole, participation in management gives the worker a sense of importance, pride and accomplishment; it gives him the freedom of opportunity for self-expression; a feeling of belongingness with the place of work and a sense of workmanship and creativity. WPM has its roots in Human Relations approach to management which views the workers as human beings and values them as productive assets of the organization. In the modern era, WPM is a vital component of industrial democracy. International Labour Organization (ILO) encourages its member nations to promote the concept of WPM.[1]

ILO defines WPM as: "Workers' participation, may broadly be taken to cover all terms of association of workers and their representatives with the decision-making process, ranging from exchange of information, consultations, decisions and negotiations, to more institutionalized forms such as the presence of workers' member on management or supervisory boards or even management by workers themselves (as practiced in Yugoslavia)."[2]

The main implications of workers' participation in management as summarized by ILO:

- Workers have ideas which can be useful.
- Workers may work more intelligently if they are informed about the reasons for and the intention of decisions that are taken in a participative atmosphere.

Types of Managerial Decisions Affecting Workers

There are certain managerial decisions that affect the workers in the organization. Thus, it is essential that the workers have a say in it, they should be given the right to discuss the related issues and contribute to the ultimate decision-making.

1. **Economic decisions:** These are the decisions related to lay-offs, mergers, production methods, automation, shutdown of factory, etc. which deeply affect the workers.
2. **Personnel decisions:** The personnel decisions naturally affect the human resources of the organizations. Examples of these are recruitment and selection decisions, promotion and transfer decisions, etc.
3. **Social welfare decisions:** These are decisions related to employee welfare activities such as workers' safety, health, hours of work, benefits, etc.

Objectives of WPM

1. To encourage better relations between management and employees and establish industrial democracy.
2. To promote increased productivity for the benefit of the workers and the organization as a whole.
3. To facilitate the growth and development of individual workers by giving them a chance to participate in decision-making.
4. To help the employees understand their role in the setting of and achieving the organizational goals.
5. Fulfil the esteem needs of the workers by treating them as valuable contributors to the organization.

6. To create a just workplace where principles of equality and cooperation are upheld.
7. To elevate the social status of the worker through his participation in the important managerial activities.

Importance of WPM

1. **Better industrial relations:** Industrial unrest results because of conflict of interests between the management and the workers. But if decision-making takes the form of a collective effort where the interests of both the management and employees are accounted for, then industrial tension can be minimised. If the parties cooperate to arrive at the optimum decision, then decisions based on common interests can be taken.
2. **Reduced misunderstandings:** When there is open two-way communication between the workers and management, both the parties can clarify their doubts and clear any misunderstandings among them.
3. **Higher productivity:** Mutual understanding between the employer and the employees coupled with better industrial relations creates a work environment conducive for growth. Employees tend to work harder and more sincerely when their views are respected by the superiors. Thus, their productivity rises.
4. **Decentralization of authority:** When the decision-making process becomes a group effort instead of being concentrated at the top level, it encourages decentralization of authority. In WPM, the workers are informed about organizational problems and are asked to suggest solutions. Their views and opinions are given due importance while taking the final decision.
5. **Industrial democracy:** Industrial democracy refers to the involvement of employees in decision-making and sharing of authority and responsibility related to important industrial matters. WPM brings about equality in the organization and provides a degree of industrial balance.

6. **Commitment towards goals:** When the individual worker is involved in decision-making and gets an opportunity to express his thoughts and opinions, he feels a deeper sense of belongingness with the organization. He realizes that he has a role to play in the management of the business, and therefore is more committed towards the organizational goals.
7. **Individual growth and development:** Individuals get a chance to develop their skills and capabilities while participating in the management processes. They are required to be creative, innovative and responsive in their interaction with the management and this helps them to develop more as a human being in the process.
8. **Responsiveness to change:** Normally, workers in any organization are resistant to change. They are reluctant to adopt the changes that the management forces upon them. But when they get a chance to participate in the decision-making process, they can clear their doubts and insecurities regarding the proposed changes. If the workers are made aware of the consequences of the change, then they will be more responsive towards it.

Essential Conditions for Successful Implementation of WPM

1. Open communication should be encouraged between the parties and such an environment should be created where free and frank exchange of ideas, views and opinions is possible.
2. The management as well as the workers should be informed about the concept, and interest should be created in their minds regarding this.
3. The wholehearted cooperation of both the parties should be garnered. Management and workers should have faith in each other and be ready to work together for the advantage of the organization.

4. WPM will be successful only if peaceful industrial relations prevail in the organization. Strikes, lockouts, etc. are detrimental to this process.
5. Realistic and achievable objectives should be set. Objectives should not be vague, ambiguous or impractical.
6. The workers' participation should be real. The participation of workers in management should not be just a theoretical concept, but should be implemented practically also.
7. There should be a strong trade union that can effectively take part in collective bargaining. But multiple unions in the enterprise should be restricted as they can disrupt the peaceful management proceedings.
8. The employees' participation should take place at two or three levels in the management.
9. Proper training and education should be provided to the labour to make them capable of participating in the management productively. Continuous efforts should be made to enhance the skills and knowledge of the workers.
10. Management should have trust in the employees and must provide them the information regarding the working of the industry and the problems faced by it.
11. There should be a proper follow-up mechanism for taking actions on the decisions taken during the WPM meetings.

Levels of WPM

1. **Information participation:** It is the most basic level of WPM. At this level it is ensured that the workers receive all necessary information relevant to the organization and are given a chance to express their views regarding the general issues.
2. **Consultative participation:** The workers are consulted on matters that directly affect them such as work, safety

and health. The workers' role is only advisory; the final decision is always taken by the top management. They may or may not consider the workers' suggestions.

3. **Associative participation:** Under this arrangement, the managers and workers jointly take decisions. The management is obliged to consider the decisions of the employees and implement them. This is a natural extension of consultative participation.
4. **Administrative participation:** In this kind of participation, the decisions are already taken by the management, but alternative ways of implementing them are discussed with the workers. The workers review the different ways of putting the decisions to action and choose the best option.
5. **Decisive participation:** This is the highest level of participation where the management and the employees interact on a regular basis, discuss issues related to various aspects of management and jointly arrive at decisions that are beneficial to all the parties involved.[3]

Methods of WPM

1. **Works committee:** Every establishment employing 100 or more workers is required to constitute a works committee as specified by the Industrial Disputes Act, 1947. This committee would include equal number of representatives from the employer and the employees. The purpose of Works Committee is to serve as a platform for joint consultation and for promoting peaceful industrial relations. It is the duty of the Works Committee to promote measures for securing and preserving amity and good relations between the employer and workmen. Work committees are concerned with issues regarding the day-to-day working in the factory, such as:
   (i) Administration of welfare and fine funds.
   (ii) Educational and recreational activities such as libraries, reading rooms, cinema shows, sports, games, picnic parties, etc.

(iii) Safety and accident prevention.

(iv) Protection against occupational diseases and protective equipment.

(v) Conditions of work such as ventilation, lightening, temperature and sanitation including latrines and urinals.

(vi) Adjustment of festival and national holidays.

(vii) Amenities such as drinking water, canteen, dining rooms, medical and health services.

(viii) Implementation and review of decisions reached at meetings of works committees.

The Works Committees function actively in some big organizations like Tata Steel, Hindustan Unilever, etc. but they could not make any progress in many smaller organizations due to the following reasons:

(i) Indifferent attitude of both the management and the workers.

(ii) Lack of interest on the part of the workers' representatives.

(iii) Managers consider it below their dignity to interact with the workers.

(iv) Lack of follow up actions on decisions of Works Committee.

(v) Delays and loopholes in implementing the decisions.

2. **Suggestion schemes:** Under suggestion schemes, workers are invited and encouraged to offer suggestions for improving the working of the enterprise. A suggestion box is installed at a convenient place in the organization and any worker can write down his suggestion and drop it in the box. There is a Suggestion Screening Committee that scrutinizes these suggestions periodically. This committee has an equal number of representatives from management and workers. Good suggestions are considered for implementation and the concerned workers are awarded accordingly. Suggestion schemes

encourage workers' interest in the working of the enterprise. Such schemes sound good theoretically, but are rarely implemented in real business situations.

3. **Joint Management Councils (JMC):** The Industrial Policy Resolution adopted by the Government in 1956 declared that in a socialist democracy, labour was a partner in the common task of development, and should be asked to participate in it with enthusiasm. The setting up of JMC at all organizations employing 500 or more employees was recommended in the second five-year plan. These councils consist of equal representatives from the employers' and the employees' sides, not exceeding 12 at the plant level.

   The Indian Labour Conference (ILC) in its 15th session in 1957 made the following recommendations:

   (i) Workers' participation in management schemes should be set up in selected undertakings on a voluntary basis.

   (ii) A sub-committee consisting of representatives of employers, workers and government should be set up for considering the details of workers' participation in management schemes. This committee should select the undertakings where workers' participation in management schemes would be introduced on an experimental basis.

   The JMC discusses various matters related to the working of the industry. This council is responsible for activities related to the following: safety and health schemes, working hours, training schemes, accident prevention, canteen, water, sanitation facilities, absenteeism, indiscipline, etc. Problems related to wages, bonus, etc. are outside the scope of this council.

4. **Joint councils:** Any industrial unit employing 500 or more employees should have a joint council. One joint council is constituted for the whole unit. Only those people who are actually engaged in the organization

shall be members of the joint council. This council deals with issues related to production, productivity and efficiency of the various resources of the organization. A joint council shall meet whenever necessary, but at least once in a quarter. The term of the council will be two years. The chief executive of the unit will be the chairman of the council and vice chairman will be nominated by worker members. The decision of the council will be based on consensus and not on voting.

Functions:

(i) Ensuring optimum use of raw material and high quality of finished products.

(ii) Dealing with issues regarding the production efficiency and productivity of men and machinery.

(iii) Preparing production schedules of working hours and of holidays.

(iv) Developing the skills of working and providing adequate facilities for training.

(v) Rewarding the workers for their valuable and innovative suggestions for improvement of the organization.

In 1977, the concept of joint council was extended to Public Sector Undertakings (PSU) like commercial and service sector organizations employing 100 or more persons. These include hotels, hospitals, railway and road transport, post and telegraph offices, and state electricity boards.

5. **Collective bargaining:** This is a process which enables the representatives of the employees who are members of labour unions to negotiate with the employers to reach collective agreement regarding rules for their terms of employment and conditions of service including pay, benefits, working hours, leave, health and safety policies, etc. Such agreements are not legally binding upon the employers, but still they do have some impact. For collective bargaining to be successful,

the representatives of both the employers and the employees need to bargain in the right spirit. But this does not happen in reality as each party tries to take advantage of the other. But if administered properly, collective bargaining can be used to bring both parties together and develop mutual understanding so that decisions that are in the best interests of both can be taken.

6. **Unit Councils:** After implementing joint council scheme in the manufacturing and mining sectors, the government in 1977 introduced the concept of unit councils in commercial and service organizations in the public sector having large scale operations. Unit councils are to be set up in units having 100 or more workers. These councils would discuss day-to-day problems and find solutions. The council shall be composed of an equal number of representatives from management and workers, and the total number of members shall not exceed 12. All the decisions of the council shall be taken on the basis of consensus and not by voting and such decisions shall be implemented by the parties concerned within a month unless otherwise stated in the decisions. The council is normally constituted for a period of three years. Council meetings shall be held as and when considered necessary, though a meeting should be held at least once a month.
7. **Shop council:** The concept of shop council was announced by the government in 1975. In every industrial unit employing 500 or more workers, the employers shall constitute a shop council for each department or shop. Each shop council would consist of an equal number of representatives from both the employers and the employees and the total number shall not exceed 12. The employers' representatives will be nominated by the management and must consist of persons within the establishment. The workers' representatives will be from among the workers of the department or shop

concerned. All the decisions of the council shall be taken on the basis of consensus and not by voting.

Functions of shop councils:

(i) Improve production, productivity and efficiency.

(ii) Study absenteeism in the shop/department and recommend steps to reduce it.

(iii) Suggest safety measures and improvement in physical conditions of working.

(iv) Assist in maintaining general discipline in the shop/department.

(v) Suggest welfare measures to be adopted for efficient running of the shop/department.

(vi) Ensure proper flow of adequate two-way communication between the management and the workers.

(vii) Suggest technological innovations in the shop.

(viii) Assist in the implementation of cost reduction programme.

(ix) Ensure a periodic review of the utilization of the critical machines.

8. **Worker directors:** Under this scheme, the representatives of the workers would be taken on the board of directors of public sector enterprises. This is the highest form of WPM. The participation would be limited to companies employing 1000 or more workers (excluding temporary or seasonal workers). The representatives of the workers should be those actually working in the organization. The worker director will be elected by all the workers of the company through secret ballot. The purpose of introducing this method was to improve employer-employee relations, encourage industrial democracy and safeguard workers' interests. This was aimed at increasing the active role of the workers in formulating policies and taking decisions in areas that directly concern the workers. This scheme was implemented in public sector enterprises like Hindustan Antibiotics

Ltd., Hindustan Organic Chemicals Ltd. and in some nationalized banks. However, this scheme could never be successful in India due to poor industrial relations, multiplicity of labour unions, role conflict of the worker director, lack of management support, etc.[4]

QUESTIONS

1. What is WPM? Why is it important?
2. How do economic and social welfare decisions affect workers?
3. What are the essential conditions for successful implementation of WPM?
4. What are various levels of WPM? Which one is the highest?
5. What is a Joint Council? What are its various functions?
6. Write a note on Worker Directors. Was this concept successful in India?

NOTES

1. http://www.mbaknol.com/human-resource-management/workers-participation-in-management/
2. http://www.projects4mba.com/human-resource-management-hrm/
3. http://learnmba.blogspot.in/2011/06/workers-participation-in-management.html
4. http://labour.nic.in/lcomm2/2nlc-pdfs/chap12-I-II.pdf

Chapter 26

Grievance Handling and Redressal

In an organization, employees have complaints against their employers such as dissatisfaction from the quantum of wages, mode of payment for overtime work, working conditions, promotion, transfer, dismissal or discharge, poor quality of food in the canteen, etc. These types of complaints should not be allowed to aggravate. An HR manager should try to identify and resolve them as they come to his knowledge. Identification of grievances and their proper handling is necessary for maintaining harmonious industrial relations. A grievance can be any discontent or dissatisfaction, whether expressed or not, whether valid or not, arising out of anything connected with the company that an employee thinks, believes or even feels is unfair, unjust or inequitable.[1] This dissatisfaction may be stated or unvoiced, written or oral, legitimate or ridiculous, but the only thing is that the discontent must affect performance. A grievance is anything that an employee thinks or feels is wrong and is generally accompanied by an actively disturbing feeling. It is not to be justified.[2] There is a difference between the word 'grievance' and 'complaint'. A complaint is a discontent or dissatisfaction that has not, as yet, assumed a great measure of importance to the complainant. Complaints are more in numbers than grievances at the workplace, e.g. it is too hot in the shop; a colleague is not cooperating, etc. Often, the complaints are submitted in a very informal way. But a complaint becomes a grievance when the employee feels that an injustice has been done. When the supervisor or manager ignores the complaint and thereafter dissatisfaction that grows within the employee usually assumes the status of a grievance. A grievance is always expressed whether verbally or in writing. A grievance may be submitted by a worker or several workers. Where a grievance is transformed into a general claim—either by the union or by a large number of workers—it falls outside the grievance procedure and normally comes under the purview of collective bargaining.[3] In other words, where the issue is of a wider or of general nature or of general applicability then it will be outside the purview of grievance machinery.

Causes of Grievance

The causes of grievance may broadly be classified in the following categories:

1. **Working conditions:** A large number of workers' grievances are related with the unhealthy and bad working conditions such as non-availability of proper tools, equipment and machines to perform the job, bad physical conditions in the factory, frequent breakdown of machines, tight production standards, more rejection of goods, unjustified and continuous cuts in wages, disruption in the supply of material, lack of proper discipline, etc.
2. **Difference of opinion:** The difference of opinion or thoughts on any particular point between workers and management also becomes a cause of grievance. Also, different interpretations of legal provisions lead to difference of thoughts.
3. **Doubts and fears:** In some cases, the doubts and fears in the minds of workers regarding any injustice committed to them may also give rise to grievances.
4. **Management policy and practices:** Various policies of management may contribute to grievances such as harsh supervision, victimisation, discrimination, ignoring suggestions from subordinates, authoritarian management style, promotion, transfer, demotion,

discharge, leave, overtime, holidays, lack of career planning and employee development plan, non-recognition of trade union, hostility towards a trade union, non-adherence to policies or procedures, etc.

5. **Status of trade unions:** The age and status of trade union is also a leading factor in grievance bearing. If a trade union is comparatively young and it has substantial strength, naturally it will be more militant and it will give air to the slightest grievances of the workers in a big way.[4]
6. **Social injustice:** Grievances may be due to social injustice. For instance, if a facility is provided in one department of the company, the employees of the other department where that facility is not provided may feel dissatisfied.
7. **Personal maladjustment:** Personal maladjustment may also give rise to grievances, e.g. excessive self-esteem, impractical attitude towards life, over-ambition, etc.
8. **Violation:** Grievances may be caused due to the alleged violation of central and state laws, collective bargaining agreement, past practice, company rules, etc.
9. **Wages:** Grievances may arise due to wage inequalities, payment system, complicated compensation systems, problems relating to calculation of incentives and overtime, fines, increments, stagnation and recovery of dues.[5]

Need and Importance of Grievance Handling Machinery

There is hardly a single organization which functions absolutely smoothly at all times. Employees' grievances in any form will invariably always be present. For the maintenance of harmonious industrial relations, it is essential for the management to identify the causes of grievances and redress them in the best possible manner. Thus, setting up of proper grievance handling machinery is necessary for maintaining peace. The grievance machinery or procedure is a problem-solving or dispute-settling device. It has other benefits too. The mere fact that such a procedure exists is satisfying even though an employee never has an occasion to use it. In brief, it can be said that a grievance handling procedure is essential in an organization because of the following:

(i) It encourages all the problems faced by workers should come out.

(ii) It provides a channel through which the aggrieved employee may put up his or her case forward.

(iii) It provides an opportunity to all workers to express their doubts, fears, feelings and dissatisfaction.

(iv) It improves the morale of the employees, as they know that if any injustice is done to them they will be listened to by the authorities.

(v) It helps the management in knowing the attitude and behaviour of the superior and the supervisor towards their subordinates.

(vi) A proper and formal grievance handling procedure ensures that every grievance will be handled in a systematic manner.

(vii) It restricts the immediate boss and supervisors from acting in an arbitrary and autocratic manner.

(viii) It helps the management in knowing the drawbacks in the present practices, policies, procedures, styles of functioning, rules, etc.

(ix) It ensures that the supervisors and the management show more concern towards human aspects at workplace.

Model Grievance Procedure

The National Commission on Labour suggested a model grievance procedure. The model grievance procedure has successive time-bound steps, with access to the next stage, if the satisfaction was not obtained. The stage or the level at which settlement takes place is an index of the climate or the spirit that prevails in the firm. The lower the level of settlement, the quicker the redressal of a grievance.[6] At the first stage, the supervisor is in a position of give and take but at the subsequent stages he comes under the glare of publicity and thus his position is likely to harden. From the aggrieved employee's point of view, the delay would only increase his anxiety and frustration. In turn, this affects his morale and productivity. If an employee prefers this procedure for the redressal of his grievance then the formal conciliation machinery shall not intervene till all the stages outlined in this procedure have been exhausted. A grievance shall be presumed to take the form of a dispute only when the final decision given by the top management in respect of the grievance is not acceptable to the worker.

The grievance procedure is as follows:

Stage I: Firstly, the aggrieved employee shall convey his grievance verbally in person to the officer designated by the management for this purpose. The officer has to answer within 48 hours of the presentation of the complaint.

Stage II: If the worker is not satisfied with the decision of this officer or he fails to receive the answer within the stipulated time, then, he shall along with his departmental representative, present his grievance to the head of the department. Usually, a fixed time is specified during which an aggrieved employee could meet the departmental head. The head of the department shall give his answer within three days of the presentation of the grievance.

Stage III: If the decision of the head of department is unsatisfactory, then the aggrieved employee along with the departmental representative may forward his grievance to the grievance committee. The grievance committee shall make its recommendations to the manager within 7 days of the employee's request. If the recommendations of the committee are unanimous then the management shall implement it. If there are differences of opinion among the members of the committee then the views of all the members shall be placed before the manager for the final decision. In either case, the final decision of the management shall be communicated to the employee within three days from the receipt of the recommendations of the grievance committee.

Stage IV: If the decision of the management is not in time or unsatisfactory then the worker may appeal to the management for revision. The management shall communicate its decision on appeal within a week.

Stage V: If still no agreement is reached, then the union and the management may refer the grievance to voluntary arbitration within a week after the decision of the management. In the model grievance procedure there is a time limit within which an appeal shall be taken from one stage to the other. The aggrieved worker shall, within 72 hours of the receipt of the decision at one stage (in case no decision is received then on the expiry of the stipulated period), file his appeal with the authority at the next higher stage.

Pre-Requisites of a Successful Grievance Handling Procedure

1. **Conformity with the prevailing legislations:** The grievance procedure should be in conformity with the existing legislations. It should be designed in such a way that it supplements the statutory provisions.
2. **Acceptability:** The grievance procedure should be developed with the mutual consultation among management, workers and labour union. In other words, it must be acceptable to all the concerned parties.
3. **Simplicity:** It should be as simple as possible. It should involve steps only to encourage the employees. Otherwise if there are so many steps or stages the procedure will become complex and the workers get discouraged.
4. **Clarity:** Each and every step in the procedure should be clear-cut and unambiguous. An aggrieved employee should be well-informed to whom he should make representation, the form of report, the time limit for making request, appeal, etc.
5. **Promptness:** A grievance procedure must make speedy redressal of grievances as unnecessary delays add to frustration of the workers.

6. **Based on facts:** At all the stages, the officer in charge of handling the grievance should make full search of facts and maintain his records properly. Getting the relevant facts is very essential and equally important is the analysis of the facts after taking into consideration the economic, psychological, social and legal issues involved in it.
7. **Training:** Proper training of supervisors and union representatives is essential for the effective working of grievance procedure.
8. **Follow-up:** The working of grievance handling procedure should be reviewed at periodical intervals. To make it more effective necessary improvements must be made.

Grievances of Management

Employers and management too have grievances against their workmen and trade unions. These are generally the following:[7]

1. **Indiscipline:** This includes non-observance of the plant rules, disregard for supervisor's orders, non-observance for safety rules, absenteeism, late coming, irresponsible attitude, etc.
2. **Output:** This includes low speed of doing a work, less output, poor quality of work, etc.
3. **Collective bargaining agreements:** This includes wrong representation of the clauses of the contract, violation of contract, non-fulfilling of assurances by trade unions, etc.
4. **Miscellaneous:** This includes failure to take action by the trade unions for the acts of indiscipline by their members, misrepresenting management's actions and attitudes, undesirable methods of soliciting union members, irresponsible charges and statements by union leaders against management, inciting workers against management, illegal strikes, etc.

QUESTIONS

1. What is a grievance? What are the causes of employee grievances?
2. What are the pre-requisites of an efficient grievance handling machinery?
3. Explain the steps in the grievance handling procedure.
4. What will happen if the management fails to handle workers' grievances effectively?
5. Not just the workers, but also the management has some grievances against the workers. Explain.

NOTES

1. Edwin B. Flippo. *Personnel Management.* McGraw-Hill, Kogakusha Ltd., Tokyo, 1976, p. 429.
2. P. Calhoon. *Managing the Personnel.* p. 319.
3. Arun Monappa. *Industrial Relations.* Tata McGraw-Hill, New Delhi, 1985, p. 149.
4. D.C. Sharma and R.C. Sharma. *Personnel Management and Industrial Relations.* First Ed. S.J. Publications, Meerut, p. 435.
5. Ratna Sen. *Industrial Relations in India: Shifting Paradigms.* Macmillan, 2003, p. 462.
6. Arun Monappa. *Industrial Relations.* Tata McGraw-Hill, New Delhi, 1985, p. 155.
7. D.C. Sharma and R.C. Sharma. *Op. cit.*, p. 436.

Chapter 27

Human Resource Information System

The Human Resource Information System (HRIS) is a system which merges the activities associated with Human Resource Management (HRM) and Information Technology (IT) into one common database through the use of Enterprise Resource Planning (ERP) software.[1]

The ERP software that forms the basis for HRIS originates from the software that integrates information from different applications into one universal database. It aims to provide an online or computer-based system for dealing with various HR issues like payroll, management, accounting functions, labour productivity, etc. It is also known as Human Resource Management Systems (HRMs). The HR department has to acquire and manage different kinds of important information related to various HR activities. In the past this work involved maintaining a large number of files and documents. Any wrong information, entry or misplacement of files would cause much disruption and unnecessary delays in work. Also manually searching for required information was a time consuming process. Thus, in order to help the HR manager in managing these documents more efficiently, the system of HRIS was developed. HRIS helps the HR personnel to streamline their work, save time and eliminate excess paperwork. Not only does HRIS facilitate smooth functioning of the HR departments, it also helps in improving communication of the HR department with other departments like finance and IT. HRIS solutions are generally administrative in nature and are therefore useful for all types of organizations. The needs and requirements of different organizations vary and the HRIS systems can be adapted according to organizational needs. The management may avail of the services of an external IT professional to create an HRIS specifically catering to the requirements of the particular organization. An organization having a formalised procedure for recruitment, selection, performance appraisal and payroll process will have different needs from an organization that still functions in an informal and traditional manner. Even though a HRIS system will help any type of organization in streamlining its operations, the management should take care to implement a system that best suits the organizational needs and can be easily integrated with the already existing systems within the organization.

Areas Covered by HRIS

1. **Human resource management (HRM):** HRM has a wide scope covering areas from recruitment and selection to career development and separations. HRIS facilitates HRM activities by maintaining records about the demographic profiles of the employees, recruitment and selection procedures, information regarding training and development programmes, compensation system records, and other important data. HRIS makes the administrative processes in an organization more systematic and well-organized. The ready availability of up-to-date information helps the HR manager to formulate policies and take important HR decisions in a timely manner.
2. **Recruitment:** Online recruitment, i.e. handling the organization's employment needs electronically is one of the most popular applications of HRIS. This includes posting job advertisements on websites/job portals. Posting the jobs online ensures that the advertisement reaches a very wide, geographically dispersed audience. These job portals allow the candidates to search for relevant employment opportunities and apply online.

Candidates' data are stored on a database that allows searching, screening and filtering of applications. The profiles of the candidates are compared with the requirements of the company and the candidates meeting the criteria are selected for interview. Online recruitment system saves a lot of time, energy and costs associated with the traditional recruitment process. This system is also known as 'Applicant Tracking' system.

3. **Training:** The training module of HRIS provides a system for tracking and managing the organization's training and development efforts. It provides an open environment where the trainees can access training content at their convenience. Training material can be shared through online methods with trainees at branch offices all over the world. Video conferencing, email, voice chat, etc. can be used for interactions between the trainers and trainees. E-training concept also provides for a more efficient system of training evaluation. Participation of employees in training programmes and the competencies acquired by them can be tracked from time to time. This would help to update the trainees' competency reports periodically. The aim of HRIS is to make the training and development process more efficient and cost effective. Further, the organization can provide learning material to its other stakeholders like customers and investors by uploading relevant information onto its website.
4. **Employee self-service system:** HRIS manages all the basic information about the employees. It maintains a database where each employee's individual profile is saved. This profile contains their personal details, attendance, overtime, performance appraisal, training reports, and résumés. Therefore, the employees can clear many of their minor HR-related queries by accessing the system's information database. The employees no longer need to disturb their supervisor regarding such trivial matters. Some companies may empower their employees to update their profiles regarding change of address,

self-appraisal, resumes, etc. by themselves in order to save time and efforts of the HR manager.

5. **Payroll:** This is one of the oldest uses of HRIS. Information technology and computers have been used for long to manage payroll processes. HRIS fully automates the procedure of calculating the amount payable to the workers. The payroll model collects the data regarding the attendance, leaves and overtime of the employees. Formulae for calculating employee salary are inbuilt in such systems. These modules compute tax and other deductions to generate periodic salary reports. By performing the payroll functions using information technology, the administrative and paper work of the accounts department is greatly reduced. The system also enables the employees to view their individual details and salary slips for their personal clarifications.
6. **Benefits administration:** All the organizations have to provide certain benefits to their employees such as employee benefit programmes, medical and health care, retirement benefits, insurance, etc. Online automation of the benefit management system will enable the HR manager to improve the benefit support system by reducing time and costs involved in the process. Use of HRIS in this area will also increase the reliability and efficiency of benefits administration.
7. **Work time management:** HRIS provides for the online record keeping of time and attendance records of the workers. The information regarding time and attendance is collected from virtual time cards and evaluated using Information Technology. These systems also have policies for leaves, holidays and over-time, therefore they can define rotation and shift plans for the employees. The work time management system is automatically integrated with other HRIS areas like payroll and benefits. It helps to maintain a single database for storing detailed information about the employees which can be accessed by the management for formulating labour policies.[2]

Advantages of HRIS

(i) HRIS is managed by technologically qualified professionals who help to streamline processes like recruitment, payroll, benefits administration, etc.

(ii) HRIS enhances the productivity and workflow of the HR department through maintenance of important information in a centralized database.

(iii) HRIS helps to save precious time. Employees are no longer required to manually perform time-consuming administrative functions, and they can use this time for productive activities.

(iv) Accuracy and credibility of important HR information is maintained. Files and folders can be manipulated or damaged, but information in HR database is secure.

(v) HRIS helps to improve the overall efficiency of the working of the HR department by providing a proper structure for functions, processes and information.

(vi) HRIS provides for better communication as all employees can access information from the database. HRIS helps in better dispersal of important information throughout the department.

Challenges Associated with HRIS

(i) There is always the risk of a computer system crash which may temporarily disable HRIS in an organization.

(ii) Security risks are inherent in an HRIS. Unauthorized people can hack the system and gain access of important information.

(iii) Implementation of HRIS is an expensive process. Small organizations cannot afford it.

(iv) Technical staff with specialised knowledge is required to efficiently manage HRIS. But such experts are hard to find.

(v) Errors in data entry can drastically reduce the usefulness of the system. Human errors can occur while inputting or updating the information stored in the database.

(vi) The effectiveness of the system is highly dependent on the competence of the staff maintaining the system and of the HR personnel using the information for decision making.[3]

QUESTIONS

1. What is HRIS? How does it facilitate the smooth functioning of the HR department?
2. Explain the role of HRIS in recruitment and training.
3. Write a note on work time management and benefits administration.
4. What are the advantages of HRIS?
5. List some challenges associated with HRIS. How can they be overcome?

NOTES

1. http://www.businessdictionary.com/definition/Human-Resource-Information-Systems-HRIS.html
2. http://www.comparehris.com/HRIS-overview/
3. http://www.ehow.com/list_7395393_disadvantages-human-resource-management-system_.html

Chapter 28

International Human Resource Management and Workforce Diversity

The concept of HRM as we are familiar with today began to evolve from the early 19th century. But the concept of International HRM is of a recent origin. Increased international trade and widespread globalization over the past few decades have given rise to a contemporary branch of HRM, i.e. international HRM, also known as global HRM. It deals with the typical HRM functions like recruitment, selection, training and development, performance appraisal, etc. at the international level. According to Hugh Scullion, International HRM (IHRM) involves the HRM issues and problems arising from the internationalisation of business, and the HRM strategies, policies and practices which firms pursue in response to the internationalisation of business.[1]

IHRM is concerned with the management of all the human resource activities in global organizations without regard to geographic boundaries. It is the process of procurement, allocation and effective utilization of human resources in international business. It is the interplay among the three dimensions—human resource activities, types of employees and countries of operation. In other words, the basic human resource processes such as HR planning, procurement, training and development, induction, compensation, performance management and industrial relations are influenced by two other groups of variables. First group of variables consists of types of employees; these may be host country nationals, parent country nationals and third country nationals. Second group of variables consists of countries involved—the host country where a subsidiary may be located, the home country where the company has its headquarters and the other countries that may be the source of finance or labour.

Differences between International and Domestic HRM

The practice of HRM in the international context is different from its domestic counterpart in the following number of ways:

1. International HRM is responsible for a greater number of functions and activities such as the selection, training and management of international assignees. Domestic HRM deals with such functions only in the domestic context.
2. International HRM has to address issues like international taxation, foreign country employment laws, international orientation of the employees, etc. These issues are not applicable to domestic HRM.
3. HR managers working in an international environment have to deal with a highly diverse workforce as people belonging to various countries and multiple cultures work in the same office. Domestic HR managers deal with a less diverse workforce.
4. International HR managers have to get closely involved in the employees' personal life when posting them to foreign locations. Issues like relocation of the employee's family, ability of the employee to adjust to new environment, cost of relocation, etc. have to be dealt with. Problems regarding relocation of families are less severe in case of domestic HRM.
5. International HRM functions are impacted by foreign cultures and laws. Only the parent nation's culture and laws have to be considered in case of domestic HRM.
6. There are more risks involved in international HRM as compared to domestic HRM. These risks include health

and safety of employees, protection of intellectual property rights, threats of terrorism, etc.

7. Compensation planning is more complicated in International HRM as compared to domestic HRM because a variety of allowances and adjustments have to be taken into account while fixing remuneration of international employees.
8. Training in International HRM includes aspects of pre-departure and post-departure cultural training, imparting knowledge of international taxation, currency fluctuations, diversity management, etc. which are not a part of domestic HR training.

International Recruitment and Staffing

Recruitment and staffing for international organizations requires the HR manager to have a thorough knowledge of the business processes in the particular country it is located in, the culture and language of that place, and the skills and knowledge the employees posted there would be required to possess in order to perform their duties efficiently. The job requirements will have to be matched with the availability of potential employees with adequate capabilities to fill the posts. In international staffing, employees may be of three types:

1. **Expatriate (Parent country national):** An expatriate is a person employed in a foreign country. In other words, it is an employee who is not a citizen of the country in which the organization's operation is located but is a citizen of the country in which the organization is headquartered. For example, an US citizen employed in a subsidiary of a US company located in Germany.

Advantages

(i) Familiarity with the home office, goals, objectives, policies and practices.

(ii) Easy organizational control and coordination.

(iii) Promising managers are given international exposure.

(iv) Expatriates are the best people for foreign assignments because of special skills and experiences.

Disadvantages

(i) Difficulty in adapting to the foreign language and the socio-economic, political, cultural and legal environment.

(ii) Excessive cost of selecting, training and maintaining expatriate managers and their families abroad.

(iii) Promotional opportunities for host country nationals are limited.

(iv) Expatriates may impose an inappropriate Headquarters style.

(v) Compensation for expatriates and host country nationals may differ.

(vi) Family adjustment problems, especially concerning the unemployed spouses.

2. **Host country national:** It refers to an employee who is a citizen of the country where the subsidiary is located, for example, an Indian citizen working for a Japanese company in India.

Advantages

(i) Familiarity with the socio-economic, political and legal environment and with business practices in the host country.

(ii) Lower costs incurred in hiring as compared to parent country nationals and third country nationals.

(iii) Promotional opportunities to locals and consequently their motivation and commitment.

(iv) Responds effectively to the host country's demands for localisation of the subsidiary's operations.

(v) Languages and other barriers are eliminated.

(vi) Continuity of management improves, since host country nationals stay longer in positions.

Disadvantages

(i) Difficulty in exercising effective control over subsidiary's operations.

(ii) Communication difficulties in dealing with home office personnel.

(iii) Lack of opportunities for the home country's nationals to gain international and cross-cultural experience.

(iv) Host country nationals have limited career opportunities outside the subsidiary.

(v) Hiring host country nationals may encourage a federation of nationals rather than global units.

3. **Third country national:** It refers to the citizen of one country, working in a second country, and employed by the firm headquartered in a third country. For example, an Indian working for a Korean company in England.

Advantages

(i) Salary and benefit requirements may be lower than for parent country nationals.

(ii) Third country nationals may be better informed than parent country nationals about host country environment.

(iii) Third country nationals are truly international managers.

Disadvantages

(i) Host country government may resent hiring third country nationals.

(ii) Third country nationals may not want to return to their own countries after assignment.

(iii) Host country's sensitivity with respect to nationals of specific countries is an issue of concern.

(iv) Host country nationals are impeded in their efforts to upgrade their own ranks and assure responsible positions in the multinational subsidiaries.[2]

International Staffing Approaches

There are four major approaches to international staffing. These are the following:

1. **Ethnocentric staffing:** This staffing policy means hiring home country individuals for higher/senior level foreign positions. The major logic behind this staffing policy is that the managers are well aware of the organization's policies and programmes and they can implement these policies and programmes efficiently. This policy is commonly followed by the Japanese. The expatriate selection criteria should include cultural adaptability, strong communication skills, technical competence, professional or operational expertise, global experience, country-specific experience, interpersonal skills, language skills, family flexibility and country or region specific consideration.[3] The difficulty in adjusting to a foreign country by managers often leads to 'culture shock', which means that the expatriates feel uncomfortable in a foreign country environment. Their psychological orientation changes and they become irritable, home sick and low performing. Culture shock refers to the problems arising out of cultural differences faced while working in a foreign country. In some cases, expatriates are able to successfully adapt themselves to the local environment in the host country and become accustomed to the ways of life in that country. In such situations, they find themselves unsuitable for the home country environment after working abroad for some time, and prefer to stay abroad instead of returning home. And if they are compelled to return home, they suffer from 'reverse culture shock'.
2. **Polycentric staffing:** In this approach, more host country nationals are used throughout the organization, from top to bottom. Each subsidiary is managed on a local basis, and the culture and business practices of the host country are predominant. The underlying belief supporting this approach is that every country is different and the operations in any one country can be successfully managed only by employees having in-depth knowledge about the local practices. Employing

the host country nationals is also less expensive than employing expatriates. The host country nationals would be familiar with the region's social, economic and legal environment which would not be so in the case of expatriates. Polycentric approach also facilitates the development of the human resources in the countries where the subsidiaries are located.

3. **Regiocentric staffing:** The regiocentric staffing policy supports hiring of managers from a region that is culturally and economically similar to that of the country in which a subsidiary is located. For example, hiring an Indian manager for the subsidiary of a Dutch company located in Sri Lanka. This policy is based on the logic that regional insiders understand the business environment of neighbouring countries. An organization implements a regional staffing strategy when synergetic benefits can be obtained by sharing functions across regions.
4. **Geocentric staffing:** This staffing approach uses a worldwide integrated business strategy. The ultimate objective of the organization is to hire the best person available for a position, regardless of where the individual comes from. The company is not concerned about the nationality of the employees, only the job requirements and the skills and potential of the employees are given significance. This approach facilitates the development of a global perspective towards staffing. Adoption of this policy enables the company to build up a pool of highly talented managers from different cultures and nationalities. The global giant Coca Cola is one of the major companies adopting this policy with great success. In geocentric approach, a majority of the workforce is composed of third country nationals rather than parent country nationals or host country nationals. Though this model of staffing seems to be the ideal one for MNCs, there are certain inherent problems in this approach too. The process of HRM becomes more complex in this case as nationals from so many different countries work

together in one office. The chances of cultural clashes, language problems, problems in adjusting to foreign locations, etc. are greater. Also complications arise in formulating training and development programmes, fixing remuneration packages, etc.

Training and Development in an International Scenario

The international workforce comprises professionals of varied national origins who may not be very familiar with the work culture and practices of the country where they work. Even though the employees would be highly competent in their professional fields, problems may arise due to cultural differences. While having a diverse workforce brings along many associated benefits, the full advantage of diversity can be enjoyed only if the differences between the employees are skilfully managed. The aim of training and development is to enhance the capabilities of the employees in their respective fields so that they are able to perform better in their work.

Objectives of International HR training and development:

(i) Training and development of employees working in subsidiaries throughout the world.

(ii) Motivating and encouraging employees from a variety of cultural backgrounds.

(iii) Specialised training to prepare expatriates for foreign assignments.

(iv) Development of a pool of highly skilled and mobile managers who are capable of working anywhere in the world.

(v) Special training to marketing people to enable them to negotiate deals and make sales to customers of different nationalities.

(vi) Extensive Development of HRD personnel so that they are able to effectively train a diverse workforce.

(vii) Cross-cultural training to all the employees so that they understand and respect cultures and beliefs different from their own.

(viii) Imparting knowledge about international laws and codes of ethics to employees so that they are familiar with the socio-economic, political and legal environment of the country they would be working in.

International training and development may be carried out in two ways:

(i) **Centralized approach:** In the centralized training approach training originates at the headquarters. The modules and techniques of training are developed at the headquarters and these are modified according to local requirements at the subsidiary levels. This approach is used in the ethnocentric and geocentric methods of staffing. In the ethnocentric model, citizens of the parent country are employed in the company's subsidiaries in the various parts of the world. Thus, the employees are provided training at the headquarters as part of their expatriate preparation and development programme. This includes pre-departure orientation and training, continual development and repatriation orientation and training. In a geocentric approach also, the training is centralized. But in this case, the training programmes are developed through the interactions between the headquarters staff and the subsidiaries staff. Experienced trainers are sent from one location to another to develop the international managers originating from different nations.

(ii) **Decentralized approach:** This method is followed in a polycentric model. Development of training modules is not centralized at the headquarters, but is decentralized at the local subsidiaries. In a polycentric staffing approach, the citizens of the host country are employed at various levels in the organization. The work culture and practices of the host country are predominant. Therefore, training programmes are also designed at the local level, keeping in view the peculiar requirements of the business environment of that particular country in which the subsidiary is located. This approach recognizes the fact that every country is different and that training programmes need to be customised according to the business environment of each nation.[4] In order to maximise training effectiveness, it is vital to consider the HR practices and cultures followed in the different countries. In the US, it is common for trainers and trainees to use each other's' first names and interact on an informal basis. But in Asian countries, subordinates address their superiors as 'sir' or 'madam' and are more formal with their colleagues. These differences should be understood by the trainer while imparting training to employees from different nations of the world.

International Compensation

The compensation packages offered by any company play an important role in attracting and retaining talented employees. In case of organizations involved in international operations, the process of fixing remuneration for the parent country nationals and third country nationals becomes even more complex. A truly international company has employees originating from different parts of the world. Such organizations need to formulate a clear international pay philosophy and develop a comprehensive compensation plan in line with their overall global business strategy.

Objectives of international compensation plans:

(i) Developing an international and local salary structure.

(ii) Formulating special compensation policies for expatriates.

(iii) Fixing incentives and benefits programmes for employees working in different nations.

(iv) Designing customised pay packages appropriate for specific countries.

(v) Developing a system of Employee Stock Ownership Plans that is applicable globally.

(vi) Setting up a system of effective compensation management for managing issues related to international compensation.

The complexity of international compensation arises from the fact that the factors which influence compensation like employment laws, living costs, tax policies, etc. vary from country to country.

Components of International Compensation

The compensation package for expatriate employees consists of four components.

(i) **Base salary:** Base salaries are the foundation of the compensation package. The base salary of an employee depends upon the nature of the job and the responsibilities involved. The base salary must be competitive enough to attract and retain employees to work on international assignments. While determining base salary for an expatriate, the company can either follow the policies of the parent company, or may choose to follow the practices prevalent in the country where the expatriate works. The compensation programme should comply with the laws and regulations of the host country while being aligned with the parent company's overall strategy.

(ii) **Indirect monetary compensation (benefits):** Expatriates need to be provided attractive benefits as part of their compensation package. The benefits package given to the expatriates is often similar to the ones provided in the home country. But the organization should keep in mind that certain host countries may legally provide for benefits normally not offered by the home country. In such cases, the organization may choose to give these benefits also to its expatriates. For example, in France, organizations are legally required to provide 25 days of vacation to every employee each year. A US company with a subsidiary in France may also decide to give its expatriates this benefit enjoyed by French nationals. Similarly, different countries have different rules and regulations regarding unemployment benefits, retirement, lay-offs, etc. which the organizations have to follow.

(iii) **Equalization benefits:** These benefits are meant to help the expatriates maintain a similar financial condition they were in before moving to a foreign country on an overseas assignment. These benefits intend to minimise the negative aspects of living in a foreign country. Some of the equalization benefits include:

(a) Tax equalization benefits.

(b) International medical insurance.

(c) Housing allowance.

(d) Language training.

(e) Foreign service premium.

(f) Spousal employment.

(g) Club membership.

(h) Educational allowance for dependent children.

These are just a few of the benefits that an organization may provide to its expatriate employees. The actual benefits offered by a company may vary from organization to organization.

(iv) **Incentives:** Organizations provide a variety of benefits to expatriates as incentives in order to motivate them for their foreign assignment. These incentives may be in the form of cash bonuses, stock options, performance-related payments, etc.[5]

An effective international compensation plan takes into consideration the job responsibilities of the expatriates, nature of the assignments, and the rules and regulations of the nation where the subsidiary is located.

Workforce Diversity

Workforce diversity refers to the variety of differences between the employees in an organization. Diversity can be based on age, sex, ethnicity, physical abilities, race, educational background, financial background, religious beliefs, work experience, etc. Diversity in a workplace should be valued and the differences among people should be respected. The unique contributions of the diverse employees should be recognized and an environment of mutual cooperation should be fostered to utilize the workforce to the maximum of their capabilities. Diversity not only involves people's perception of themselves, but also their attitudes towards other groups which are different from them. These attitudes and beliefs affect the way employees interact with each other and the manner in which they perform their jobs. Diversity in the workplace can bring about a lot of benefits to the organization though it may give rise to many challenges also. Managing diverse workforce requires the HR manager to deal with issues like communication, adaptability and resistance to change.

Factors Promoting Workplace Diversity

1. **Social responsibility:** Many groups and communities in the society face discrimination and are underprivileged. Providing employment to such people would be a socially responsible action which helps the downtrodden to live with dignity. For example, providing employment to rural women and differently abled people.
2. **Composition of available manpower:** People from different backgrounds, religions, regions and physical abilities comprise the available talent. Indian working population used to be dominated by males in the past, but now the scenario has changed with more and more women choosing to study and work.
3. **Legal requirement:** Many companies are legally required to be non-discriminatory in their employment practices. A certain per cent of positions in public companies are reserved for some underprivileged classes of people.
4. **Marketing requirements:** Companies which need to interact with different varieties of customers need a workforce which would understand the unique needs of the customers. Thus, they employ a diverse workforce so that they can cater to their customer needs in a better way. Banks employ people from a rural background for their village branches because they would have a better understanding of the rural situations and challenges.

5. **Better communication strategy:** The stakeholders in a business are often very diverse. The vendor, suppliers, customers, etc. of any particular company are composed of many different categories of people. Thus, it is beneficial for a company to have a diverse workforce which can effectively communicate with the external parties.
6. **Scope of future development:** The business environment is ever changing and only those organizations which adapt themselves accordingly can survive and grow. The capacity to identify emerging opportunities and take quick action depends upon the knowledge, experience, insight and talents of the workforce. A varied array of workforce brings a wide range of experiences and opinions to the organization.

Benefits of Workforce Diversity

1. **Increased adaptability:** People from diverse backgrounds have different experiences, perceptions, thoughts and opinions. This creates flexibility regarding acceptance of innovations and new ideas which help the organization to adapt to changing circumstances.
2. **Richness in the workplace:** Having workplace diversity adds a degree of richness to the work environment. People try harder to achieve cooperation and put in extra efforts which enrich the workplace.
3. **Better understanding of national and global culture:** Having employees from different religions, races, and capabilities broadens the organization's understanding of the national and global culture.
4. **Variety of ideas and viewpoints:** The employees can contribute their unique and different perceptions towards business situations and help to generate a variety of ideas and opinions.
5. **Better customer services:** Customers of any organization are invariably a heterogeneous population. A diverse workforce can help the organization in understanding

the different categories of customers better and provide improved customer services.[6]

Challenges to Workforce Diversity

1. **Communication:** Effective communication may be a problem for a workforce that is culturally diverse. Differences in languages and culture can be a hurdle in proper communication and may give rise to misunderstandings.
2. **Management of diversity:** The management should create and promote an atmosphere which encourages diversity and respects the differences in the behaviour and habits of the employees. In the absence of proper management, good relations between the employees cannot be achieved.
3. **Workplace policies:** It is a challenge to prepare workplace policies that are suitable for, and accepted by the diverse groups of employees.
4. **Resistance to change:** If a workplace has traditionally had a homogeneous workforce, then the older employees may be resistant to the concept of diversity. Many male employees may feel intimidated to work under a female boss.

Facing Challenges of Diversity

1. While managing diversity, the manager should look for similarities and not for differences among the workforce. This will help to create a healthy working environment.
2. The organization should promote effective communication and try to minimise confusion caused due to language and cultural barriers.
3. Special care should be given to the emotional and psychological well-being of the employees.
4. All employees should be treated with dignity and respect. Problems like discrimination based on gender, religion, ethnicity, etc. should be dealt with strictly.

5. An open atmosphere should be provided and no employee should be stopped from voicing his opinions and views.
6. The organization can arrange for diversity training to help the employees understand each other better and work together productively.
7. Diversity in top positions and leadership should be encouraged.

QUESTIONS

1. Define International HRM. Differentiate between domestic HRM and international HRM.
2. What are the three categories of employees in international staffing?
3. What do you mean by ethnocentric staffing? What are the problems associated with it?
4. Compare the centralized vs. decentralized approach in international training.
5. Describe various components of international compensation.
6. What do you mean by workforce diversity? What are the factors promoting workplace diversity?
7. How does diversity benefit the organization?

NOTES

1. http://www.ebooks.com/231840/international-human-resource-management-in-retrospect-and-prospect/morley-michael-ed—scullion-hugh-ed/
2. K. Aswathappa. *Human Resource and Personnel Management,* Tata McGraw-Hill, New Delhi, 2006, p. 648.
3. C.M. Solomon. "Success Abroad Depends on More than Job Skills", *Personnel Journal*, April 1994, 73, pp. 51-59.
4. http://www.citehr.com/13375-ethnocentric-approach-recruitment.html
5. http://www.winstonbrill.com/bril001/html/article_index/articles/551-600/article557_body.html
6. http://lifestyle.iloveindia.com/lounge/diversity-in-the-workplace 1595.html

Chapter 29

Human Resource Accounting and Audit

Human resources are the most valuable assets of an organization, and the ultimate success of any enterprise depends upon the skills, competence and knowledge of its employees. The human resources contribute a lot towards building the total wealth of an organization; therefore it becomes necessary to formulate a measure for evaluating the worth of the human capital. But due to the peculiar nature of human beings, the value of the human capital cannot be measured in the same way the value of other assets can be measured. Human Resource Accounting (HRA) is the process of quantifying and measuring the value of the human resources. HRA can be defined as the assigning, budgeting, and reporting the cost of human resources incurred in an organization, including wages and salaries and training expenses.[1]

It measures the costs incurred in order to recruit, hire, train and develop the personnel employed at various levels of the organization. HRA also evaluates the present economic value of the employees. An HRA report is prepared after calculating the costs incurred in acquiring and maintaining the employees and the value obtained from them.

Some definitions of HRA:

1. The American Accounting Association's Committee on Human Resource Accounting: "The process of identifying and measuring data about human resources

and communicating this information to interested parties."

2. Eric Flamholtz: "The measurement and reporting of the cost and value of people in organizational resources."
3. Woodruff: "Human Resource Accounting is an attempt to identify and report investments made in human resources of an organization that are presently not accounted for in conventional accounting practice. Basically it is an information system that tells the management what changes over time are occurring to the human resource in the business."
4. Davidson and Well: "A term used to describe a variety of proposals that seek to report and emphasize the importance of human resources—knowledgeable, trained and loyal employees in a company earning process and total assets."
5. Stephen Knauf: "The measurement and quantification of human organizational inputs such as recruiting, training, experience and commitment."

HRA involves not just the measurement of costs involved with acquiring employees, but also the qualification of the economic value of the people in an organization. In many countries, furnishing of information regarding HRA by organizations is a common practice though this trend is yet to catch up in India. Since proving HRA related information is not a legal requirement in India, there are only few companies which do it. However, some companies like Bharat Heavy Electricals Ltd (BHEL), Steel Authority of India Ltd. (SAIL), Oil and Natural Gas Commission (ONGC), etc. provide HRA information in their annual reports.

Purposes of HRA

In the year 1971, renowned management expert Rensis Likert specified the following purposes of HRA.

(i) It furnishes cost/value information for making management decisions about acquiring, allocating, developing, and maintaining human resources in order to attain cost-effectiveness;

(ii) It allows management personnel to monitor effectively the use of human resources;

(iii) It provides a sound and effective basis of human asset control, that is, whether the asset is appreciated, depleted or conserved;

(iv) It helps in the development of management principles by classifying the financial consequences of various practices.[2]

Approaches to HRA

There are different angles to HRA, regarding components of costs, investment and value related to employees of an organization. There are two approaches to assign monetary values to these aspects, the cost approach and the economic value approach. The cost approach involves the expenditures incurred by a company regarding an employees like costs of recruitment, selection, placement, training and development, etc. On the other hand, the economic value approach regards employees as assets and measures the economic value added by the employees to the organization's total worth. It aims to measure the benefits created by HR.

The Cost Approach

1. **The historical cost method:** According to this method, all the costs incurred in recruitment, selection, placement, training and development of employees are taken into account while evaluating the value of human resources. Some of these costs are direct costs like salaries while costs in terms of time spent in training and development are indirect costs. This method is simple and easy to understand, though it suffers from many demerits; the biggest one being that since training and development costs are taken into account while valuing employees, highly skilled employees requiring lesser training will be valued lower than those requiring more training.

2. **The opportunity cost method:** This method calculates what would have been the returns if the money spent on HR was spent on something else. It was Hekimian and Jones who had advocated this method, also known as the Market Value Method. This is not a very objective method and therefore is only used for internal reporting. One serious limitation of this method is that it totally disregards the fact that well-trained employees can be easily hired from outside sources, and it would be difficult to measure the opportunity costs related to them.
3. **The replacement cost method:** Replacement cost refers to the costs that would have to be incurred if the existing employees were to be replaced by identical ones. When an employee leaves the organization, costs of recruiting, selecting, placing and training the new employee would have to be incurred in order to replace him. The replacement costs can be viewed from two angles: personal replacement costs and positional replacement costs. Personal replacement cost is the cost that would have to be incurred to replace an employee with a substitute who can provide the same set of services that the employee being replaced might have rendered at various positions he would have occupied during his tenure. Positional replacement costs are the costs incurred to replace the set of services rendered by an employee in a particular position. This takes into account the position the employee is currently holding as well as the future positions expected to be held by him. The major weakness of this method is that it is highly subjective.[3]

The Economic Value Approach

1. **Flamholtz's model of determinants of individual value to formal organizations:** According to Flamholtz, the value of an individual to an organization is determined by the services he is expected to render. The current

value of an employee is the present worth of the services that he is likely to render to the organization in future. As an employee moves from one position to another within the organization, the set of services provided by him changes. While calculating the current value of the individual, the present cumulative value of all the possible services that may be rendered by him during his tenure with the organization is taken. There are two dimensions to this value.

(i) *Expected conditional value*: This is the worth that could be possibly realized from the services of an individual over the period of his productive work life in the organization.

(ii) *Expected realizable value*: The expected realizable value depends upon the expected conditional value of an employee and the probability that the individual will remain in the organization for the duration of his productive work life. Since the employees may leave the organization any time they wish, it is important to ascertain the chances of their turnover.

2. **Flamholtz's stochastic rewards valuation model:** This model considers the movement of employees in an organization through various roles. This process of progressing through organizational states is called a stochastic process. The stochastic rewards valuation model measures a person's expected conditional value and expected realizable value. In any organization, employees generate value as they move along organizational roles and render a set of services in different capacities. It is presumed that any employee would move from one state to another over a duration of time; in this model the separation of an employee from his workplace is also considered a state. This is a very sophisticated and complex model that requires extensive information for determining the value of individuals.

3. **The Lev and Schwartz model:** According to this model, the value of human resources is calculated as the present value of estimated future earnings discounted by the rate of return on investment (cost of capital). The mathematical formula for calculation of value of human resources is as follows:

$$Vy = \frac{I(t)}{(1+r)^{t-y}}$$

Where,

V_y = the value of an individual 'y' years old.

$I(t)$ = the individual's annual earnings up to retirement.

t = retirement age.

r = a discount rate specific to the cost of capital to the company.

This is the most commonly used method for HRA used by most companies in India.

4. **Hekimian and Jones competitive bidding model:** In this method, the managers bid against each other for the human resources already available in an organization. The highest bid is taken as the value of the employee. This is a highly subjective method as there are no set criteria to evaluate the employees. The value of an employee is based solely on the judgement of the managers.

Non-Monetary Methods

The value of human resources can be measured by non-monetary methods as well. These methods may be used to supplement monetary methods.

1. **Skills inventory:** This is a simple listing of the education, knowledge, experience, skills of the organization's human resources.
2. **Performance evaluation methods:** This includes methods like simple ranking method, paired comparison, check lists, graphic rating scales, etc.

3. **Potential assessment:** It refers to the identification of hidden skills, talents and abilities in a person which even he may be unaware of. It determines an employee's capacity for promotion and advancement.
4. **Attitude measurements:** These measurements assess employees' attitudes towards their jobs, remuneration, work environment, etc. in order to determine their levels of satisfaction or dissatisfaction.[4]

Advantages of HRA

(i) It provides useful information regarding the costs and values associated with HR for manpower planning.

(ii) HRA helps to predict about the prospective availability of skilled human resources in the long run, and thus the corporate plans for the future can be mapped according to this.

(iii) HRA helps to prepare and successfully implement a system of succession planning for filling key leadership positions in the future.

(iv) HRA provides information for designing meaningful training and development programmes for the employees and therefore lead to their advancement.

(v) HRA ensures that the organization's human resources are utilized to their full potential in a way that is beneficial to both the organization and the employees.

(vi) HRA helps the management to prepare a comprehensive system of recruitment, selection, placement and training so that the best possible candidates are hired and maintained in the organization.

Limitations of HRA

(i) HR valuation methods assume that employees would remain with their organizations for a specified period of time. But this assumption is wrong because in reality employees do not remain with one company for long and often change jobs.

(ii) It is very difficult to establish standards for HRA as in case of other fields of accounting such as financial accounting or management accounting. Every organization uses its own standards, and thus the HRA data of no two organizations can be compared.

(iii) HRA dehumanises the employees by evaluating them in monetary terms. Human beings cannot be owned or used like machines.

(iv) There is no model of HRA valuation that can be said to be ideal. Each model has many practical drawbacks.

(v) The life of a human being is uncertain. The lifespan of an employee can never be predicted accurately, and therefore values can never be assigned to any employee with surety.

Human Resource Audit

The term audit is normally associated with financial accounting and refers to the official examination and verification of a company's financial and accounting records. HR audit is a similar concept in the field of Human Resource Management. HR audit involves examining and reviewing the organization's existing policies, procedures and practices regarding recruitment and selection, orientation and placement, training and development, job analysis and design, job evaluation, compensation, morale and motivation, employee health and safety, social welfare, industrial relations, etc. According to Eric Flamholtz, "Human Resource Audit is a systematic assessment of the strengths, limitations, and developmental needs of its existing human resources in the context of organizational performance."

Normally, in an organization, not all HR policies are formal and written; there are many informal policies, not officially documented. The HR audit involves the review of all the HR policies, procedures and practices currently adopted by the organization, irrespective of whether they are formal or informal. The audit also helps to check that the company complies with the legal requirements and regulations regarding employees as laid down by the government of the country. By means of an audit, the company can determine its strengths and weaknesses in the area of HRM and plan accordingly to improve its processes and procedures related to the human resource function.

Objectives of HR Audit

(i) Check whether the existing HR policies are actually being implemented in a proper sequence with positive results.

(ii) Identify those processes and procedures that need to be updated according to changing organizational requirements.

(iii) Find out whether any of the informal/unwritten policies being followed are harmful to the well-being of the organization.

(iv) Determine if there is any policy that is not being followed properly and find out the underlying causes.

(v) Identify the needs and opportunities for new policies that will lead to betterment of the HR in the organization.

(vi) Check if there is any requirement for updating the training and development processes currently followed.

Scope of HR Audit

(i) Recruitment and selection.

(ii) Orientation and placement.

(iii) Training and development.

(iv) Employee communications.

(v) Morale and motivation.

(vi) HR policies and procedures.

(vii) Job evaluation and design.

(viii) Industrial relations.

(ix) Grievance handling and redressal.

(x) Employee health and safety.

(xi) Legal compliance.
(xii) Employee compensation/remuneration.
(xiii) Separations (retirement, resignations, death, etc.).

Process of HR Audit

1. **Determining the scope and type of audit:** Since HR is a very wide field, the company may either choose to conduct a comprehensive review of all HR functions or it may decide to review a few specific areas as it deems necessary. For example, a company may choose to review only the policies and procedures related to recruitment, selection and orientation policies.
2. **Determining the audit method:** HR audits are usually conducted by using a questionnaire that elicits information about the relevant HR areas. The audit may also be conducted by interviewing managers and employees of the HR department to analyze how well they have understood the company's policies and how efficiently these policies are being implemented. When using a questionnaire, care should be taken to design it in such a way that it elicits all necessary information regarding the areas to be audited.
3. **Data collection:** This step includes the actual process of collecting data about the organization and its HR practices. Information is collected by using the questionnaire and by interviewing relevant HR personnel about the HR procedures and policies being used in the company.
4. **Setting the standards:** To assess the efficiency of HR functions, the information collected has to be compared with some pre-determined standards. These standards have to be pre-set and any acceptable level of discrepancies should be specified clearly. Comparing the actual results with the standards will give an idea about the efficiency with which the HR functions are being performed.

5. **Feedback about the results:** After collecting information and comparing the results, the audit team summarises the findings and provides feedback to the company's HR personnel and senior management in the form of an audit report. The results of the audit should be discussed with the employees of the HR department so that they are made aware of the present condition of the HR functions in the company. Discussion with employees will also throw up new ideas for improving the policies and procedures in future.
6. **Develop action plans:** Once the results of the audit are out, this information should be used for improving the working of the HR department. The findings of the audit should be categorised according to order of importance: high, medium and low. The organization should examine the areas of weaknesses as revealed by the audit and find ways to overcome them. Conducting HR audit would serve no practical purpose if no actions are taken.[5]

Advantages of HR Audit

(i) HR audit helps the company to identify the areas where improvement is required.

(ii) It helps to ascertain the proper contribution of the HR department towards the organization.

(iii) HR audit facilitates the development of HR plans for the future based on the current performance of the HR department.

(iv) It helps to motivate the employees to perform better and boosts their morale.

(v) HR audit keeps a check on whether the company is complying with the required legal rules and regulations.

(vi) The weaknesses of the HR department can be pin-pointed by way of HR audit so that remedial measures may be taken.

(vii) It enables the HR manager to evaluate the job positions and the employees in order to formulate promotion and transfer policies.

QUESTIONS

1. What is Human Resource Accounting? What are its various cost approach models?
2. Write a note on Flamholtz's stochastic rewards valuation model.
3. What are the non-monetary methods of human capital evaluation?
4. Define HR Audit. Why is it necessary?
5. Enumerate the steps in HR Audit. What are the data collection methods used for this purpose?
6. What are the advantages of HR audits?

NOTES

1. http://www.businessdictionary.com/definition/human-resource-accounting.html
2. http://www.whatishumanresource.com/Human-Resource—accounting
3. www.charteredclub.com/what-is-human-resource-accounting/
4. http://www.egyankosh.ac.in/bitstream/123456789/ 35602/1/unit-18.pdf
5. http://www.shrm.org/TemplatesTools/hrqa/Pages/basicstepsinanHRAudit.aspx